OVER MY HEAD

OVER MY HEAD

*A Doctor's Own Story of
Head Injury
from the Inside Looking Out*

Claudia L. Osborn

**Andrews McMeel
Publishing**

Kansas City

www.andrewsmcmeel.com

98 99 00 01 02   RDH   10 9 8 7 6 5 4 3 2 1

Grateful acknowledgment is made to the following:
"Getting On with It" by Grace Butcher and "If I Had My Life to Live Over" by Nadine Stair from *If I Had My Life to Live Over I Would Pick More Daisies*, edited by Sandra Haldeman Martz, © 1992 Papier-Mache Press. Used by permission.
"If I Live," © 1977 by Cris Williamson, Bird Ankles Music (BMI). All Rights Reserved. Used by permission.
"Let's Face the Music and Dance," words and music by Irving Berlin, from *Follow the Fleet*, 1936.
"Wild Grapes" from *The Poetry of Robert Frost*, edited by Edward Connery Lathem. Copyright 1923, 1951 by Robert Frost, © 1969 by Henry Holt & Co., Inc. Reprinted by permission of Henry Holt & Co., Inc.
"Dropkick Me Jesus," words and music by Paul Craft, © 1972 Screen Gems-EMI Music Inc. and Black Sheep Music. All rights controlled and administered by Screen Gems-EMI Music Inc. All rights reserved. International copyright secured. Used by permission.

Library of Congress Cataloging-in-Publication Data

Osborn, Claudia L.
   Over my head : a doctor's own story of head injury from the inside looking out / by Claudia L. Osborn.
     p.   cm.
   Includes bibliographical references.
   ISBN: 0-8362-5419-8 (hbk.)
   1. Brain damage—Patients—Michigan—Biography. 2. Internist—Michigan—Biography.
 I. Title.
RC387.5.083   1998
362.1´97481´0092
[B]—DC21
                                          97-40542
                                           CIP

ATTENTION: SCHOOLS AND BUSINESSES

Andrews McMeel books are available at quantity discounts with bulk purchase for educational, business, or sales promotional use. For information, please write to: Special Sales Department, Andrews McMeel Publishing, 4520 Main Street, Kansas City, Missouri 64111.

For Mama, who gave me life, then helped me find it again;
and for Marcia, my tenacious lion in winter, who held the door open
and waited for me

$\ast\{$ $\}\ast$

Contents

Foreword by Yehuda Ben-Yishay, Ph.D.   ix
Author's Note   xi

PROLOGUE   *March 8, 1989: New York*   1
CHAPTER 1   *Friday, July 8, 1988: Detroit*   7
CHAPTER 2   *Monday, July 11, 1988*   14
CHAPTER 3   *Twist of Lemon*   18
CHAPTER 4   *Monday Night*   21
CHAPTER 5   *Not Adding Up the Score*   27
CHAPTER 6   *Who Is This in Here with Me?*   35
CHAPTER 7   *What If I Need Them and They Won't Take Me?*   40
CHAPTER 8   *March 8, 1989: New York—*
             I'd Rather Have a Root Canal   47
CHAPTER 9   *Mopping Up a Flood*   57
CHAPTER 10   *There Goes the Neighborhood*   64
CHAPTER 11   *Dropkick Me, Joanie*   73
CHAPTER 12   *In the Same Boat*   84
CHAPTER 13   *Don't Charge the Battery, Fix the Generator*   92
CHAPTER 14   *Halfway Home*   99
CHAPTER 15   *Meltdown*   108
CHAPTER 16   *The Collapse of My Dreams*   116
CHAPTER 17   *Waking Up Is Hard to Do*   122
CHAPTER 18   *Recycled Brains*   130
CHAPTER 19   *What I Did on My Summer Vacation*   138
CHAPTER 20   *I'm Out of Sorts. Please Send Sorts.*   150
CHAPTER 21   *Getting Better*   161
CHAPTER 22   *Turning Leaves*   173
CHAPTER 23   *Not as I Wish, but as I Am*   184

Contents

CHAPTER 24   *Moving On*   195

CHAPTER 25   *Occupational Trials*   204

CHAPTER 26   *Living in the Real World*   216

EPILOGUE   *March 20, 1997: Grosse Pointe*   229

Special Thanks   233

A Head Injury Primer   235

References and Resources   239

Foreword

In world literature, there are a number of awe-inspiring accounts of exceptional individuals who—in the face of severely incapacitating physical disabilities—have attained extraordinary achievements. One example is Stephen Hawking, the world's foremost cosmologist, whose formidable mind is imprisoned (due to a motor neuron disease) in an emaciated, utterly helpless, and now also voiceless body. And yet, Hawking continues to transmit his profound ideas about the universe through eye movements which are converted by a computer and voice synthesizer into audible words. Douglas Bader is another example: This double-amputee World War II British fighter pilot, by the sheer force of his will and amazing skill, became one of the heroes of the Battle of Britain.

In contrast, there are few stories about remarkable comebacks following devastating injuries to the brain—the very engine, guidance system, and repository of a person's mind, experiences, and personality. The present autobiographical account is one such inspiring story.

A gifted young professor at a medical school, an accomplished physician and mentor of other young physicians, chronicles her rehabilitation process from the moment of her brain injury in a motor vehicle accident to the resumption of medical school teaching and research.

This is the story of a triumphant personal journey from deep despair to philosophical acceptance, from perplexity and occasional incoherence to an examined life, from greatly hampered, often short-circuited thought processes to effective reasoning and problem-solving ability, from an impatience with her less gifted intellect to a genuine empathy with her new self.

Here is eloquent proof that—with the right kind of rehabilitation—there can be a productive and meaningful life after a head injury.

Yehuda Ben-Yishay, Ph.D.
Professor of Clinical Rehabilitation Medicine
Director, Brain Injury Day Treatment Program
New York University Medical Center
New York, April 1997

Author's Note

It is a daunting task for me to make my thoughts clear. My difficulty in telling this story was compounded by the deficits in my memory, language, and organizational skills. I have no memory of being injured and only a dim recollection of the nine months preceding my rehabilitation in New York. To compensate, I relied upon the memories of those close to me, copious notes from my journals, video- and audiotapes, and the assistance of my mother, who organized boxes of my papers and edited my manuscript.

Some journal entries quoted in the book have been edited by me for clarity. My intention is to candidly portray what it is like to live with a head injury, not to require you to decipher my language at that time. The essays between chapters, entitled "Piece of Mind," are excerpts from my journals, written at various times and used here to illuminate an idea or capture a feeling, and are unrelated to the story line.

As to the latter, I took creative license in setting scenes and recreating conversations in order to tell this experience in the first-person voice, as a story, rather than as a medical documentary. The prologue is an example. During this period I was virtually incapable of registering detailed or structured information and recorded nothing beyond the essential. As a result, the circumstances and details used to describe some situations may have actually occurred later. However, the situations *occurred*—often over and over. Because those most involved have read this account and occasionally supplied a missing detail I am reassured that, while details and conversations may not be *exact*, they are nonetheless true.

The names of my fellow trainees and the professionals responsible for my rehabilitation are used with their permission. I have provided some anonymity to my pre-injury medical work environment. All patients and certain minor characters have been given pseudonyms to protect their privacy.

This book is, of necessity, about the grief accompanying the loss of one's self. More important, it is about the process of rehabilitation and the building of a new life. It is also an attempt to provide insight into what happens when neural pathways in the brain are damaged and the most sophisticated computer in the universe goes awry.

I hope to show the effect head injury has on behavior and personality, and how thinking and problem-solving ability can be so altered that the simplest actions require extraordinary conscious effort. My purpose is to forever change the way you see someone you love, know, or employ who has experienced a brain injury.

We are different, we know it, and we would give much to have the dimensions of that loss understood, and thereby bridge the chasm between those of you who have not had this experience and those of us who have.

C.L.O.

OVER MY HEAD

March 8, 1989

NEW YORK

Hello . . . I'm in a phone booth at the corner of
Walk and Don't Walk.
ANONYMOUS

✙

A blast of music from WABC-FM blew my eyes open. I lay still, fully awake if not informed by what I saw. My eyes surveyed the room searching for a hint of something familiar.

Nothing.

I struggled upright, my protesting back announcing the quality of my sofa hide-a-bed, reached out, and tapped the clock radio into silence. Traffic noises wafted in through the open window, so I knew I was in a city.

If I had thought about it at all, I would have been surprised at how someone as curious as I am by nature could feel so little interest in waking up in a clearly alien place. Yet I sat quietly, devoid of wonder, serene in my disorientation. The most familiar part of waking up was its unfamiliarity. I was accustomed to it. I had become one of the fortunate few who could be catapulted through a time warp and arrive unruffled in Never-Never-Land in the twenty-third century. I wouldn't know it wasn't a typical day.

Rustling noises behind me caught my attention. A sleepy face appeared over the back of the sofa and mumbled, "Good morning."

Lori. I knew Lori. We had been roommates at Vassar years ago. Apparently, we were again.

Drawn by the noise of traffic and the billowing curtains, I struggled free of the covers and went to the open window, leaning far enough out to make Lori gasp. Forty-three floors below, tiny people scurried and toy cars multiplied to jell traffic. "Manhattan," I said. "I'm in Manhattan."

"Right," she said. "It's not Tuesday; this can't be Belgium. How about closing that window."

I realized I was shivering. "This must be wintertime," I informed her.

"Whatever," Lori said absently as she headed for the bathroom.

I returned to the sofa and snuggled under the covers, seeking warmth, not wanting Lori to feel hurried to free up the shower. I lounged contentedly while she moved briskly about the large, airy studio apartment. Notes on the end table by my sofabed spelled out the directions to 24th Street under big block letters:

BE THERE AT 9:45 A.M.!!!

I should start to get ready. It was almost six-thirty.

"You have your keys?" Lori said. "Remember, I won't be home till late this evening, I have a long deposition today, but the doorman knows you if you have a problem."

"Is it with a doctor?"

"No. Are you listening? You're sure you're set for the day? Money? Directions? My phone number, in case?"

"I'm set," I said. "I have everything written down."

It wasn't like I didn't know my way around. I'd stayed in this city many times . . . maybe years. I was adept at navigating the streets and subway system.

She was cramming files into an already bulging leather briefcase. "All right then, as long as you're sure."

"I'm glad it's not a doctor," I said. "You'll win the case, Lori."

"From your lips to God's ear. See ya." And she was out the door.

I arose and began my own preparations, striving to imitate the efficient routine I had just witnessed.

I put my suitcase on Lori's bed and opened it. Nice. Marcia would have packed everything I needed. Blouses were neatly folded on top. I put one on. Underneath were little piles of underwear. Deodorant, shampoo, miscellaneous toilet articles were tucked in on the side.

Shampoo. I needed to shower. I closed the case, put it under the bed, went into the bathroom, took my blouse off, turned on the water, and stepped into the shower. Damn. No shampoo. I stepped out of the shower, dripping wet, returned to the main room, but couldn't spot the suitcase.

It was okay, I'd use Lori's shampoo.

I lathered and rinsed my hair several times before I felt assured I'd remembered to use the shampoo, but as I towel-dried my tangled hair, I realized I had missed the conditioner.

From the bathroom doorway, I spotted the suitcase sticking out from under the bed. I opened it and took out underwear, stockings, and another blouse and dressed myself, putting on the shoes I had worn yesterday. Then I took a pair of wool slacks out of the suitcase and, after some difficulty getting them on over my shoes, removed my shoes and finished my dressing.

As I dressed, I checked then rechecked the notes on the end table so I could remember why I was alone in this strange apartment in this strange city. They also reminded me about food. A note from Lori suggested I have a bagel and orange juice. I went into the tiny kitchenette, buttered a bagel, and poured some juice. Then, satisfied that I had done everything I was supposed to do, I locked the door and left.

I had allowed almost two hours to make the two-and-a-half-mile trip to 24th Street and First Avenue. I hoped it was enough. Time, I had learned, tended to evaporate inexplicably. Best to build extra minutes—even hours—into any plan.

The needle-sharp March wind whipping down the street stung my eyes. I shivered, pulled up the collar of my coat, and realized my scalp felt like ice. I must not have blow-dried my hair. Too late now. I'd write it down for tomorrow.

I immediately pulled a scrap of paper from my pocket and wrote a reminder to myself while standing in the middle of the sidewalk. For the most part, I was oblivious to the buffeting of passersby hurrying to their jobs, but I responded courteously to a shabby man who touched my arm and asked with a putrid, alcoholic breath for assistance.

Poor old man. I supposed he thought he knew me. Maybe he did, but for the life of me I couldn't place his face. He asked for help several times while I tried to figure out what kind of help he needed; then he gave up and abandoned me to speak to someone else.

Just as well. I wouldn't have wanted to misdirect him, although I had no trouble following my own directions to the bus stop, where I stood, shivering, in line. As we moved forward for boarding, I reached into my coin purse for my bus money.

"Damn!" I said.

There was only the solitary quarter I kept for an emergency phone call. I needed a dollar in change or a token to ride the bus.

I stood stiffly at the curb, struggling to find a solution to my problem, barely aware of the drunk who had apparently followed me until he stepped right into my face and said, "I need money."

I promptly put my quarter into his outstretched hand.

He turned away in disgust. "You need it worse than me," he said, but he didn't give it back.

What did I do now about change for the bus? I was numb with cold and bewilderment. There had to be an easier way to fix my trivial thinking problems than subjecting myself to living for months in New York City.

I comforted myself that many of my friends back in Detroit wouldn't have a clue about how to maneuver their way around Manhattan either. It was a condition I now shared with them. Temporarily, that is.

In the old days, I would have hopped into a cab, or gone into a store and gotten change, or even walked to 24th Street. None of those answers occurred to me.

When I calmed down, my thinking cleared and one idea emerged—return to the apartment and get change. It seemed a reasonable choice. More to the point, it seemed to be my only choice.

I walked back into the warm apartment building. Which was good. Now I could dry my hair and put myself together to look professional.

When I used the mirror to style my hair, I realized I'd never combed it that morning. A tangled mass of brown curls stuck out in every direction—as though I'd stuck my wet finger in a live socket, my grandmother would have said. The mirror also revealed the fact that I wore just one earring and had forgotten a belt.

I searched my luggage for ten minutes for a belt and discovered the mate to my sapphire earring, all by itself in the middle of the bathroom counter. I was definitely going to have to remember to look carefully in a mirror. Still, I left the apartment feeling much more in charge.

The bus change still sat on the dresser.

Fifteen minutes later, after a third trip to the apartment, I deposited my change in a crosstown bus farebox and clung to the pole, swaying with the motion of the bus, rigidly attentive to street signs. It was only a mile to Second Avenue, where I would transfer to a downtown bus. I was not going to miss that stop. "Second Avenue," I whispered fiercely to myself. "You want Second Avenue."

I made the transfer seamlessly and settled into my new bus seat, now relaxed. I watched the teenager across the aisle apply another coat of mascara. Her face was a kaleidoscope of color, buried under layers of beige pancake; cheeks of an improbable pink and eyes ringed with a violet that matched her jacket. The lipstick was a harmonizing fuchsia.

I licked my own lips, which were chapped. I wasn't much on makeup, but surely I must be wearing some. I wanted to look attractive. My fingers assessed the dryness of my face. No moisturizer. I felt a trickle of sweat roll down my side. Could I have actually forgotten deodorant? No makeup, maybe, but deodorant? It was part of showering. Still, this situation was vaguely familiar.

I ran over my notes again. After *shower and dress* came *bagel and juice.* My stomach growled. I was starving, so I must not have eaten the bagel. What if it was still in the kitchen, attracting roaches? Lori would kill me. I pushed my way toward the door and jumped off at the next stop.

The street signs read 14TH ST. and SECOND AVENUE. Whoa, I was nowhere near that bagel. I sat down against a store wall and tried to collect myself. When my thoughts began to clear, I read my notes again. I was supposed to have gotten off the bus back at 24th Street and then walked a block east to First Avenue.

I still had enough time if I forgot about that bagel. Maybe it was still in the refrigerator. Maybe it never existed despite what the note said. Notes in my experience were often wrong. I didn't know why, but nothing in my life could be taken for granted anymore. I knew I was doing everything as usual, yet here I was hungry and probably stinking as much as the old man dozing next to me. Go figure.

I rose and headed back up Second Avenue at a brisk pace. I should have skipped the buses and walked the whole route that morning. Exercise always made me feel better.

The traffic lights that decorated each Manhattan intersection frustrated me at every block. I would barely reach my stride before I had to stop at a crossing. As I reached 20th Street the light turned red against me. Again!

Ah, but the WALK sign lit up across Second Avenue and the person next to me turned quickly and headed toward Third. I followed, obeying the command—WALK. I swiftly overtook fellow pedestrians and made good progress till I caught a red light at Park Avenue.

Wait, what was I doing? I had faithfully read all the street signs, but their clear message that I was heading in the wrong direction hadn't registered. Somewhere I had forgotten that the point of this trip was not continuous motion, but reaching a destination. I was no longer early. I would have to hurry while maintaining course. That should be easy.

But would it? Success had such a random quality.

I was flushed, sweaty, and ragged when I arrived at the beige brick dental school on 24th Street, one of many undistinguished-looking buildings accommodating a sprawling New York University. I threaded my way through the crowded lobby to the elevator bank. When I stepped off at the eighth floor, I was a tad disheveled to be sure and, at a mile-per-hour speed, not your average marathon walker, but as I pushed open the door labeled HEAD TRAUMA PROGRAM, NEW YORK UNIVERSITY, I glanced at my watch with grim satisfaction.

I was right on time.

1

Friday, July 8, 1988

DETROIT

The practice of medicine is an art, not a trade;
a calling, not a business.
SIR WILLIAM OSLER

⚕

The hospital where I practiced was an old one with new trappings. Indirect lamplight made the most of featureless beige wallpaper picked to complement newly carpeted halls. Most patient rooms now had pastel walls and updated lighting. VIP rooms were papered and furnished with blond, painted-metal furniture meant to create a hotel-like ambiance. The administrators deserved high marks for effort, but on the whole, the redecoration of this old inner-city institution was more ambitious than successful. The elevators were still slow, which dictated that I run up and down staircases to save time, and there was no central air-conditioning.

It was only six-thirty in the morning when I whipped down the corridor leading to Three East enjoying the relative calm between the hospital's night and day. I had seen my ICU patients already and it would be an hour before my house staff tracked me down for morning rounds, time enough to review the charts of two new patients admitted during the night. I was actually ahead of schedule. For the moment.

My lead vanished when I arrived at the nurses' station, which sat like a NASA command post, dead-center of the intersection. There Ms. Rollins nailed me, wearing that smarmy nurse smile which heralds the transfer of burden from nurse to physician.

"Dr. Osborn," she said. "Mrs. Jones, your patient in 301-A? She's refusing her surgery prep."

7

Because getting to the point was my usual style, I couldn't resist saying, "Whatever happened to 'Good morning'?"

"It hasn't started yet. I get off in an hour." She suppressed a grin that quickly turned into a frown. "Now, Dr. Osborn, I don't know what's gotten into Mrs. Jones. She accepted everything yesterday."

"What did the night intern have to say about her change of mind?" I suspected the answer.

"I didn't tell him." She folded her arms across her starchy chest. "He has an attitude. That young man couldn't convince a starving man to eat free food. Besides, I knew you'd be along."

"Give the new interns a chance, Ms. Rollins. They've only been doctors for a week. They're insecure. Some of them cover it by being a bit assertive."

Despite my defense, I was relieved the intern hadn't spoken to Mrs. Jones. Her surgery was essential, and an impatient, exhausted intern still flushed with his new authority wasn't what an anxious, frightened patient needed.

"I'll see Mrs. Jones now."

I tried to inch by Ms. Rollins, but she reeled me back.

"That's not all, doctor," she said. "Here are the lab results for 309, and I wish you'd do something about Mr. Samuels. Last night, he was hopelessly confused and drove the nurses crazy and . . ."

Ms. Rollins's list was long, especially since I interrupted her recitation to answer overhead and beeper pages from Five South, the wife of a patient, the Urgent Care Center, and two interns. It was seven o'clock before she and I were satisfied that everything was in hand and I could sprint to Mrs. Jones's room.

I hesitated a moment outside the door so I could appear to stroll in. It's counterproductive for patients to feel their doctors don't have enough time for them.

When I emerged from her room twenty minutes later, Mrs. Jones was still apprehensive but once again understood her critical need for the surgery, and I was half an hour behind schedule. My entourage was lounging against the far wall engaged in desultory conversation punctuated with a lot of yawns, waiting for me to start rounds. They were a good group who seemed to get along with each other. Jeff, a short redhead with a down-home accent, was a second-year resident in internal medicine. My two interns, Susan and Brian, had joined my house staff a week ago at the same time as the two medical students, Paul and Madeline.

Brian had a chart in his hand.

"What have you got?" I said.

"Mrs. Wilson. I've written out her discharge instructions. I knew you'd want to see them."

"Sure." I quickly reviewed his directives and medication list on the sixty-six-year-old newly diagnosed diabetic. "You did a good job with her diet and insulin. I think she really understands what she needs to know."

He straightened. "Thank you."

"But your discharge instructions? Especially this line about swimming or taking walks in her neighborhood every day?"

"She's fat. You said exercise is the best way to lose weight."

"Brian, she lives on social security in an area so dangerous she's scared to go to her clinic appointments. She can't afford to join a club to swim, and a stroll in her neighborhood poses a greater risk than her disease."

"I can only tell her what to do. I can't help it if she doesn't do it."

"Stop a moment." I stretched out my arms, stopping the group in the middle of the hall. "The art of medicine is as essential as the science. You're not helping her if you suggest something she can't do. How about talking to her about walking in the mall? Her transportation can be taken care of through a car pool, maybe through her church or the diabetic classes or our Cardiac Rehab Program. Or maybe she could buy a secondhand stationary bike."

"I don't want to get that involved."

"Well, you'll have to for the month you're on my service. It's a central ingredient of internal medicine." And even more in my practice, which was composed largely of the medically disenfranchised—especially the elderly poor and the foreign-born.

His face flushed. "That's my point. Internal medicine requires too much interaction with patients. That's why I want to be an anesthesiologist."

He looked so serious, I had to suppress my grin. "It's true we internists tend to be pleased when our patients stay conscious."

"Look, Dr. Osborn," he said, "I know what you're saying, but medicine isn't in my blood like it's in yours. It's exciting when we're saving someone's life or solving a diagnostic problem or even doing rounds—you liven things up. But most of the time, it's just me and the patients, and they bore me."

"I think—"

"Dr. Osborn to the ICU, stat. Dr. Osborn, stat, ICU."

At the sound of the overhead stat page, the six of us sprang to life. My emergency was also their emergency. I felt the familiar rush of adrenaline. No time to preview the other charts. It didn't matter. The day was in full swing.

Brian had me dead right. The patient care that irked him charged my life. I didn't ask my house staff to follow in my footsteps, but I wanted them to be enthralled with medicine, the stimulation of diagnosing, the challenge of helping a patient attain a better quality of life, the sheer joy of nurturing. It was possible to become disenchanted with medicine in a poor, inner-city hospital. Our patients' stays were seldom uncomplicated, and rarely elective. Nor did our patients look like the ones in TV commercials who leave the hospital smiling, loaded down with flowers, a doting family at their side, everything put to rights.

Our patients were usually the chronically ill. Most were elderly with precious little money. Many had end-stage diseases—cancer, failed kidneys, heart, lungs, or liver. Often, their suffering was compounded with alcoholism, drug abuse, and AIDS.

The day whizzed along at its usual dizzying speed. At five o'clock, I was in the outpatient department with my resident, Jeff, and it seemed possible to predict when I would be leaving the hospital. My housemate, Marcia, and I had dinner plans that evening.

I dialed her clinic number, balancing the receiver between ear and shoulder while I added the finishing touches to my recommendations on a consultation.

"It looks like I can get out of here by six tonight," I told her when she answered. "I'll be home in time to go to Stephen's with you so we don't end up with two cars."

"Great," Marcia said. "I can't remember the last time we both made an evening event on time."

I nodded to the EKG technician to go ahead and do my patient's graph and took the blood gas results from the respiratory therapist at my elbow.

"Are we supposed to bring anything?" I said into the phone, handing back the results to the therapist and adding, "Three liters, nasal canula, please."

"No," Marcia said. "Got to run. See you at six-thirty."

My beeper went off, paging me to a number outside the hospital, one I didn't recognize. "I hate mystery numbers."

"Especially at five on a Friday night," Jeff said. "It could be another hospital wanting to transfer a patient."

"I'm leaving here in an hour," I said. "Think positively."

I walked over to a cubicle where I would be less accessible to disruptions and punched the number into the phone. I was relieved to hear my cousin Nancy's voice.

"How are you?" I said. "It's nice to hear from you."

"Listen, is this a bad time or do you have a minute?"

"All the time you need. What's up?"

"Do you remember my friend Jenny Langton," she said, "from high school days?"

"Sure do," I said, dredging up a sixteen-year-old memory of a petite blonde girl.

"Well, she's sick, really sick. I saw her two weeks ago and she looked bad. I saw her again today and I'm really frightened at how much she's changed."

"I'm very sorry, Nancy. Who's her doctor?"

"Nobody, that's the problem. She's handling it with prayer at home. Her religion doesn't go along with much medical intervention. Her mother told me it's liver failure. The situation is pretty hopeless—short of a miracle—and she's suffering terribly. She's bright yellow, she can't eat, she can barely breathe." Nancy's voice began to crack. "We have to do something. Help her, will you? Please."

"I will if she'll let me," I said gently. "I can't force her to get help, but if you can get her to agree to see me, I'll try to persuade her to at least let me make her comfortable."

"She already said she'll come see you as a favor to me. I told her you wouldn't make her do anything she didn't think was right. When should she come?"

"Well, the way you describe her condition, someone better bring her to the hospital now." I hung up the phone knowing that Marcia and I would be taking two cars to Stephen's tonight. Emergencies are never convenient; it would be nice if you could schedule them.

Half an hour later, I confirmed how gravely ill Jenny Langton was. She allowed me to examine her thoroughly and do a chest X ray, but what she needed was aggressive medical intervention or she would soon die.

My natural desire was always to jump in and lead the charge to save a life. Holding back was hard and I detested being shackled. So did Jeff.

"Why aren't we doing anything?" Jeff punched his fist into his other hand. "Do we just stand by and watch her die? How the hell can we respect her wishes at a time like this?"

"If I break her trust," I said, "how long do you think I could keep her alive? She has liver failure. She has the right to make her own choices." I walked away but called back over my shoulder, "Wish me luck."

I entered the examining room and sat down on the cushioned stool next to the bed where Jenny was propped up to keep her from drowning in the fluid that filled her lungs. The small, quiet room magnified the sound of her raspy breathing and involuntary cough. In the light streaming from the wall fixture behind her, her saffron-yellow skin was startling, as though she had been dipped in a dye bath. Her medium-length, ash-colored hair hung limply, her eyes were half closed and dull, the whites yellow.

Numerous open sores, most of them on her legs and abdomen, oozed fluid, the body's response to the enormous pressure of fifty pounds of excess water that had collected in her tissues, swelling her malnourished frame to a huge size. She looked nine months pregnant. All water.

"I'm in pretty bad shape, aren't I?" she said.

"If we do nothing, yes," I said. "Your heart can't take the strain much longer. You're not getting enough oxygen into your lungs. Your whole body is shutting down."

"I suppose it's God's will."

"Prayer plays a vital role in medicine," I said, "but I can't imagine that God intends us to remain passive when we can help ourselves." Let me say the right things, dear God. Let her hear me. "If you saw your three-year-old niece run in front of an oncoming car, I know you'd pray hard that she would be spared. But I bet you'd run after her to sweep her out of harm's way and not just wait on the curb hoping God would do all the work."

"Of course, I'd try to save her."

"I know this seems very different to you, but I'm asking you to do the same thing for yourself. Let me help you. We would take one step at a time. No surprises. First, we'll focus on just making you comfortable and allowing your body to get more oxygen and nutrition. I know it's a lot to ask, but I can't do this unless you're admitted to the hospital."

She said nothing. Even if she was willing to listen to me, there was a problem. She was now so ill, I feared it would be all too easy for her to give up her will to live. Yet she had come to me. I played my last card.

"Your mother and your friends are grieving. Your body is very sick and your energies are depleted. It is a difficult time to make decisions. But I can buy you time, and once you're more comfortable and rested, your thinking will be clearer. You can decide then what you want to do. Everyone will respect your wishes. Please don't say no tonight and tie my hands."

She cried and nodded. "Thank you."

A heavy weight lifted off my chest.

Ten minutes later, Brian threw himself heavily into the chair next to the desk where I was writing orders on Jenny's chart. I was almost done. Maybe I could get to Stephen's in time for dessert.

"I heard your liver failure patient agreed to be admitted," he said. "She doesn't stand a chance without a liver transplant, does she?"

"Probably not," I said. "But that's not the issue now. Tonight I'm just grateful she agreed to stay."

"Yes, but if she turns out to be a candidate for a transplant, and she says no, she'll die anyway."

"Don't be hard. Just let me savor the peace I'll have tonight knowing she has gained a little time. We don't know yet what we can hope for down the line."

2

Monday, July 11, 1988

If I had my life to live over, I would start
barefoot earlier in the spring and stay that way
later in the fall. I would go to more dances. I
would ride more merry-go-rounds.
I would pick more daisies.

NADINE STAIR
If I Had My Life to Live Over

❧

Monday afternoon at the clinic, Mattie, my nurse, observed warily that "everything's goin' smooth as silk." She and I were an efficient team. "We oughta be," she boomed when I said that. "We've been a two-step for a year now."

At five I packed my case, preparing to return to the hospital. If I could keep my time there short, I could pick up the dry cleaning.

An early close to the day seldom occurred. My job was filled with unpredictable interruptions and crises. Even so, there was a basic schedule. In my dual role as a clinician and a trainer of young doctors, my mornings were filled with leading daily teaching rounds, conducting a weekly lecture, and presiding over a Morning Report session. My afternoons were spent in this nearby clinic, seeing patients but mostly supervising internal medicine residents. Sandwiched in between were committee meetings, hospital patients, medical records, consultations, meeting with patients' families, and preparing seminars.

I relished the interweaving of tasks, the satisfaction derived from juggling multiple (at times, simultaneous) demands on my time and felt my happiest on the days when it was six o'clock before I realized my bladder might burst if I didn't stop soon, and that I'd missed lunch. Again.

This had been a good day. For that matter, it had been a good weekend. Saturday morning, Marcia and I got in an early game of tennis, which we played against the backdrop of a glorious dawn. Because the lawns of our city's public park border Lake St. Clair, the courts afford a full view of passing Great Lakes freighters. That morning, five of them steamed by. Afterward, back home, I made omelets while we discussed an Anna Quindlen piece in the *New York Times.*

My reverie evaporated when Mattie came in and shut the door behind her. She was wearing a mock-frown that narrowed her expressive eyes which normally were, with Maybelline's help, as large as Lena Horne's—a comparison Mattie relished.

"Don't be fixin' to leave, Claudia. We got a delay." Delay, pronounced *dee-lay,* was one of Mattie's favorite words. "Miz Phillips is here. Today's Monday, I told her, not Wednesday. Her appointment's Wednesday at four. There's no telling her. You'll have to see her."

"Can you persuade her to come back Wednesday?"

"Before I do that, you oughta know. She hitchhiked here."

"You're kidding." Mrs. Phillips was in her seventies and lived in a neighborhood that wasn't safe for an eighteen-year-old karate black belt.

"No, ma'am. She says it's all on account of you."

"Of course, hitchhiking therapy. It's quickly replacing medication as the first-line therapy for Alzheimer's disease. It's part of a geographic cure."

Mattie giggled. It was an improbable sound, light and girlish, and a surprise every time I heard it emanate from that chest, which was worthy of an opera diva.

I moved the files on my desk to one side and put my white coat back on. "Grab her chart for me and bring her in. And please give Jeff a call and tell him I'll be late."

"He can tell hisself if he looks at the clock. I knew the day was too good, you weren't meant to get to the hospital on time."

"Thank you for that valuable insight."

A moment later, Mrs. Phillips strode into my office, shook my extended hand, and sat dignified and erect on the edge of the chair I offered her. As always, she was impeccably dressed in a beautifully tailored blue wool suit with a pillbox hat. Her ebony face was unlined, much younger than her seventy-two years. She did not return my smile.

"Your young lady said I do not have an appointment."

"That's right, Mrs. Phillips."

"I've forgotten more than they'll ever learn, but that doesn't mean that there isn't plenty I still know."

"That's true, Mrs. Phillips."

It was hard watching her agile mind slowly deteriorate. She was still a board member of several prominent organizations in the city, but only because they hoped she would recognize her diminished abilities and fade away without their having to request her resignation.

"I want it back."

I waited, unsure of our subject.

"My daughter says you're the one responsible," she said. "You took my driver's license from me. How can I get to my board meetings? You have taken away my access to my work when there is so much yet to be done. How could you?"

"I understand your frustration—not being able to drive in Detroit is a serious hardship. But, I explained before, Mrs. Phillips, the secretary of state's office took your license away because it's not safe for you to drive. I agree with them. I've been frightened for you each time you've had trouble. Much as I want you to keep your independence, you have to start using other people for your transportation."

"I've driven for more than forty years and never had so much as a ticket."

"Two months ago, you stopped in the middle of an intersection. Again."

"That man struck my car, you know."

"Yes, after you stopped. The light was green. You weren't making a turn. You just stopped."

"A little common courtesy and patience and it never would have happened."

"I'm sure you're right, but someone could have been badly hurt. And last month you were a bit confused and drove almost to Cincinnati."

"I hardly think I went that far. My daughters exaggerate at times. When I've got so much business on my mind, I can be absentminded about where I'm going. You know I've forgotten more things than most people ever learned."

I sighed. "How did you get here today?"

"I flagged down a car on Boston Boulevard and asked if they'd be so kind as to bring me over here."

"Did you know these people?"

"No, but I'm a good judge of character. I've worked with every kind in the union, from the man on the line to the top brass, since before your time. I choose carefully."

"You know you wouldn't want someone you love to take a chance like that. Please promise me you won't hitchhike again."

"Then give me back my car."

Dear God, if I could give her back something, it would be her memory. But once again I explained the dangers in continuing to drive. I concluded with "I'll speak with your daughter about helping you arrange transportation."

"It's not the same, you know," she said. "You don't know what it's like to have other people run your life."

"It must be very hard, Mrs. Phillips." I prayed I'd never have to know how hard. I took her hands in mine and willed her attention: "It is not safe for you to drive. Trust me on this. I'm on my way to the hospital. Come, let me drive you home."

My log says the day ended neatly at seven with a last-minute consultation on an elderly woman with dehydration and a dangerously high sodium level. After advising my interns on her care that night and promising a talk on hypernatremia tomorrow, I walked rapidly down the hall till I was around the corner and out of sight. Safe from view, I tapdanced out the double doors and headed home.

3

Twist of Lemon

*Life is what happens while you're
making other plans.*
JOHN LENNON
⊼

When I arrived home, Marcia was already there, sitting at the
kitchen counter sipping a Diet Coke and sorting the huge stack of
mail we received every day. Medical journals, professional literature, bills,
business mail, and personal correspondence were laid out on the counter
in "yours," "mine," and "discard-without-opening" piles. Marcia's stack of
personal mail was usually higher than mine. Although she, as I, telephoned
her family frequently, she also communicated through long letters with a
half dozen old friends in widely scattered places. One pen pal was my
grandmother, TuTu, who loved Marcia as one of her own.

Marcia wrote for the most part very late at night at a huge desk in the
basement made out of a door balanced on two file cabinets. It was big
enough to hold an old electric typewriter, stacks of "I'll do it later" work,
lines of reference books, and jars of colored pens used for doodling during
protracted phone sessions with patients. It was a threadbare but cozy retreat that suited her, and it was a mini-playground for our three cats, who
shared her nocturnal life.

It worked out fine for me. I used the bright, carpeted former bedroom
on the first floor for my office, though it had a second desk in the corner
for Marcia's Nintendo game.

"Here's your mail," Marcia said with the satisfied voice of one who had
been able to dispose of a chunk of her own into the trash. "I've got a great
idea. How about a short bike ride after dinner?"

"Well, I'd love to . . ."

"But, what?"

"I was going to work on my lecture tonight."

"It's always something. You missed dinner yesterday and a great party Friday night." She waved aside my beginning protest. "I know, I know, you had a good excuse, and I don't doubt you made a difference being there, especially Friday with Jenny. But there will always be someone who needs attention day and night. I'm just saying it doesn't always have to be you who gives it."

She was right. I had vowed to take time off.

She echoed my thoughts. "In May, you said you wanted to play more this summer. I'm just pointing out that it's July and you haven't started yet."

I mentally scanned the next eight weeks. "There isn't anything I want to give up. Too bad we waste so much time in sleep."

"The only person I know who can pack more into a day than you is your mother, and I think she lives a second life when others sleep."

"I have a great idea," I said. "Let's go for a bike ride after we eat."

She laughed. "Good. We'll come back early so you can hit the books." She was referring to my nightly study session for my internal medicine board exams. They were scheduled for early September and I was systematically working my way through the medical subsections.

I ran upstairs to my room and quickly washed my face and hands and changed into shorts, T-shirt, and track shoes.

Meals were my domain, one I loved. Although Marcia would willingly wash dishes and shop for the groceries, cooking was a chore she performed only if she was faint from hunger and no one else could possibly do it. She couldn't imagine having a culinary urge. Labeling herself "a creative eater" was the closest she came to the art of gastronomy.

Supper tonight was a make-do of leftovers. The best part was the crisp Rome apples given to me by a grateful patient. So we could be home before dusk, Marcia rinsed and stacked the dishes while I got the bicycles from the garage.

Our house was in an old residential suburb of Detroit known as Grosse Pointe Farms. It was a beautiful and favorite place to bicycle, especially if we rode along Lake Shore Drive and watched the freighters moving through Lake St. Clair bound for Chicago, Detroit, Duluth, Cleveland, or any of a dozen other ports ringing the Great Lakes.

This evening, because we were both on call, we stayed closer to home, devoutly hoping our beepers would not call us back and remind us our time was not our own.

Our part of the "Farms" was away from the water and wealth that translated into manors and mansions. Even so, our streets were beautiful, the homes well kept, and the gardens neatly tended. The houses for the most part were built in the thirties and forties and were a mix of styles—modest brick bungalows, colonials, Cape Cods, and Tudors lived side by side on tree-lined streets. Summer flowers were everywhere, bunched around trees and edging evergreen shrubs, but the scent we caught most often was that of newly mown grass. It was a restful contrast to the hospital's frenetic pace and fluorescent lights.

We didn't feel like talking. This wasn't the time to talk about a patient of mine who'd died that morning or to hear whatever grim story Marcia might produce from her day. This was Eden and speech would have interfered.

We were on Chalfonte, a pretty side street that leads to our house. Marcia was in the lead, half a bike length ahead and to my right, hugging the curb. Up ahead, we saw an old Chevy round the corner and come toward us. His turn was too wide, putting him on the wrong side of the street and directly in our path.

He reached us in seconds. Marcia threw herself to the right, over the curb and onto the grassy tree bank. The grille of his car struck my bike full force, catapulting me over its roof and into the air.

Marcia says she will never forget that night. I will never remember it.

4

Monday Night

*I like living. I have sometimes been wildly,
despairingly, acutely miserable, racked with
sorrow, but through it all I still know quite
certainly that just to be alive is a grand thing.*
AGATHA CHRISTIE
⊼

I opened my eyes and saw my friend Maggie sitting by my bed. Only it couldn't be my bed. The wall behind her was a white canvas curtain. Her face was almost level with mine and framed by silver bars. And there was that faint familiar smell of . . . what?

"Hospital?" I said. The one word was an effort.

"Yes," she said. "A hospital."

"Oh," I said and drifted off to sleep.

When I opened my eyes, I was looking directly into Marcia's anxious ones about fifteen inches away. "Hi," I said.

"Hi, yourself."

Looking slightly to my left and just beyond her, I could see white shoes and legs sheathed in surgical scrubs moving beneath a drawn white curtain. Everything looked familiar but the perspective was wrong. This was a hospital but I was *in* the bed. A hospital bed. Dear God, did I fall asleep in an empty room? Overworked doctors do that sometimes.

"Why are you here?" I asked her. "Why am I here? This is a patient's bed."

"Yup, and you're the patient. You were in an accident. Do you remember that?"

"This is an IV."

"You're in the ER."

"What happened?"

"You were in an accident. We were riding our bikes. Right after work. Remember?"

"No, tell me. Please."

"We went out bicycling after dinner. When this kid drove right at us, I was barely able to jump over the curb." Her voice was steady and her face impassive. "I heard the crash when he hit you and, um . . . a thud when you hit the pavement . . ."

"My head?"

"Uh . . . Anyway you were lying there behind his car . . ."

She told me the details, but I took in nothing of what she said—not then or any of the next half dozen times I asked her. Over time, I learned the story.

Marcia had scrambled to my side in seconds. I lay sprawled and disjointed, "like a rag doll," she said. She spoke my name repeatedly, aware that I was unconscious. My pulse, she found, was irregular and thready, my breathing shallow. "But," she said, "at least you were breathing."

"Call 911," she yelled to the driver who'd hit me. "Keep breathing," she irrationally implored my unconscious body. When the driver returned, she leapt to her feet. "What in God's name have you done?" She grabbed him by the shoulders and shoved him backward. "Keep away from her."

Marcia had spent hundreds of hours trying to save lives in hospital emergencies. A gratifying part of such experience is gaining the knowledge with which to act—the know-how to stop bleeding, electrically restart a heart, provide essential drug therapy. She wanted to do something, anything but kneel helplessly, watching, praying, impotent to effect any change, knowing there was nothing she could do for my brain.

A neighbor, Dale, and his young son, Daniel, ran across the street to our aid. Daniel took off his shirt and placed it under my head. Dale held my hand between both of his and silently prayed. Marcia raged inwardly and willed me to live. The ambulance wait was an eternity.

Dale told Marcia that he was a policeman. He said that for several minutes prior to the accident, he and Daniel had been talking together on their front lawn and had casually noted us on our bikes when we were almost abreast of his house. It was Daniel who actually saw the grille of the car smash into my bike and boot me into the air like a ball. They both saw me catapult over the top of the car and land on my head.

"She moved," someone said. Marcia said nothing. I had brought my arms rigidly up to my chest in a reflexive posturing of the body typical of injury to the brain stem. The involuntary gesture was usually a sign of serious damage. It was never one of hope.

My tongue extended outside my mouth and I was repetitively biting it. Marcia moistened my dried-out tongue with her own saliva and pushed it away from my teeth.

"You are going to be all right," she said over and over into my unconscious ear throughout the ambulance ride. "I'm right here and you're going to be fine."

Seconds after the ambulance pulled under the porte cochere on the renovated side of St. John's Hospital, the attendants wheeled my stretcher over the cement walk and through the glass-walled entrance.

"In here," the triage nurse directed the attendants while barring Marcia's way. "Who are you?" the nurse asked.

"A friend."

"Then go through those doors to Admitting and give them all the information you can. Then, if you sit in the waiting room, we'll call you."

"The waiting room?" Marcia was in Alice's looking glass, without credentials in a foreign land, powerless to act at a time when she had a desperate need to be involved.

The waiting area was the typical nine-at-night mess. Two dozen chrome chairs minimally padded in black leatherette were in ragged rows, back to back like in a shoe store. Tattered, opened magazines of indeterminate age spilled across tables littered with half-empty paper cups. One next to the THANK YOU FOR NOT SMOKING sign contained several cigarette butts. Harsh fluorescent lights emphasized the tatty, slightly dirty industrial carpeting.

Marcia sat down next to a mother whose arm was around a thin little boy whose extended leg was supported by an empty facing chair. An ice pack rested on his swollen ankle. On the other side, a young couple flanked an elderly man, their faces somber, their silence underscored by mindless supermarket music from a wall speaker, a crying baby, and an old lady with spasmodic coughing. The few who talked did so in hushed voices.

After fifteen minutes of fidgeting while the room filled to capacity, thinned out a little, then filled again, Marcia went over to the high desk in the corner guarding the double doors leading into the Emergency Room.

"Excuse me, I'm Dr. Baker." she said. "May I go in there and check on Claudia Osborn?"

"Are you her doctor?"

"No, I'm a friend."

"I'm sorry, doctor, but you'll have to take a seat in the waiting room."

She turned away, exasperated at herself for failing to give the magic password for admission. As she returned to her seat, one of the two beepers on her belt sounded. My beeper. She remembered removing it from my belt and putting it on her own when we were in the ambulance. She now read the number and went to the pay phone hanging on the wall and returned the call.

"Hello, this is Dr. Baker answering for Dr. Osborn."

"Hi, this is Jack Sinclair, a night intern. Dr. Osborn wanted to be notified when Mrs. Randall's hemoglobin dropped below seven grams. It's six point eight so we're going to start her blood transfusion."

"I'll let her know," she answered, wanting nothing more than the ability to walk up to my bedside, wake me from my coma, and tell me about a real patient.

Marcia then called Stephen Miller, my associate, to ask him to take my calls. Because she didn't work in the same hospital system as I, she couldn't take responsibility for my cases even if she had had the emotional energy to care for my patients in addition to her own that night.

Her next call was to our close friend Maggie, an internist who lived in the neighborhood.

"Maggie, I need you to act as Claudia's doctor."

"I *am* her doctor."

"I know, but that's not why I called. I don't need you to treat her, just to get me into her room. She's in St. John's, and after I said I was just her friend, they won't let me in. Will you come over? Now?"

With Maggie as the passport, Marcia gained access to my bedside.

"Hi, Claudia."

"Why am I in a hospital?"

"You were in an accident. A car hit you when we were biking. Dr. Wallace, here, is the ER resident. He's been taking care of you."

"Hello, Dr. Osborn. Do you remember we spoke earlier?"

"No."

"I'll leave your head injury for the neurosurgeon but everything else seems pretty good. Your right shoulder is sprained and may have a tear in the rotator cuff, but there's no fracture. There's quite a lot of external swelling behind your right ear and you're developing a cauliflower ear that, best I can tell now, would do justice to a heavyweight fighter. The road rash—the abrasions on your ear and shoulder from the pavement—look pretty grim now but they're superficial. We can tell more when we take your neck brace off. Right now, we can't even clean you."

"Okay," I said and was gone again.

When I roused, Marcia was resting her head on the side rail.

"I have an IV," I said for my benefit, not Marcia's.

"Yes, you have an IV. You were in an accident. You're in St. John's ER. We've been waiting for you to wake up."

"I'm awake. Let's go home."

"Do you know where you are?"

"I have an IV?"

"Yes, you're in the hospital. This is Dr. Simjin; he's a neurosurgeon."

I turned my eyes toward his face and watched him talk.

" . . . CAT scan doesn't show a bleed," he was saying. "It's too early to see swelling. From what Dr. Baker says about your reflexive movement right after your head struck the pavement, you could have had a seizure. It sounds more like decorticate posturing. Since that's often a sign which accompanies significant brain-stem injury, I'm sure glad you woke up. We know, at the least, you have a concussion, so obviously you need observation. I'm going to arrange for your admittance to the hospital."

"Why? I live with a doctor." I'd had concussions before. This was not a problem.

"I'd be more comfortable with you in the hospital."

"I'll come back if I need to."

"You're safer here."

"I'm a doctor."

"I'm not going to argue with you, but I will remind you that you may be sleeping a lot, and I expect to hear from you if you have a seizure or any other problem. Your headache isn't going to get better for some time, maybe days . . ."

He continued his instructions, speaking slowly and clearly, but it was impossible for me to register any meaning. I tried to focus, but even as I registered the meaning of each word, the import of the sentence as a whole disappeared. I stopped listening. All that mattered was I was going home. I would certainly know, wouldn't I, if anything major was wrong.

Doctors as patients often get their own way, a situation that often leads to less than the best treatment. I was discharged.

When we arrived home, pink and yellow streaks glowed in the eastern sky. First light, a favorite time of day for me. Marcia picked up the *New York Times* and the *Detroit Free Press* from the porch and unlocked the front door.

We had no bathroom on our second floor, and she worried aloud that I wouldn't be able to manage the stairs in my groggy condition, especially at night. Over my insistence that I go to my own bed, she had me wait in the dining room while she solved the problem. I slept at the table, my head cradled on my arms, while she wrestled a futon into the room and made it up into a bed. She helped me undress and get between the sheets, and set an alarm so she could do neuro checks hourly. Then she telephoned my parents.

"Last night was a nightmare," she told my mother. "I can tell you I was terrified about brain damage, but she woke up. She seems fine, just fine."

5

Not Adding Up the Score

If it walks like a duck and quacks like a duck,
it ain't Bambi.

A POLITICAL CAMPAIGN DOCTOR

⊼

Throughout the first two weeks following my injury, I slept, usually about twenty-two hours out of every twenty-four. I could be roused without difficulty but I could not stay awake, not even to finish a meal. Although Marcia's plan had been for me to sleep in the dining room for only a few days, I was still there.

Marcia's clinic office was twenty minutes away, which allowed her to come home midday to prepare lunch and check on me.

"Claudia," Marcia prodded from the kitchen doorway. "I want you to finish your sandwich before I go back to work."

"I'm just going to lie down for a minute." Only a minute. I had to practice staying awake so I could go back to work.

"That's what you said this morning, but your cereal's still here from breakfast."

My friend Mary, a doctor who specialized in sports medicine and osteo-pathic manipulation, often stopped by on her own lunch hour. She used cranial osteopathy, so useful after trauma to free restricted motion of bones and other tissues, to treat my head. One side benefit of her work was that she made my headache disappear. She also treated my right shoulder injury, but I still wasn't making use of that arm.

"Claudia," Mary said one afternoon, "I don't think you're doing your shoulder exercises."

"She's not," Marcia said. "Till the last couple days, she's slept most of the time and the little she is awake, she uses her left hand."

"Marcia, I'm right-handed. I use my right hand."

Marcia nodded. "You should know. Have some chips and salsa while I heat up the carry-out."

I dipped my tortilla into the salsa with my left hand.

Marcia tapped my arm. "A case in point."

"I'm tired," I said.

"I see that, but ordinarily we'd have to tie you down to keep you from overexercising an injury. It isn't like you to ignore this. Mary and I think it's time you see a neurologist to make sure you're progressing all right."

"Yes, I'm all right."

Marcia made an appointment anyway. When I insisted I didn't need her as an interpreter, she arranged for taxi transportation and I went alone. The entire episode—from my shower until my return home—took over three hours, the longest period I had been awake since the accident. When I got home, I was exhausted.

"What did the neurologist say?" she asked, awakening me at her lunch hour.

I couldn't recall a thing.

"Did you tell him you aren't doing or saying much of anything?" she said.

"Oh, yeah. I told him I'm very tired."

"How about your memory?"

"What memory?"

"Exactly. Did you tell him you are having problems with your memory?"

"My memory's fine. I'm just too tired to pay attention."

Eventually, Marcia called the neurologist. He told her I was experiencing a postconcussive syndrome and was having several problems, but he felt they were most likely transitory. To Marcia's surprise, he agreed with my assessment of my ability to return to work. I could go back to my job as long as I didn't overdo. I should do only what I was capable of doing. My problems, he felt, would resolve with time.

Marcia was less confident. That evening, she tried to explain her concern by talking to me doctor to doctor.

"Do you remember one of your favorite teaching stories?" she said. "The one about the injured bowler?"

"Yeah, sure. It's a funny story."

She was referring to a case from a Morning Report session which Sam, a medical student working in the Urgent Care Center, presented.

"Yesterday," Sam said from the podium, "this forty-five-year-old white woman came in. Her chief complaint was 'My bowling game is way off. I thought I should see someone.'" Over the laughter, he added, "Honest, that's just what she said."

He went on to say her left arm was limp and she was dragging her left leg, but when asked, she said they were fine. "I figured her left side was dysfunctional from an old stroke because she insisted those limbs weren't bothering her. She just rambled on about her game and her low scores. I don't know anything about bowling so I thought, at first, we should just send her home."

Then the intern got a thorough history from the husband and learned she had struck her head on a bathtub three weeks earlier, which is when her left-sided paralysis began. A CAT scan revealed a large blood clot compressing her brain and causing her dysfunction.

But the point of the lesson was to understand both her lack of concern and her lack of awareness about the functional loss of two limbs. It's a common situation in brain injury.

"When someone's injury causes them to ignore a side of their body," I told my students, "it is termed inattention and neglect. Since it's the brain which communicates and interprets our mental and physical functioning, we shouldn't be surprised that the brain-injured patient may be oblivious to changes in function and unconcerned by the few problems they do notice. Moreover, such a patient is almost incapable of giving a history or assisting in her own diagnosis. Why? Because when the brain is injured, there is no objective mechanism to understand what's been lost.

"After the clot pressing on her brain was removed, Sam's patient's paralysis and left-sided neglect cleared up. It did wonders for her bowling game and that will be what she remembers and thanks her doctor for."

Now I listened to Marcia reminding me of this.

"So?" I said when she was done. "I don't have those problems."

Marcia just looked at me.

A few minutes later, Marcia followed me into the bathroom, where I was turning in circles trying to recall what I'd come in for. She handed me my toothbrush. "How are you going to practice medicine when you can't brush your teeth without guidance?"

"I don't need guidance," I said as I layered the toothbrush with hand lotion from the pump bottle by the sink. "I know medicine."

The following evening my mother called just as Marcia and I were finishing dinner. She spoke at some length. I didn't keep up.

The previous year, she and my stepfather, Richard, had decided to change their lifestyle. They now spent winter in Naples, Florida, and summer in Northern Michigan, where they'd built a beautiful house on the shores of the Leelanau Peninsula. A heart attack prompted Richard to retire from his job as a development director. My mother's resignation from her job was a commitment to stop working twelve-hour days, six days a week, as the head of a large television station. The biggest change in her life was her new ability to take time for her family and to entertain a stream of houseguests. My mother has always lived in overdrive and even her newly slowed pace was warp speed.

"Claudia?" Her voice grabbed my attention. "Is that a yes or a no?"

Even if I'd known the subject of the question, I couldn't have chosen an answer. "Marcia would know," I said and carried the phone into the dining room to Marcia.

"I know, Jeanne," Marcia said. "I'm troubled too. It has been three weeks. . . . Well, as I told you last night, we're going along right now with what the neurologist said yesterday. Meanwhile, I'm living with a stranger. Tonight, when I told her to microwave the frozen dinners, she put them in a cold oven and set the timer on the microwave. And she's still not using her right hand. . . . No, you're lucky to have caught her awake. She's still out of it nearly all the time. Without question, she needs more convalescence."

❧ My mother called often, although it was of limited value to either of us. Even though I was awake more frequently, I couldn't connect with others for long. It didn't make for meaningful conversation.

"I'm soaked," Marcia said one Saturday morning. "Look at me, this wet, just from going out to get the papers."

"It's a good paper," I agreed pleasantly, stroking Anon, the youngest of our three elderly cats.

Marcia pulled a hand towel from the drawer and mopped her hair. She nodded toward the receiver lying on the kitchen counter. "Are you on the phone with someone, Claudia?"

"Oh, right, it's Mama. She wants to talk to you."

Marcia snatched up the receiver. "Sorry, Jeanne, I didn't know you were on the phone. . . . Yeah, I know, she doesn't take in much of what I say either. I'm learning if there's something I want her to know, I have to convey it in two- or three-word sentences. If I say more, her eyes lose focus and she drifts off. . . . I don't know if she doesn't try or simply can't follow conversation. She latches on to a few words and assumes it's the point. . . . She's still preoccupied with her need to get back to work. It is the only thing she talks about. . . . I know she's not ready. . . . I'll try, but I'm her friend, not her doctor, Jeanne. I can direct her to some degree, but I can't make someone who thinks she's superwoman stay home anymore than you can."

A week later I announced to Marcia, "I'm going to work today. At the clinic."

Marcia sighed and put down the morning newspaper. "You tried that two days ago. It didn't go well, remember?"

"I'll take a cab."

"Claudia, you took a cab. Driving is only one problem. You had to come back almost immediately. You were confused. You didn't accomplish anything. Relax. You're covered at the hospital, and the clinic can get along without you awhile longer."

"I was tired, I think."

What had gone wrong last time? I didn't see any patients, only discussed them with my residents. Maybe there hadn't been a problem.

I had Marcia call me a cab.

My small office at the clinic was warm. I took off my jacket and sat at my desk trying to decide what it was I wanted to do.

Mail was stacked in high piles at one end. I opened the top piece and read it, then put it down, not knowing what it said. I tried again. Nothing. I opened another letter with no better results. Every word was clear at the moment I read it, but the meaning of the sentences disappeared while I was reading the words.

I tried to do it out loud, sounding out the words, "The . . . lab . . . results . . . on . . ." and it was lost.

Try it again. "The lab." Got it. "Results." Results was clear, but of what? X ray? "The lab." What about the lab?

It was no better with my residents. I could call up medical knowledge with no difficulty, but I couldn't stay focused on their presentations. Because I lost track of the conversation, I couldn't respond in a meaningful way. Instead, I answered their questions or comments with "Sounds good" or "Interesting case." I faked understanding because I couldn't believe I didn't understand. I knew I must know, so I acted as though I did.

Even when I was aware of my immediate confusion and exhaustion I couldn't grasp that these were recurring problems. Each incident was a fresh dilemma. I didn't grasp that I couldn't follow conversations, I only understood that *this* conversation was a difficulty. I could make the same error six times over and see each instance as a first occurrence. Such insight as I could dredge up was fleeting. Just as it took shape and I almost clutched its meaning, it disappeared through the holes in my thinking.

My family perceived my problems more clearly than I did, but they attributed them to my need for additional convalescence. On the evening of my visit to my clinic, my mother answered my vague worry that the day hadn't gone well with "Give it time, darling. It's only a month."

But she said to Marcia, "Doesn't she see she's not herself?"

"I don't think so. If she did, she'd be horrified that she is a doctor who can no longer read a newspaper or do simple multiplication. Look at her language skills—when she speaks, that is. Mostly she doesn't. One good thing about having tried going to work is that she's discovered she's not ready to return and she's agreed to wait a little longer before trying again."

"Good," my mother said. "I'm sure she'll be fine. She just needs enough time to heal."

~ We were all busy weaving a net of delusion. As commonly happens, be it with head injury, Alzheimer's disease, stroke, or mental illness, Marcia and my family were becoming accustomed to my dysfunction. With loving tolerance, they began supporting my failures with their crutches.

"Remember, just concentrate on doing what's on the note and don't try to accomplish anything else today," Marcia said a week or so after my second unsuccessful attempt to go to the clinic. Nothing had changed since then except I had resumed driving.

"I can do a lot more than these two things," I said.

Marcia gulped the last of her coffee on her way out the door. "Trust me, Claudia, start with these two. I really need you to pick up this text at the medical bookstore, and our lawn is not going to survive in this heat if you don't water it."

I was sure I belonged at work, but I was pacified by my mother's rationale that there were plenty of long-neglected jobs I could tackle in the house now that I had all this time. I was not able to sort out what, how, or when to do these tasks, but I had no doubt I could do them.

Marcia refrained from adding that, despite her daily reminder, I had failed to water the lawn even once all week. All she said was "Please. Just follow the note and please drive carefully."

"I got it," I said. "No problem."

I left soon after for the bookstore, but with the force of old habit and despite Marcia's written reminder dangling from the dash, I drove directly to the hospital. And then home again. Three times.

It was noon when I drove out of the hospital parking lot for the third time. I was determined it wouldn't happen again.

Now, as I turned onto the main road, Marcia's note clutched in my hand, I chanted, "Bookstore, go to the bookstore."

I was still saying it thirty minutes later as I turned into our driveway. When I got into the house, I reread Marcia's note. Lord, the bookstore.

Well, I would definitely get the book tomorrow. Right now, I could still do the second item on her list—water the lawn.

I love working in my garden, and a directive to go outside to do so was like sending a child to a candy store. Actually, that was part of the problem. Each time I read the note, I went out into the yard. Each time I did, I forgot why I was there but found plenty of small distractions to keep me occupied—pulling a weed from the begonias, plucking a dead rose, watching Punkin, our black and white cat, climb the plum tree, or walking aimlessly through the garden. On my last trip, I sat down for a moment in a chair on the shaded patio and went to sleep.

That night, Marcia and I watered the lawn together.

Despite these problems, my determination to return to work persisted. And, in the end, I once again got my way.

"Good grief," my mother said to Marcia, "I don't understand how Claudia can be working at the hospital when she sounds so disconnected on the phone. How is she managing to get through the day? I can't believe she's lasted four days."

"Well, she's exhausted but we both know that's not the problem."

"What do you suppose her patients think? Or her house staff?"

"She only sees an occasional patient and never alone. And the house staff are loyal and supportive. They like her. They're being supervised by Claudia's colleagues, so she's covered. But your concerns are valid, Jeanne. I don't know what's going on with her. I only know she needs to see another neurologist. Soon. She's just not getting better."

6

Who Is This in Here with Me?

I have had just about all I can take of myself.
S. N. BEHRMAN
✦

At eight A.M., the long hospital corridors were a frenetic ballet of activity and color. Figures in white and pink and green walked purposefully, lounged on desks with phones to ear, leaned against counters engaged in conversation, pushed carts piled high with trays of food or supplies or linens, or threaded their way between obstacles while wheeling gurneys, pushing chairs, or toting baskets or trays filled with red, blue, and green vials. One's nose was assaulted with odors and scents that pleased or offended depending on what they were and one's previous experiences. The whole was accompanied by a low-pitched cacophony of clanking metal, squeaky wheels, suppressed laughter, loud instructions, and whispered words.

It was so hard to concentrate even in the quiet of my own living room that I had forgotten what real distraction was.

It was two months since my injury and my second week back at the hospital. My house staff had changed, which meant three new names to learn. With my new group flanking me, we leaned over the Formica-topped counter dominated by Ms. Bromley, the punctilious charge nurse. I stared at the top of her russet-gray head, waiting for her to hang up the phone and turn to the notes concerning my patients.

I tried to concentrate on what it was I needed to know, to shut out the commotion around me and avoid catching the eyes of passing staffers.

An older man I didn't recognize clapped me on the back. "Been on holiday, doctor?"

"Uhm, sort of."

I turned from this man I couldn't place into a barrage of words being leveled at me by Bromley. Each time she looked down at her charts, she had to use the forefinger of one hand to hold her glasses to her nose. The pencil in her other hand tracked her notes. She rat-a-tat-tatted away, determined to say her piece before she was interrupted. Which she was again. And again.

I nodded a lot. I hoped I looked interested even though I was less transfixed by her monotone than by the flashing HOLD buttons on the telephone near her hand. I tried to recall if one or two of those blinking lights were for me. If so, who were they? I heard my beeper sound and reached absently into my coat pocket and shut it off. Lord, another one. Is that two? Three calls?

When I began to walk away from her station, Ms. Bromley startled me with "So, are you stopping her aminophylline, doctor?"

"What's the problem?" I asked.

"I just told you her IV came out and—"

"We were just going to make rounds on that patient," my resident intervened. "Right, Claudia?"

I looked at him. What is his name anyway? I tried unobtrusively to read it on his white coat. I missed Jeff.

"We'll give you an answer, Ms. Bromley, before we leave the floor," he said.

The overhead page blared my name and a medical student leapt to answer it. "Is he on our service?" I asked my resident.

"Yeah, that's Mark Williams. You met him Monday. You said you were going to quiz him today on asthma drugs. He's ready."

"Great." I smiled weakly. I had to learn to keep my mouth shut.

A passing woman paused long enough to ask with a chilly smile, "Did you forget your lecture yesterday, Claudia? Again?"

I apologized while desperately trying to recall what it was I had promised to do and whom I had made the promise to. When the woman was gone, I made a note and crammed it into my pocket with the dozen other notes.

My entourage and I started down the hall. It was hard here to tell which of us was the leader. A passing administrator stopped me with a touch on my arm. "Missed you at the meeting this morning, doctor."

I didn't know which meeting I had forgotten, but I didn't want him to think I treated any of the committees I sat on lightly so I vaguely indicated an emergency. And maybe there had been one. I had no idea what I'd done early that morning.

I tried to refer to the dozens of notes stuffing my pocket—I didn't know when I'd lost my notebook—but they said things like *9:00!!, Be there!!, Get file,* or *Room 512, Dr. Smith needs info, Ask John.* All were equally cryptic. Orders without details, details without purpose. I did not know what might be important, so I put the confused, crumpled mess back in my pocket and hoped their meanings would become clear later.

"Let's start at the top and work down," I said to my house staff.

"We're at the top," my resident said. "You only have two patients. Come back down the hall this way."

The new medical student gestured to the right. "Ah ... doctor, I think you want this room."

"Sure," I said. "Who's room is this?"

"Mrs. Brown," the student said. "You admitted her on Monday."

"What is her chief problem and where is her chart?" I asked.

"This is the asthmatic Ms. Bromley was asking about," my intern said. "You have the chart in your hand."

"Of course." I opened the chart. It didn't look familiar and none of the notations or orders were in my handwriting. "Let's just go in and see the patient."

This was the stuff of an attending doctor's nightmare. Too many things that needed doing at the same time, too much information coming at me too quickly, all the presentations unclear, disjointed—I was overwhelmed by this maelstrom of constant noise, rushing people, jarring interruptions, urgent questions, flashing lights, incomprehensible charts, and sheaves of paper.

I made a Herculean effort to concentrate on all the competing voices and perform as doctor-teacher. I admonished myself for not staying more alert and attentive, without knowing just how to do that. But I must not be trying very hard. Why else would I appear to be stumbling? Just when I thought I was doing fine, others would indicate I was off target.

It was as if I was cast in a play without ever having read the script. Sometimes my ad-libbing brought applause, other times gasps and boos. I knew I was out of step. I didn't know why.

I appeased myself, if not the situation, with platitudes: "Sounds good." "By all means." "Call in a consulting doctor." "Write that up." "Set up a meeting." Do it, sweetheart, whatever it takes.

The rules had changed and everyone but I was privy to key information. I alternated between moments of anger and despair because I could not will myself to improve; then I quickly forgot both emotions until the next mishap, when I would relive the emotional cycle.

Reality broke through when my intern hung up the phone and turned toward me. "Good news. Mrs. Owen made it through surgery."

"Great," I said. "Who is she?"

"She's the elderly woman who needed her leg amputated. You supervised my placement of her subclavian catheter this morning. I missed going down to read the X ray with you, but I want you to know I dutifully followed your procedures and personally checked the X ray with Dr. Maikowski."

"Good, that's good." I forced myself to stop nodding. "Excuse me now." My words commanded his hasty retreat.

I moved to a deserted desk in the back corner of the nurses' station and sat down, my heart racing, my hands in a sweat. I fingered a patient chart lying on the desk, wondering if my vague memory of a warm, motherly woman was accurate. She needed an amputation of her gangrenous leg to survive. Surgery was risky enough and I doubt she would have made it through if her lung had collapsed. Obviously it hadn't and she was stable for now, but not because of me.

I hadn't checked her X ray. It was an error I thought I was incapable of making, an omission as unthinkable as walking out of the house naked in the morning. I quickly looked down and checked my clothing.

I had ignored my mother's pleas that I take a sabbatical from work. Marcia shook her head every day as I walked out the door. I had thought they were crazy. Now I wondered what they knew that I didn't. Was I the one who was crazy? What could possibly be this wrong with me? Maybe this was what a mental breakdown felt like.

I would know if a head injury was to blame, wouldn't I? I had to find out. I couldn't live with myself if I were to jeopardize the life of a patient, and I just had.

When I regained a semblance of control, I picked up the phone book. I couldn't sort through the alphabet or figure out the first letters of the words "Ford" or "Hospital." I enlisted the assistance of our telephone operator, a good soul, to look up the number and dial it for me.

Two rings were followed by a cheerful, "Neurology."

"This is Dr. Osborn. I must speak to Dr. Shatz. Now, please."

When I heard Rhonna Shatz's "Hello," I charged right in. "Sorry, it's not an emergency exactly, but I need an appointment as soon as you can."

"Oh? Who's the patient?"

"I . . . ah . . . I am."

We spoke briefly and she agreed to see me the next day at three. Her parting words were "Do not practice medicine again until I examine you."

I didn't protest. It isn't hard to walk away from something you love if you think you are coming right back.

7

What If I Need Them
and They Won't Take Me?

You must do the thing you think you cannot do.
ELEANOR ROOSEVELT
❈

"New York is another country altogether," I said.

Marcia and I were folding the laundry. She took two mismatched socks from my hands. "Are you trying to say you won't go?" Marcia asked.

"I don't have time for New York. I have to get back to my job."

"That's the point, remember? You can't go back to your job unless you get help. That's what your doctors say."

I sank down on the bed. "But five months! You could make carrots sprout."

"Excuse me?"

"You know. Brussels sprouts. No, I mean grow, learn. You could teach Mr. Potato Head in five months."

Marcia sat down and took my hand. "Claudia, listen to me. No one is calling you a vegetable. Let's look at this one step at a time. Dr. Shatz has said you have a moderately severe head injury. Right?"

"Right. But I can still think. I still know medicine. That's the important thing here. It's only the little pieces causing trouble."

"What do you call 'little pieces'?"

"Memory problems, according to them."

"Right," Marcia said, quoting my neuropsychological evaluation, " . . . 'severe and wide-ranging difficulties including attention/concentration problems, short-term memory impairment, visuospatial impairment, impaired motor coordination, and general organizational problems,' and . . ."

She lapsed into her *Saturday Night Live* mode. "... I haven't even gotten to the good stuff."

I said nothing. She stood and went back to the laundry basket. Marcia is nothing if not practical and direct.

"You do want help, don't you?" she said. "Do you know a better place than a rehabilitation clinic?"

"No. Yes. Yes. No. Yes. But I only need a little program. Sort of a crash course in ... you know ... memory stuff. I'm a fast learner."

"You may be dead right, but you and I don't have the expert knowledge to make that call. This Head Trauma Program is, best any of us can tell, the finest rehabilitation program offered."

I was no longer listening. Five months!

"Claudia, look at me. I understand living alone in Manhattan is a frightening idea. It will be a major dislocation, especially under these circumstances."

"I can do circumstances."

"That's true, and you have friends there—"

"Everyone's stuck doing my job."

"No one's complaining. They understand and they care about you. Everyone wants you to get well."

"If I'm gone ..."

"What?"

"If I'm gone five months, they'll replace me."

"Let's take one thing at a time. At least go get the two-week evaluation in January." Marcia did not point out that it had already been four months since my accident in July and the rehab program would not even begin until March. She knew I usually thought of my injury as if it had happened only days ago. "These rehab people can tell you if you're improving on your own, and whether there's a simpler way to get on with your life than moving to New York."

Then she clinched the argument with "You don't have to agree to five months of therapy, Claudia. You're still in charge. They'll tell you if there's an alternative to the full program. Tell them you want an opinion."

"Okay." I brightened, no longer focused on the conversation now that I had discovered something Marcia didn't know: "Your shoelace is untied."

"Thank you."

∾ Several hundred rehabilitation facilities for the head-injured exist in the United States. The one Dr. Shatz recommended is associated with the Rusk Institute of Rehabilitation Medicine at New York University.

I was told the Head Trauma Program, or HTP, as I came to know it, accepted only twelve individuals each term. The candidates for the slots were first examined by the staff to determine if they were suitable for training. Potential trainees must have progressed as far as they could on their own, or as far as their previous rehabilitation programs could take them. For some, that meant years of treatment elsewhere learning how to walk or speak clearly before they reached a functional level high enough to benefit from the program.

I made the appointment for the evaluation and went to New York in January when the director of HTP said I could come. When I told Lori, my old friend from college, she invited me to stay with her in her West Side apartment. It not only made the idea of the trip palatable, it really made it possible.

I knew the process would take two weeks. No one told me it would be so exhaustive.

"They want everything in my head," I told my mother at the end of the first day when I called her at her home in Florida, a practice I repeated daily.

"What do you mean, Claudia?"

"All the tests. There are interviews. My mind is so tired. The good part is that this search will show that I'm basically okay."

"That is true, darling. All the tests will reveal your strengths. Eat *now*, please don't forget."

I wrote *EAT* on my phone pad and underlined it. "Lori has food here."

"I'm sure. Why don't you make a simple list. It would remind you to eat and help you choose the menu."

"Why? I know what I'm going to eat." I've done it often enough. Who needed a plan to eat?

"You often forget. Tell me, what will you eat tonight?"

"I'm too tired to think."

She was silent. I tried again. "Uhm . . . twisted juice, for one thing." I'd become better with multiple-choice questions than essays.

"I've never heard of it."

"Well, it's common." I had an image of the carton with the picture of oranges. "You know, flattened oranges."

"Ah! Squeezed, not a concentrate. What else?"

"Postage . . . crumbled cereal." I added quickly, "That's not quite right. I only have the brand name right."

"Postage isn't a brand. It's Post, like Post Raisin Bran."

I rolled my eyes and said with studied patience, "Mama, I was using past tense."

"What past tense?"

"Postage...past tense for Post."

She laughed. "That would be fine. You could even have it for breakfast *if* Lori has any. Humor me. When we hang up, go to the kitchen and see what's in the refrigerator and cupboards. Write down two things. Then fix them, then eat what you fixed. Will you do that?"

I curled up on the couch and closed my eyes. "Okay, Mama."

"Then you'll go to bed. Right?"

I didn't need to write it down. I did it first.

 Richard, my stepfather, called at the end of the first week. "I was thinking of you. I'm making your favorite quiche, chèvre and tomato." He spoke over the swelling passages of *La Bohème*. Richard appreciates good food and loves to prepare it for others. When he says let's make pasta for dinner, he doesn't reach into the cupboard for a box of linguini, he gets out his pasta machine. He's a renaissance man we always associate with art, music, food; low-key and comfortable like a favorite jacket, and yin to my mother's high-energy yang.

"What's wrong, my dear?" he asked.

"Sometimes I think I'm doing well. Today, I'm not so sure."

"The important thing is to just do your best."

"Yeah, but what if I don't pass? And they don't let me go home?"

"This isn't about passing," he said. "This is about learning about you, about what kind of help you need."

True enough. In those two weeks I'd experienced brief interludes of il-lumination that spawned a growing yet vague uneasiness that what was wrong was much more serious than I had previously been able to see.

A telling moment occurred in the second week. I had completed a test earlier that day in which I was required to insert pegs into a board as quickly as I could with one hand, then with the other. In response to one of my rare probes for information on how well I performed, Dr. Laurie Freeman, the neuropsychologist testing me, said, "You know, Claudia, you've said several times that the problems with your right hand are triv-ial. However, although you are right-handed, you executed that peg test far better using your left hand. In fact, you are now actually left hand–domi-nant and far more dexterous in the use of it than of your right hand."

I had been told by Dr. Shatz and Marcia that I was neglecting my right hand in favor of my left, but until Laurie showed me the test results, I didn't know my right hand was significantly impaired. Pre-injury, that dysfunction would have horrified me. Now, like the bowler in my favorite story, I simply thought I'd play tennis with my left hand.

I was also emotionally disassociated from my right hand. It felt like an artificial appendage. I didn't like to use it. I wanted to use my own left hand even though it lacked the coordination of my former dominant right.

My discovery that I had this physical problem was more enlightening than any information I had been told thus far. Not because I now saw it as a serious problem but because I could not discount this data. This was ob-jective evidence and it held more meaning for me than any cognitive test result. I could see it—at least for brief periods when it was pointed out to me.

The two weeks of testing at HTP generated in me a curious ambiva-lence. I longed to have this staff of professionals reassure me I wasn't in-jured enough to require their high-level care. On the other hand, I became increasingly anxious that, if they did determine I could benefit from their program, they wouldn't take me. I feared falling through the cracks— needing their program but not getting one of their limited spaces.

On the last day of my evaluation, I was told the bittersweet news: I did need their help. And they would take me.

My relief in being accepted lasted only seconds. It was erased instantly by the naked fact that my brain was injured enough to need serious help. Sometimes, it's only when you're thrown a life jacket that you grasp the horrific truth that your ship is sinking. The pain threw me off guard. Grief drowned any feelings of gratitude I had. I hope I remembered to say thank you.

None of the arrangements was palatable. Every aspect of the plan was problematic—months more of lost time, having to leave my home, living independent of Marcia, learning to cope in a strange place when I could not manage in the place where I had lived all my life.

My family urged me to go. State Farm said they would pay for it. All that remained was for me to accept the situation with grace.

Five months sounded like forever.

Ultimately, it wasn't that hard to say yes after my neuropsychologist sketched out my alternatives: What would I rather do? she asked. Stay home and stay disabled? Or pursue my only hope of returning to normal life and to medicine?

There was a twisted humor to the plan. Rehabilitation at HTP is designed to provide elementary education in living, yet it's taught in a city where a useful prerequisite is an advanced degree in urban stress management. Learning to master my personal life in the sturm und drang of New York was like learning to ride a bicycle in the Tour de France.

I spent the day before I was to leave packing for my trip to New York. Underwear, a toothbrush, a medical textbook, and a large teddy bear sat in a row on the bed awaiting Marcia's approval. I was satisfied with my choices until she arrived home.

"This is it?" She looked around the room as if other stacks were hiding in the corners.

"You said to pack light and you'd make sure I didn't forget anything."

"Well, then, let's talk about light. That medical text must weigh ten pounds and, as I recall, you're not reading the newspaper yet."

"I've seen you pack heavy things."

"Yes, and you will again. For now, let's concentrate on bare necessities."

She obviously didn't mean "bear." There certainly wasn't room left in the suitcase for it once she included clothes and toiletries.

When Claudia woke up in the hospital, the worst nightmare of my life seemed just another small crisis. It was like a daytime television drama where it is so unbearable for the heroine to be dead that they recant and say it was only a dream. I didn't know my relief would be a brief interlude. The misery was to come.

I blame the injury, not Claudia, for the shell of a person that awoke after two weeks of round-the-clock sleeping. In the acute stages of an illness, it's easy to be a good friend—exhausting but rewarding to nurse a loved one back to health. But her health never returned and chronic care takes tenacious strength when you're also battling grief. I often feel unequal to the challenge.

The Claudia I knew was dynamic, articulate, compassionate, and funny. She had a thriving career. She was a gifted, empathic doctor with an analytical mind; a generous, loyal friend; a diplomat; a caring healer whose passion for life was inspiring. This looks like a job recommendation. It feels like an obituary.

Surely I have seen flashes of Claudia these last eight months, but, in truth, she is gone. The friend I send to New York for rehab is an enigma who has lost all. When I talk with others who are close to head-injured people, we discuss the big losses: Claudia can't be a doctor, Terry will never finish college, Brian cannot support his wife and children.

But it's the everyday losses that get to you. Claudia is a boring conversationalist. Her language is no longer fluid and she lacks ideas to discuss with me. It doesn't occur to her to ask how my day was, and she wouldn't remember what I told her anyway.

Our friendship is now a one-way street of her need. Knowing that increases the burden. I miss her support, our shared memory, and her thoughtfulness. She lacks the energy, imagination, and insight of my old friend. My time with her is lonely. I feel guilty when I'm angry and I try not to blame Claudia for problems she cannot fix, but I wish there was a fall guy to scream at. I'm not going to move out of Claudia's life, although I know she fears it when my frustration and disappointment show through. She would never abandon me.

I have hope that this Head Trauma Program can help her. If anyone can relearn cognitive skills, it will be someone of Claudia's grit and motivation. I will support her efforts to improve and be here when she comes home, but I cannot endlessly play the selfless, devoted friend. I do not believe the emotional truth of those who watch their relationship change from that of equals to one of parent-child without protest, sorrow, and rage.

I have not the patience and this process is hell.

M.E.B.

FEBRUARY 1989—EIGHT MONTHS POSTINJURY

8

March 8, 1989
NEW YORK:
I'd Rather Have a Root Canal

I was gratified to answer promptly.
I said, "I don't know."
MARK TWAIN
⊀

The New York University Head Trauma Program is hidden away in an anonymous corner of the eighth floor of the NYU School of Dentistry. It would be weeks before I could equate a dental school with rehabilitation.

My second day there, I gritted my teeth and turned the handle on the glass-frosted door that opened into a narrow corridor. Immediately to my right was a tiny waiting room crammed with about a dozen people. A man seated directly across the room was speaking animatedly, punctuating his conversation with boisterous laughter, willing the attention of the others.

"It could be worse," he said in a voice too loud for the room, "we could be here to have root canals. Instead, we're only getting our brains fixed."

The remark produced polite smiles, but it seemed enough to encourage him. I knew we had all met yesterday. I thought I remembered him as someone who seemed to find everything funny. He appeared to be no more than thirty, tall and muscular. When he saw me, he struggled to his feet, came over, and welcomed me with a courtly bow and a wink. I noticed he did not have full command of his left leg and he held his left arm rigidly flexed at waist level.

"Ah, another lovely lady has joined us," he said. "Hi, I'm Scott. I'm an Army captain and I'm head-injured."

I was taken aback by a macho-acting personality announcing his dysfunction with so much AA-meeting openness. I thought of myself as someone who needed to resolve a few vexing problems. That my difficul-

ties stemmed from a head injury was not something I acknowledged publicly and I could not imagine why anyone else would choose to do so.

A tiny, dark-haired woman seated next to the door smiled sweetly up at
me. I moved closer to her. Perhaps she sensed my discomfort, or just took
in my breathless, harried arrival.

"Are you by yourself?" she asked. "I'm Dean, Lenny's mother."

She nodded her head in the direction of an impassive, bearded young
man standing apart, or as apart as you can get when fifteen people are
crowded into a small room with ten chairs. Even with my reduced deduc-
tive powers, I had no trouble discerning which of these two needed this
program.

"I'm here by myself," I answered, acutely aware from yesterday's session
that most of the others were brought to this rehabilitation program by a
parent, spouse, or friend.

"Did you have trouble getting here today?" Dean said in a softly ac-
cented voice. "I only ask because I know it can be difficult. We're from Tennessee and it's going to take some doing to get used to this city."

"I know the city pretty well," I said, ducking the question. Her concern
for me was evident and I wanted to say more. I simply had no idea what or
how. I not only lacked the words, I could not gather my thoughts. What
would I say to make sense of the three-hour struggle to get here?

A gray-haired man next to Dean nodded to me and introduced himself
as Bernie. "I'm a patient too."

"We're not patients." A curly-haired, bespectacled teenager got to his
feet. "They call us trainees and they're not doctors. Well, they are, but they
call themselves staff or coaches and we can call them by their first name."

"Yeah, train-nee," Scott said. "Just like the Army, man. I'm a train-nee."

"So am I," said the teenager. "Trainee David."

"Trainee" suited me. I loathed the image of myself in the role of patient.
I also understood HTP's tactic. They didn't want us to think of ourselves
as patients, not only for reasons of self-esteem but to enable us to become
active participants in our rehabilitation.

Dean looked beyond me, drawing my eyes to the doorway where a slim,
elegantly dressed blonde woman stood, quietly waiting for our attention.
Although I couldn't recall her name, I remembered meeting her yesterday

and knew hers was the first office inside the entrance to the HTP suite. I thought they must have given her the office near the door because she radiated friendliness and empathy.

"Good morning. I'm a coach and my name is Ellen Zide. It's ten o'clock, and it's time to get started."

Everyone silently rose. Get started on what? I neither knew nor wondered but allowed myself to be shepherded down the hall along with the others. We filed into a large, spartanly furnished room ringed with chairs. Computer terminals on long black counters lined two walls. A video camera stood in one corner. In another, an easel was stacked with large sheets of paper. The one on top was headed "Daily Goals."

The chairs were arranged in a large, ragged circle. I seated myself in one of the only two student desks—the kind you see in high school. Well, chum, this was a school. I studied my notebook intently.

Day two, I wrote. Five months to go.

The seats filled up quickly and the room felt crowded. In fact, there were a lot of us—twelve trainees, six neuropsychologists, and five visiting family members (or significant others, as they were called), all sitting on hard wooden chairs covertly looking one another over.

My eyes roved the room. This group looked like those in any assembly. They all appeared attentive and interested. If you discounted their more formal attire, you couldn't tell the coaches from the players. At least until the players spoke.

I could feel a soft bulge in my left pocket. Good, I remembered to bring Kleenex. I reached in and pulled out a wad of white cloth. Okay, it wasn't Kleenex. I unrolled it fully, spreading it out in front of me in both hands before it registered that it was my bra.

I hurriedly crushed it together and thrust it back into my pocket, only to withdraw it twice more because its strap was caught on my watchband.

Not being generously endowed, I often went braless. It was all too easy for me to put on a blouse that required one before noticing the bra still on the dresser. I must have done that this morning, then shoved the bra into my pocket so as to not interrupt some other task.

I looked down at my blouse. Yes, I needed a bra today.

I folded my arms across my chest, trying to conceal the obvious until I could dress in the women's room. Feigning nonchalance, I glanced around to see who had observed my misplaced underwear. I needn't have worried. At this moment, I could almost be pleased that the head-injured are poor observers of the passing scene. At least I hadn't blown my nose in it.

A man several seats away on my right began to address us, his voice pitched to overcome the rattling air purifier in the corner and a shrill siren screaming its way up First Avenue toward Bellevue Hospital. He looked to be in his middle thirties, about my age, although his hair was more uniformly streaked with gray.

"I will chair this first meeting," he said. "Starting tomorrow, our orientation sessions, which is the way we will begin every day, will be led by a trainee.

"Remember, everyone must raise their hand and be recognized by the chairperson before speaking. Let's begin again today with introductions from everyone so we can each increase our familiarity with each other's names. Yesterday, we each told something about ourselves. Today, we are only going to give our name and say whether we are staff, a trainee, or an SO. A person important to you is an SO—a spouse, family member, or friend. I'll be first. I'm Len Travaglione, staff member."

I intently scrawled notes, trying to link names to speakers in an effort to make identification possible tomorrow. Or ten minutes from now. Since my injury, I had found it difficult to recognize people by face, depending instead upon their voices and mannerisms. And since I was also highly suggestible nowadays, whether or not I felt I had seen someone before had more to do with how long I looked at the person than it did with our actually having met. Heck, by the end of a subway ride, everyone in the car looked familiar to me.

I had learned to not trust such faulty identifications after I had tried outside the A&P to take two grocery bags out of the arms of an elderly woman whom I was sure I knew. I don't think she even listened to my horrified apologies after she threatened to call the police.

In the last months, I had been using a system that was . . . less than perfect. I determined whether or not I'd met someone previously by the warmth of their greeting. To me, a friendly smile and hello were evidence of acquaintance rather than of their social grace or salesmanship. I responded to these overtures with a warm "How nice to see you again," rattling more than one stranger.

On the other hand, a reserved greeting from someone I knew could just as well prompt me to respond with a formal "I'm pleased to meet you." The results were only occasionally funny and, for a woman who wished to appear polished and professional, were an awkward beginning to an encounter. I was learning to wait for more clues before assuming the existence or lack of past acquaintance.

This difficulty in identifying faces, however, had its upside. By the end of the day at HTP, I felt I had known my fellow trainees for years. It was a kindly quirk of my injury that, thrust into this foreign city of eight million strangers, I could feel my new environment to be familiar.

"My name is Richard Siller and I'm twenty-five years old and I'm, uhm, pardon me, gratefully to acknowledge the pleasure which is mine to be here and this, uhm, this is surreptitiously a factor, uhm, that is to say, we are all here together and—"

"Richard?" Len said.

"Uhm, that is, of course, to say—"

"Richard?" Len waved his hand. "You have said that I may interrupt you and help you stay focused. I appreciate your graciously allowing me to step in. Our aim right now is to reacquaint each other with our names."

"Well, I just wanted to—"

"Richard, raise your hand first."

Richard's hand shot up.

"Yes, Richard?" Len said.

"My name is Richard Siller. Good morning, everyone. I am a trainee here." Richard beamed.

"Thank you," Len said. "Next. David?"

"And I'm glad to be here," Richard said.

"Me too, man. Me too," Scott chimed in.

"Hold it, guys. This is not the waiting room. If you have a comment you must raise your hand and be called upon. Now, David?" Len said.

"I'm David Dermer. I'm eighteen and I'm a trainee. Hi, everybody," said the enthusiastic and grinning young man sitting next to me.

"Go ahead." Len motioned to me.

"Claudia Osborn, trainee."

This was easier than yesterday when we had had to give a summary about ourselves. While others spoke, I had written out what to say in my notebook so that my thoughts would be organized. When it was my turn, I said, "Claudia Osborn. Thirty-four-year-old doctor. From Detroit."

"Is there anything else you might add?" Ellen had asked. "Even one more sentence?"

"No."

I was aware something else was expected, otherwise why would she have asked? But I didn't know what to do. Surely there was more to say about my life than those six tentatively offered words.

Whenever I couldn't find answers fast enough, my thinking became more limited and inflexible. As I increased my efforts, my performance worsened. My difficulties were exacerbated by my embarrassment that those who didn't know me would think me stupid, inarticulate, or shy.

Today, just names were required. I was not the only one relieved.

"To-Tommy. Trainee," said the slender, olive-skinned man on my left wearing sunglasses with almost black lenses. According to yesterday's notes, he was in his mid-thirties and a truck driver with a wife and three kids. He'd chosen the chair closest to the door and had pushed it back from the circle, distancing himself from the group. He wore tight jeans and a T-shirt that emphasized his broad chest and muscular arms. He only needed a cigarette pack rolled up in one sleeve to complete a streetwise, cocky de-meanor that seemed at odds with the discomfort he displayed. I felt an affinity for this man of few words who looked ready to bolt from the room.

After everyone had finished introducing themselves, Ellen took the floor to describe Orientation, the first of four structured periods that made up each day.

"Each morning at ten o'clock we will meet in this room and one of you trainees will volunteer to chair Orientation. Everyone will be provided with an initial goal to work on over the next few weeks. During Orienta-tion the chairperson will call on you to state your goal for that particular day and how you intend to work on it."

Ellen made the task seem desirable and doable. She spoke in a lively, relaxed manner that should have been easy to follow, although in traveling from my ears to my brain her words all ran together.

I was not able to be an attentive listener for twenty minutes. So, although Ellen explained it crisply and simply, I absorbed only that we would state something called goals.

However, you could hardly say the presentation was wasted on me. I knew from watching Ellen that I trusted her. She conveyed her confidence that we trainees could do whatever was required of us. Conclusions such as that were of greater value to me at the moment than wading through verbiage I would later forget.

I glanced at my watch. Ten-thirty. I was exhausted, but from what? Telling them my name? I hadn't yet done anything with the day. Back at the hospital, I would be halfway through rounds by now.

I was relieved when finally, at noon, one of the coaches announced we were stopping for lunch. My hunger was outweighed by fatigue. I wanted escape from this concentrated effort of thinking.

We instinctively followed Dean and the other SOs. Tagging along behind Mom like so many ducklings, we made our way to the elevators, where we had to separate for the ride down to the fourth floor. There we reassembled and moved in a ragged bunch into the cafeteria.

The large, neon-lighted room was jammed. Groups of five and six would-be dentists, some of them in white lab coats, were crowded around tables meant for four, with plastic trays, dishes, bottles, and crumpled paper napkins in a messy array in front of them. The noise of their collective voices bounced off the hard surfaces of institutional floors and furniture. To be heard, you had to raise your voice above the din.

Four of us sat off to one side. The noise didn't matter at our table, since there were no SOs to generate discussion. Our conversation was disconnected at best—just polite, filling-in-time words till we could return to our afternoon session. That is, until almost time to leave.

"So, was everybody here in some kind of car crash like me?" David asked, the congenial, if self-appointed, host.

"I was hit by a train," said Sara, "on my way to school."

"And you lived?" David asked.

"Well, I was in a car at the time."

"Oh," David said. "Still, not many people make it out of train wrecks. What about you guys?"

"I was making a delivery in my truck," Tommy mumbled. "I got hit on the head."

"Somebody attacked you?" Sara said.

"No, it fell from the ceiling."

"What fell?" David said. "The ceiling of your truck?"

"No, no, no," Tommy said, looking frustrated. "From the ceiling where I made the delivery. It fell on my head and knocked me out."

"Okay, I get it," David said. "That's weird that can happen. So, what about you? Claudia, right?"

I nodded. "Bicycle accident. I was hit by a guy coming at me who was going the wrong way. The wrong side, I mean."

"You were hit by a bicycle?" Sara asked.

"No, by a car. I was on a bicycle."

"So, it's still a car accident." David said.

I shrugged. "It's a bike accident to me."

"What's your name again?" Sara asked. "Are you really a doctor?"

"Claudia. What's yours?"

"Sara. So what kind of doctor are you?"

"I practice internal medicine and I teach it also."

"Wow, that's great," Sara said. "Who'd you teach it to?"

"Ah, well, to students. Medical students and interns and residents. You know, young doctors."

"What kind of patients did you have?"

"Sick patients. That is, at the hospital, I take care of very sick patients. Heart attacks and, ah, stuff." I momentarily could not recall any reason for being hospitalized except heart disease.

"You don't take care of patients now, do you?"

"No."

"That's too bad. I mean, with a head injury you aren't ever going to be able to be a doctor again, right?"

"Sara," David said. "I don't think you should say that."

"Why not?" Sara said. "It's true. You can't be a doctor with a head injury. Did the coaches say you could be a doctor?"

"Not absolutely. B-but that's why I came here," I said, "to, to get my job back."

"Well, I don't know everything, but it sounds dumb to me." Sara stood up, picked up her tray of empty dishes, and left.

"I say go for it," David said. "I think you'll be great as a doctor."

I mumbled an excuse and left quickly, seeking temporary refuge in the stairwell. Two kids, neither one more than twenty, had left me unnerved. What did they know anyway about who I was and what I could still do?

Here I was still trying to make sense of why I needed to be in a rehab program and there was Sara challenging my ability to continue to do what I did best.

"I don't need this," I confided to the banister, fighting a wave of nausea. I felt a lot better at home.

The New Yorkers

Manhattan's eclectic makeup and tremendous diversity make generalizations silly, but my experience seems to consistently support two conclusions: First, New Yorkers will always give you directions when you ask, even when they don't know the answer. Second, New Yorkers are not uncaring, they are just uninvolved unless you specifically ask them to help.

I was often confused on street corners and in subway stations as to which direction I was facing or what train I was boarding. If I asked someone, I was invariably given an answer. Three strangers might give three different answers, but no one said, "I don't know." I came to believe that it is part of New York etiquette to provide an authoritative response, regardless of one's knowledge. I learned that it was best to get several opinions and use the majority's choice.

New Yorkers are capable of riding a subway train without noticing a man shaving, an old woman undressing, or someone speaking in tongues right across the aisle. They do not act surprised or get caught up in the happenings around them, preferring to mind their own business on their way to work. They will ignore you, your problems, and your oddities unless you ask them to get involved. Then they jump in.

I arrived at the elevators of the dental school building one morning with two suitcases that I needed to take up with me to the eighth floor. In the morning rush, people crowded in as soon as the car reached the lobby and the doors opened. The elevator kept filling to capacity before I could make a move. I struggled to work my way onto each one in turn until I had failed for ten minutes. With a heavy suitcase in each hand, I was easily pushed out of the way by fellow riders. In a moment of frustration I announced to the remaining stragglers who had failed with me to gain a lift on the last elevator, "I have to get these suitcases upstairs. You have to let me on."

When the next elevator arrived, rather then shoving me away, they almost carried me onto the elevator. I said, "Thank you," and for a moment everyone looked quite pleased with the results of their teamwork. Then we all assumed our elevator postures, fixing our gaze on the panel over the door, which marked our ascent by illuminating the number of each passing floor. Riding in silence.

—FROM MY NOTEBOOK, SEPTEMBER 14, 1990

9

Mopping Up a Flood

We don't see things as they are;
we see things as we are.

ANAIS NIN
✢

"Good morning, everyone," Laurie said. "We will start today, as we do every day, with Orientation."

I knew that. This rehab stuff was not that hard.

It was Thursday, March 9, our third morning together. The bewilderment of the first two days evaporated in my smugness at knowing the name of the class, never mind that *Orientation* was neatly printed on the first line of my notebook and that I didn't have a clue as to the purpose of this get-together. I knew HTP would lead me through the next five hours. Having these coaches in charge gave me a sense of relief and security. Relinquishing control was surprisingly welcome. Managing the endless details of my hours outside HTP was taking a toll.

Just minutes before, in the waiting room, I had felt hopelessly inept and baffled by my mishaps. This morning, as I got off the bus on my way here, a woman on the street began screaming at me. With her nose inches from mine, she ranted about CIA transistors beaming messages into her head and making her confused. I became confused too and stepped off the curb into traffic. Horns blared, everybody was yelling. Then somebody asked me for money and I gave him what I had in my pocket, a twenty-dollar bill. So much for getting bus change at lunch. So much for lunch. I hated borrowing, I hated asking. Maybe another trainee would have extra cash. Asking a coach or SO was not worth the condescension I feared I would see in their eyes. I had enough of my own.

It was my usual emotional seesaw. A jarring experience and I knew I would never get a grip on what was expected of me. Then I could come into Orientation and realize I knew the same thing everyone else did and I would be catapulted into kidlike euphoria. Look, Ma! No hands.

In general, I seemed to register three distinct emotional states—foggy perplexity, goofy contentment, and glassy-eyed fatigue brought on by too much of either of the first two. I drifted along unaware that I was swinging from one to the other.

By midday, my spurt of confidence was long forgotten. By then, I was literally and figuratively out to lunch. I trooped along behind Lenny, his mother, Dean, and Sharon. The sunshine of the plaza was healing after the operating-room fluorescence of the noisy cafeteria.

Lenny's mother had black, short curly hair. She was small, pretty, and unobtrusive, seeming to stay in the background but always keeping an eye on Lenny. She settled us on the sun-warmed concrete steps surrounding a large, dry hollow pierced with a few metal pipes.

"Won't this be nice when they turn the water on," she said.

I turned and looked where she was pointing.

"The fountain, I mean," she said.

I had not realized what it was.

The steps provided a pleasant perch from which to watch a stream of people flowing through the plaza: students balancing books and takeout lunches, kids playing ball, a bag lady looking over her possessions, men and women hurrying by with briefcases or grocery bags, a homeless man in layers of clothes talking to his shopping cart.

Scott checked his watch. So did I. Then Lenny and Sharon looked at theirs.

"What time is it?" Dean asked.

We all checked our watches again. Lenny said, "Twelve-forty."

"When do we need to return?" Dean asked.

Sharon smiled helpfully. "I wrote it down in my notebook."

"I expect we should leave here in about fifteen minutes," Dean said. "You're supposed to be back by one." We all nodded.

I sat contentedly, absorbed in the immediacy of seeing what people did, listening to snatches of their conversation, observing their movement. I didn't analyze or question, I merely watched. For a brief period I was age-less and timeless. No cares, fears, needs, or plans. Having one's mind on holiday is a restful, intermittent feature of head injury. I enjoyed this idyll. My thinking wasn't racing with anxiety or clouded by a futile attempt to fabricate unusable plans.

Dean touched my sleeve. "It's time to go back to rehab."

Her words were an orienting and unwelcome intrusion into my mood. *What time? What rehab?* A good coach doesn't need to be a product of the professional establishment.

We silently filed back, through the wide doors, past the inscription NYU School of Dentistry, and into the crowded halls.

With that peculiar insularity to their surroundings which city dwellers and the young possess, I doubt if one in ten of the dental students throng-ing these halls had an inkling that there was an entity in their midst which had nothing whatsoever to do with problems of the mouth. On the other hand, the ordinary confusion of a head-injured person about her sur-roundings could at times turn surreal as she ascended eight floors in ele-vators crowded with white-coated would-be dentists adorned with medical instruments, reeking of formaldehyde, clutching castings of teeth or human jaws in one hand and occasionally a sandwich in the other, chat-ting animatedly and at top volume in dentalese.

By the end of a day at HTP, nothing mattered but escape from the hard work of concentration, especially when it involved focusing on material that a part of me recognized as being pretty simple by any ordinary standard.

Community session. 2:45 P.M. Fifteen more minutes and I'd be out of here. I just needed to come up with an answer to today's question. How is it they all had something to say? Scott even tried to answer the question before the coach had finished asking it. Richard talked for five minutes. I don't think one of us had any idea what he was trying to say, but at least he was responding to the assignment.

Among several career aspirations centered on the arts, Beth wanted to be an actress. Today, she was the trainee chairing our Community session. When she wasn't fiddling with her pencil, she played with her long, glossy mane of dark hair, lifting it up or tossing it about in a wholly unselfconscious way. I wonder now if Beth was aware of her beauty. "Let me repeat the question for those of you who are still thinking," Beth said, looking meaningfully at the only two of us yet to answer.

"The question is, 'What do I think about being a part of this therapeutic community?' Any more volunteers? Sharon?"

"I like being in a group setting like this," Sharon said, although the rigid set of her shoulders and head of golden brown ringlets bent low over her notebook said she might prefer to be anyplace but here. The fingers of her left hand were lightly pressed against her forehead, concealing most of her face.

"The rehab program I was in before was all individual work. I didn't like it at all." She tittered nervously. "Like David said, we can help each other here on the computers and stuff and talk about problems in Community together."

Two staff hands shot up. "Laurie?" Beth said, picking the coach who had dreamed up that day's question.

"That was a thoughtful answer, Sharon," Laurie said. "What didn't you like about the rehab you had before?"

Sharon, following the rules, waited for the chair's recognition, waving her arm over her head trying to catch Beth's eye.

Beth was busy doodling. Prompted by Laurie, she said, "Oh, ah, Sharon."

"I thought I was the only one who had all these problems. I never knew anyone else with a head injury."

I sat woodenly. The harder I tried to formulate an answer, the less clear my thoughts became. Just write down anything, I pleaded with myself. It's crazy that everyone is supposed to answer the question, but if they can, I should be able to.

"Claudia?" Beth asked. "Everyone else has volunteered. Are you ready to volunteer?"

"Sure."

I would have liked to say that a directive to volunteer was a contradiction in terms, but I never could have pulled that thought together fast enough to get it into words. Feeling no confidence, I read my answer from my notebook.

"Okay," I said. "It is fine to be here." No ad-libs came to my rescue to make my thought more complete.

Joan, another coach, raised her hand and was given Beth's go-ahead nod. "Claudia, can you elaborate on that?"

If I could have elaborated on that, sugar plum, I wouldn't be sitting here looking foolish. "No," I said.

Three o'clock finally arrived and the trainees and their family members straggled toward the exit.

David, gregarious and energetic, bounded alongside me, trying to match my long-legged stride. "Which way are you going?"

"I'm going to check that," I answered, vaguely realizing as I said it that I had no idea. "See you tomorrow."

In the cool, fresh air outside, I felt relaxed and invigorated. I would take a bus "home," which, for this first week, meant the apartment of my friend Lori. The First Avenue line uptown is a stop-and-start form of travel. I watched the street signs carefully at first, but they passed slowly and any thoughts I might have had began to evaporate. By the eighth block, I was in my vacant mode.

I returned to the world about 75th Street, a mile past my stop. Alarmed, I bounded off the bus and charged across the street in front of screeching brakes and blaring horns. At least one person took the trouble to roll down his window and communicate with me at the top of his lungs. It would have been nice—as long as we were interacting—if I could have asked him what I should do now, but I was frozen in confusion.

I stood on the curb poised for action but without a glimmer of an idea as to what to do. My thinking was on hold, my mind blank. I was "flooding." The situation was distressingly familiar.

Flooding is an organic problem caused by the injury. When it happens, my thinking becomes painfully slow and ineffectual, and I am easily confused. Trying to hear another person's words is akin to listening to a symphony with cotton plugging my ears—much is lost. In fact, I feel as though my whole brain is swathed in cotton batting that prevents my thoughts from moving, inhibiting the transmission of information. I become rigid, mentally and physically. Ideas do not come to mind. My mental switchboard is awash in strong emotions even though, at times, I am unaware of any emotion.

Since arriving in New York I had been beset with more floods than occur in an Indian monsoon. I feared I might drown in one of them.

After several minutes, I became cold and eager to get home. I tried desperately to hold on to my thoughts, to decide what to do and then to act on that decision. After an hour of crisscrossing midtown Manhattan, running impulsively for buses I didn't want, hailing a cab and, when he stopped, not getting in, I finally jumped on a bus traveling in the wrong direction. Eventually, I made it onto another bus now headed downtown. Heady with relief, I had a terse conference with the driver as to whether I could use a transfer from a line which didn't intersect with his.

It turned out to be a moot point. I had forgotten to get a transfer.

Once safely inside the apartment, fatigue won an easy victory over hunger as it often would in the months to come. I made up the sofa bed immediately. I suppose I undressed. I know I slept thirteen hours in that warm haven, contentedly unmindful of Lori's return.

In the morning, I reviewed my notes for commuting to rehab. To my pages of directions, I had added: *Exact change. Pay attention. Get a transfer.*

"Any trouble with the buses?" Lori asked before she left for work.

"I forgot to get a transfer," I said.

"We've all done that." Lori laughed. "You don't seem to realize that most of the mistakes you make, we all make. We just don't have an excuse to justify our absentmindedness. You get to blame it on the head injury."

I smiled weakly. "Lucky me."

Bedside Notes

August 9, 1989—Irish Hills:
This is Jeff and Diana's house.
The bathroom is the second door on the right.
GO BACK TO SLEEP!
Addendum—made later in the night:
Noises from other bed are by Molly—2 1/2 yrs.

March 18, 1990—Amherst
It's Friday night.
You are at Daisy's with Shirl and Marilyn.
Bathroom—right turn, go straight:
No, nothing is familiar. Yes, dogs and cat.

From time to time, I consider adding to these bedside notes, which are so necessary when I wake up in the middle of the night in a strange room. I thought I might explain my confusion to myself by noting, "You have a head injury." But I can't bring myself to do it.

The benefit of learning why I am disoriented isn't worth the price of that knowledge when I am sleepy and vulnerable. Why deflate my sweet, blessed ignorance with such a revelation? Certainly, get me to the bathroom, but let me return to my dreams believing I am the me I have always known.

FROM MY NOTEBOOK, JUNE 25, 1990

10

There Goes the Neighborhood

It's the friends you can call up at 4 A.M.
who matter.
MARLENE DIETRICH
⊤

My first bid for independence was, as all baby steps are, unsure and teetering. Though Lori was graciousness itself in offering to share her apartment to ease my transition to New York and HTP, I had promised it would only be for a week, and I was intent on honoring that promise. She understood and, with a concern befitting a mother over her kid's first trip to camp, agreed to let me execute the move by myself.

Kay, a friend and former Vassar roommate, had made arrangements for me to use an apartment owned by another Vassar alumna who spent Monday through Thursday in Boston. Because she returned to Manhattan every weekend, it meant I would move out every Thursday night. That was fine with me. Fridays, I longed to escape the turmoil of the city. Marcia had already arranged that I would come home every other weekend. On alternate weekends, I had a vague plan to stay with friends and family members who lived near New York. In that way, I could reduce my airfare costs while still escaping to home comforts every weekend.

The problem with this plan was that I did not know how unequal I was to the challenge of constantly moving from place to place. Packing an overnight bag and blithely heading off for a jolly weekend in the country was no longer in my repertoire.

But for now I had my very own apartment in New York—at least, for four days a week. So, dressed in my usual, no-decision-needed wardrobe of jeans, Reeboks, and Lands' End rugby shirt, and bowed under the burden of two suitcases and a backpack, I hopped (well, stumbled, thrust, and collapsed) into a cab.

The uneventful two-mile ride seemed auspicious except for the sour cabby who, on seeing my suitcases and bags, believed he had an airport trip. It might as well have been, given the cost of inching our way through glutted Midtown traffic to what he called a "silk-stocking neighborhood," in which, his manner indicated, I seemed out of place.

The doorman was uniformed, the lobby tastefully furnished, the hallways carpeted in deep pile. The plush ambience was wasted on me. All I cared about was getting into the lobby, hauling my things via elevator to my new abode, getting the door open (achieved eventually with the reluctant help of the doorman), and moving my things inside.

The door opened finally on a forbiddingly dark and chilly vestibule. The owner's mother had taken me through the place a few days earlier, but I had failed to make notes and recalled absolutely none of her instructions. I didn't doubt there were lights, but the location of the switches was beyond my searching. A kitchen light helped, but it didn't penetrate the living room or reach the bedroom beyond.

Should I unpack or live out of my suitcases? Looking in the dim light around the expensive furnishings and fine art pieces, I saw no place to put away my things. I was also afraid to unpack knowing I would need to reassemble my possessions three days later for my Thursday departure. I moved everything into the kitchen, where I could be sure to see them or at least fall over them.

While I was settling in—which amounted to walking aimlessly from room to room—the phone in the kitchen rang. I couldn't recall whether I was supposed to answer it or not, but just as the answering machine clicked on, it occurred to me that the call might be for me. I turned the machine off but the call was gone. Pressing a button in hopes of restarting the machine, I heard a long series of business messages for the absent owner and my heart sank. I tried to reset it so my benefactor could retrieve her messages but only managed to erase her entire tape.

I was shivering, partly from fatigue, but the temperature in the apartment was decidedly chilly and I couldn't find a thermostat. I decided to take a shower as a way to get warm. It was a mixed benefit.

Every time I let go of the faucet, the handle swiveled on its own to HOT, nearly scalding me in the stream. I decided COLD was safer if less comforting. Finally, hungry, but having made no provision for food, even if I had known where to buy any, I went to bed to escape into sleep. I saw no alarm clock but figured my stomach would rouse me in the morning.

I wrote my bedside note:

> *Today is Tuesday, March 14, 1989*
> *YOU HAVE MOVED. You live at 69th and 2nd.*
> *Turn right for the bathroom. There are no lights.*
> *If it's morning, get up. Leave for rehab by 8:30.*
> *Don't take a shower, it's a killer.*

The next evening, it took Lori all of fifteen minutes to solve the apartment's mysteries. She was matter-of-fact in pointing out the cause and effect between the two open windows and the apartment's low temperature as she closed them. At her hands, my inhospitable, dark, cold residence was quickly transformed into one of elegance and comfort. I was relieved but embarrassed that I had needed her help.

"Don't feel bad, Claudia," Lori said. "It's not as though you're not competent."

Yeah, I thought, it's not as though I'm trying out for a career as a tenant.

When Lori left I sat down at the kitchen table and wrote to my grandmother, whom I called TuTu. I tried most nights to write something to Marcia and TuTu as they faithfully wrote me. They sent epistles of encouragement, family news, and practical instruction for New York living. In turn, I told them my experiences and emotions.

At least, that was my intent, but having few thoughts, I relied on messages from my notebook and news from the radio for most content.

> *Dearest TuTu,*
> *Ninety-seven percent of Easter bunny eaters consume the ears first. I*
> *think this is part of what's wrong with America. It takes a little more en-*

*ergy and potential mess to start with a bunny's feet. But really, what is a
bunny without ears?*

*I moved into an apartment. It has a lot of tricks to it, but it's very
beautiful. Don't worry, being a tenant is not the same as having a
career.*

The next day, I was initiated into my new community by family friends
from Detroit who now lived in New York. Tina and Anthea Zonars were
petite, vivacious, and pretty—one brunette, one blonde. they didn't look
like sisters.

Both had careers in the New York art world. Anthea was an assistant cu-
rator for the American Craft Museum and Tina was a Chinese art special-
ist at Christie's Auction House. They were links to home, able to interpret
New York in Detroit terms, and best of all, they were two of the very few
people in New York who knew the pre-injury me. After a day in rehab, it
was a relief to be in the company of people who could help me forget the
person I had become because they knew the person I used to be.

"Tonight," Anthea said that evening after dinner, "my sister and I are going to teach you your neighborhood."

"I think Manhattan is awfully big," I said.

"Manhattan isn't your neighborhood," Tina said. "I don't even want you
to learn the Upper East Side. See, Manhattan is made up of a multitude of
little neighborhoods. Everything you need—the post office, the grocery
store, you name it—is within two blocks of this apartment."

"How do you know this? You live on the other side of town."

"It's like this everywhere in the city," Anthea said. "People aren't going to
walk a mile to buy a bagel in the morning. It's not like Detroit, where people drive to everything."

"So," Tina said, "let's go tour the neighborhood and see what hidden
gems are out there. Including a grocery store."

Swept up in their sense of adventure, I set forth with them on our mission of mapping the neighborhood. And they were right, I did have a post
office, a block away. And, they pointed out, a dry cleaner and a hardware
store and a fruit and flower store. The most exciting discovery was the grocery store a half block away and the bakery. I was enthralled. I identified a

real estate office, a children's shop, and a pet store among other shops which I was never to use but which I enthusiastically noted in my note-book.

It was a nice neighborhood, even a wonderful neighborhood. Walking through it with my friends at twilight, the air crisp and sweet, the side-walks still arrayed with displays of clothing, artistically arranged fruit and urns of flowers, and people strolling, made it friendly and accessible. I had everything I needed, right here. It gave me a heady sense of self-sufficiency and confidence. Typical of my thinking at the time, I equated the existence of these resources with my ability to use them.

Tina, Anthea, and I parted warmly, all of us rejoicing in my being once again in charge of my life.

∽ "I am so glad you found the grocery store," my mother said on the phone the next evening. "I know you love to cook. What did you buy?"

"Nothing," I said. "I wrote in my notebook to stop there today on my way home, but I didn't make a list. After I was in the store, I didn't know what to buy so I just came home."

"Aren't you hungry?"

"Sort of, but I bought twenty dollars' worth of Pepsi at the corner."

"I see. How did you manage to carry it?"

"Oh, it was only a six-pack. I forgot to get change."

"Tomorrow, you'll do better," she said soothingly with her good-byes. The phrase would eventually become our code for the end of a less than perfect day.

The next morning, during Orientation, I mentioned the aborted at-tempt at grocery shopping. Joan and I then discussed how to create a gro-cery list and some other simple strategies that would help me gain some control in my daily life. She reminded me of the need to follow through on my ideas, to examine the preparations for and the ramifications of my actions. It did little good to write "Go to the store" in my notebook if I didn't also include the purpose of the trip and what I should buy once I was there.

"I know that," I said, but I wrote it down anyway.

We trainees often said, "I know that." In fact, we did know many of the obvious things we were repeatedly told. However, such information existed independent of our ability to bring it into the foreground of our memory and apply it.

"Man, I'm tired," said David as we rested after lunch, once again seated by the empty fountain. "I wish we didn't have to go back in."

I watched the five faces around me nod in agreement. I was tired too, so much so that I probably didn't even think to nod.

"What are we doing this afternoon?" asked David.

Lenny looked blank. Scott laughed. "I know," Richard said.

"I don't think they told us," I said.

"They must have told us," Beth said.

"Yeah," said Scott. "They tell us everything. Didn't they tell us, Lenny?"

"Yes," said Lenny in his deep, rumbling voice.

By now, we were all nodding in agreement. Of course we knew the answer.

David looked at me. "So, what are we doing then?"

I knew they told us. On a multiple-choice test, I could pick out the answer.

"I don't know," I said, annoyed at the question.

Scott and Beth shrugged. No one volunteered an answer. When we arrived back inside HTP Ellen said, "It's one o'clock, so it's time to start Cognitive Training again on the computers."

"I knew that," Scott said.

In a loyal if misguided rah-rah support, my family enthused in phone calls and letters about my being in Manhattan, "especially with spring around the corner." Certainly I felt a fondness for this city which I'd known for twenty years as a frequent visitor. The ceaseless bustle, the rich architecture, the ready access to music, theater, and museums on a scale available nowhere else in this country—it was exhilarating. But only if you still have your head.

"It's great! Lots to do," I would respond to envious friends, but I was not a tourist. I didn't have the psychic energy, the planning ability, or the decision-making capacity to take advantage of this wonderland.

I did have one quality in common with visitors to the city. As any tourist will confirm—it's easy for things to go awry in this lusty, congested, dizzyingly high, complex city of eight million people, all of them intent on their own concerns and understandably distrustful of anyone they don't know personally. Misadventure is common in New York and you don't need a head injury to invoke it.

But I seemed to set new records for mishaps every day. Murphy's Law—if something can go wrong, it will—controlled my life.

At the heart of my difficulty was the absence of a net to catch my constant falls. At home, my problems were invisibly smoothed over by family and most of all by Marcia. It was Marcia who cued me, oriented me, and saved me a dozen times a day. She told me what to wear, where to go, sometimes what to say, and made it comfortably possible for me to avoid decisions. I could count on her to handle the details of every activity outside my home. She did such a good job that many people, even some friends, did not perceive how deep my problems ran. Most people—myself included—had no sense of the extent of my dependency on her.

These first weeks in Manhattan slammed the truth home, hard. Without a Marcia willing to take on the role of parent, I could not accomplish the simplest tasks of everyday living. My first lesson in my new home was that the management of my activities was now my responsibility. The results were usually disastrous.

Grocery shopping was typical. In Detroit, Marcia and I shopped together so I naively believed it was a team effort. I never realized she made all the decisions while I simply pushed the cart. In my New York notes, buying food figures prominently because I so often went to bed hungry. I either forgot to stop or botched my efforts to pick up food on my way home. And once home and aware of the omissions, I did not have the energy to go back out to the store, nor face the complexities of dining in a restaurant on my own, even if I could figure out which ones were affordable and nearby.

Shopping was a problem for many reasons. I couldn't decide what to put on my list. I didn't know where to go or what to buy. I would forget to take the list. I would remember the list but forget money. Decisions involving sizes and brands were most easily solved by buying nothing.

TuTu,

I was only able to find two things at the store today. It's as if they hide most things on my list. I could use some ideas for my list. Would you send me a list of items from your list?

I used your idea to draw a picture when I can't come up with the word. It almost worked. I drew a tomato, I bought an orange. Next time I will use color.

I just watched TV News for the first time. It was brutal. There were pictures of otters dying from the Alaskan oil spill. I am going back to the radio until the world announces some joyous news, and tomorrow I will buy 1 bottle milk and 3 tuna fish in cans.

If receiving my grocery lists or news commentaries or future strategies in the mail disquieted or bewildered her, my tolerant grandmother never betrayed it.

Despite my problems, I was proud of the fact that I lived alone in this huge city without anyone to look after me. All the other trainees lived with their families. Most of them lived in the New York area, which meant they could commute daily, often accompanied by a family member. Lenny was a remarkable exception in that his parents moved from Tennessee to New York for the express purpose of caring for him during his rehabilitation.

Yet my pride in my autonomy alternated with a secret envy of everyone else who had the comfort and security of someone to lean on. On days when I was incapable of completing the simplest task, when I was confused, exhausted, and hungry and unable to do anything about it, help would have been bliss. Someone to pick out my clothes, lead me home, fix my meal (and remind me to eat it before I stretched out on the sofa "for a minute"), would have been heavenly.

The Great Communicator

I am not on friendly terms with spoken language. Words elude me and refuse to come to my aid. I am incredulous, not to mention irritated, by the poor quality of my conversation. Ronald Geller has written, "Words are the clothes that thoughts wear." Frequently, my thoughts are pitifully naked.

Strangely, that is not the case with my previously acquired medical knowledge, which I can summon at will and regurgitate quite successfully. Reciting rote medical information in response to a question allows me to feel like my old self. My intact knowledge helps me to conceal my deficits—an innate, protective response of injured creatures. I am told some of my professional acquaintances—who know nothing of my injury—see this side of me and think nothing about me has changed except that I now seem to be an absentminded eccentric.

I am fascinated by Ronald Reagan's reputation during his presidency as the Great Communicator. Actually, he was a great speech reader. His deficits became evident when he was asked direct questions. For instance, when he was asked, "Can nuclear war be limited to tactical weapons?" he replied:

"Well, I would, if they realized that we—again if—if we led them back to that stalemate only because that our retaliatory power, our seconds, or strike at them after our first strike, would be so destructive that they couldn't afford it, that would hold them off."

Maybe the reason the public excuses such oddity is because we intuitively understand the thin line between abnormal and "normal." Or maybe we rationalize away the cognitive deficits in certain people because it is unthinkable that they have them. We have a need to make certain beings perfect because that person is important to us—or maybe just important.

FROM MY NOTEBOOK, NOVEMBER 10, 1989

11

Dropkick Me, Joanie

When you look inward & all the pathways
are no longer dark but clearly lighted
& shine like transparent drinking straws
then you know you'll find your way alone.
GRACE BUTCHER,
Getting On with It

The teenager sauntering along the street in front of me supported a blaring boom box on his shoulder, thrusting his musical taste on helpless pedestrians at a level high enough to distract if not deafen. Fellow citizens, depending upon their cultural orientation, were pleased, irritated, or merely indifferent. I, influenced by everything, began marching in step to the beat of "Dropkick me, Jesus, through the goalposts of life."

This simplistic portrayal of Jesus as a coach took root in my unconscious. Coaches had become a way of life these days. My mind recorded the insistent, twangy whine of the tune and replayed it noisily all day long.

It was the end of the second week and the morning I would be told by Dr. Joan Gold that she would be my coach. Early in our conversation, she asked solicitously if that was agreeable to me.

"Of course," I said.

I had no preference, if indeed a choice was possible. All the staff were nice and I didn't know one from another. I wonder now how they assigned us. Did they request certain individuals or certain personalities? Did they feel more comfortable or more competent with people of a particular background or gender or age? Did the coaches put our names in a hat and draw lots? *Hey, Ellen, trade you Claudia for Sharon.*

I was content with the match. I liked Joan's smile and warmth, her exuberant way of dressing—colorful scarves and long, full skirts. Although she may not have owned a single pair, it seemed as though she wore or should have worn sleek leather boots.

We arranged our first meeting for three that afternoon in her office. I smiled sappily as the tune coursed through my mind again, now with a slight change of lyric. With typically fuzzy association, I substituted the name of my earthly coach for the Ultimate Counselor of the song. Drop-kick me, Joanie . . .

"Nice," I said, amused by the parallel.

"I'm glad you're pleased," she said.

Coaching was integral to the HTP technique. In addition to Yehuda Ben-Yishay, the director, we had four coaches. Each had his or her doctoral degree and specialized in the neuropsychology of head injury. One or more was always present in any group or individual undertaking, unobtrusively orchestrating everything we did. We were never left to cope alone. Interpersonal Group, our most challenging joint session, would have been a circus without coaches.

We trainees were invited to consult with or to utilize the help of any coach anytime, and we occasionally did. But, most of the time, it was our own coach to whom we turned and with whom we developed our closest staff relationships. It was this person we sought out when we despaired and on whom we depended as our mentor and guide.

Throughout the day, whenever the song coursed through my semiconsciousness, I was glad I now had Joan as my personal shepherd. But almost immediately, that feeling would be replaced by another, a vague one I had difficulty hanging on to for long, though it, unlike the song, never entirely disappeared. It took various forms in response to the stimuli but went something like this: "It's all very well, team, to get my own doctor coach, but only if that luxury means full-time attention to the only item on my agenda—going back to work. I'll do anything and work unendingly, but I have to know we share the same goal. I only have one—getting repaired so I can return to a substantive life. I need to know your plans for this. I want to know how soon I will see the results."

These unclear thoughts contented me. They seemed like an action plan. I was eager for three o'clock so I could consult with my new coach and get down to the serious business of setting goals for my own personal recovery in contrast to all this "group rehabilitative" stuff we seemed to be increasingly busy doing. I mean . . . this togetherness is all very pleasant, guys, and I like the people here, but time is marching on. When I call my family at night and they say, "So, what did you accomplish today, Claudia?" (that they never asked that question was beside the point), I wanted to be able to answer, "Today, I learned X. That means my memory is five percent better. They've given me this magic formula called 'strategies.' Each one is designed to correct a particular problem. We figure if I do them religiously, I will be cured in five months. I should be able to return to my medical duties in July."

I had support in this unrealistic hope. Against their common sense, my mother and Marcia were persuaded by this dippy analysis of my situation. They had little understanding of the profound extent of my deficits, let alone how to fix them, but they had confidence in my ability to overcome adversity.

One evening, my mother said, "You're such a quick study, you'll probably complete the five-month course in three."

I was more conservative. I was willing to give it all five. The program ended Thursday, July 27; I set Monday, July 31, as D-Day. I wrote it down in my notebook. *July 31, first day back at work.*

At three o'clock, I was standing outside Joan's office door waiting for her. She invited me into the small, lamplit office made smaller still by a big desk and two visitor chairs separated by a tiny table. Books and videotapes spilled out of the wall shelves. Framed photographs of her children, husband, and a grandchild edged the desk and were almost buried by stacks of reports and papers.

She was warm, I was stilted. She spoke assuredly, I was tentative.

I was eager to discuss plans for my recovery, but it was three o'clock, the end of the day, and I was tired. I no longer had a grasp of what it was I wanted to communicate or what had seemed so important earlier.

Joan tactfully steered the conversation. I was to learn she was adroit at this. She wanted to talk about my obsessive urgency to return to medicine. She seemed to feel it was overriding other objectives and impeding my assimilation into HTP and a relationship with the group.

I was incapable of arguing the point even if I had had the energy, but I wanted to impress on her that I had a specific goal, that my difficulties might not be serious enough to require me to move at the snail's pace of the group. I probably missed saying that, even though I had written it down. I think I told her I was grateful for the opportunity to be at HTP. I was even convinced, now that I was here, that I needed their help, but I could not erase the feeling that I was losing valuable time in my medical practice. My skills might become rusty if I was separated too long from my work.

She listened serenely without interrupting. "I see," she said when I finished. "Is your deadline indelibly fixed for the end of this term? Does it have to be that soon?"

That soon? Five months? My disbelief probably showed, because she immediately changed the subject.

"Claudia, I'm concerned that you're holding back in our Community and Interpersonal Group sessions . . ." Her words flowed on. They did not seem relevant to my goals. ". . . being the objective doctor is interfering with your being a subjective patient . . . On a less conscious level, you may be resisting the role of a trainee."

She went on to gently express her opinion that I might have fallen into erroneous thinking—I know medicine, I know me, this is a medical problem, therefore, I must understand the problem in relation to me. As a result, I was getting in the way of my own treatment.

Joan then told me a story about herself, about how she underwent a mammogram after a lump was discovered in her breast. It was benign, but until she knew that, she was frightened. As a psychologist, she thought she should be able to quickly work through her anxiety so that she would appear and feel emotionally calm for the procedure. However, objectivity and professional distance became irrelevant when the problem lay within her own breast.

I realized later that by sharing an intimate experience, Joan was trying to help me find a way to give myself permission to be a patient. She wanted me to understand that it was normal, even helpful, to express fear, anger, and grief rather than wasting unproductive energy trying to be a detached, unemotional professional.

She had intuitively and correctly assessed that my many years of professional training had made my need for an objective demeanor second nature, even if, for present purposes, it was an impediment.

However, I liked being objective. I didn't *want* to feel. I was terribly disconcerted by my rare bouts of grief and despair. I certainly was not seeking permission to experience that misery. That might be okay with her; it wasn't okay with me. I also didn't want to spend time praising my current insignificant achievements. They were hardly the equivalent of, say, publishing a research paper or saving a patient's life. To hear "Claudia, you did a fine job of stating today's goal" was not a reward I valued.

I couldn't afford to waste my limited and precious energy on grieving. I wanted to pass through this program fast wearing blinders (or "blinkers," as Dr. Ben-Yishay called them). Blinkers were okay with me. They would help me focus on strategies I could take home and apply. I wished the staff shared my urgency and would give me specific remedies to hasten my recovery. I never doubted they knew how. I wanted them to focus on it now.

I felt an especial frustration at my inability to communicate all this to Joan any better than with anyone else. I was unable to translate the few pictures in my mind or the feelings welling in me into the needed words. It was a poor first session. I needed Joan to be my ally in reaching my goals. I wanted her to know me. I was irritated at being unable to formulate my thoughts. I said none of these things and we parted.

As soon as I reached home, I sat with my notebook and tried to organize my thoughts. I prayed I had communicated some of my litany: Please fix my thinking and reasoning, coach. Repair my memory. Make me a doctor again. Just get me to my job on time.

If I could have thought more cogently, I would have realized that Joan *did* understand me, if only because the way I felt and reacted was not unique. There is a universality for those in my circumstance.

Meanwhile, I had no options but to go along with them. I had no plan of my own for "getting well," no alternatives to being their trained rehab dog. I told Marcia and my mother in my calls to them that night, "I don't understand it, but if that's what it takes to get out, I will doggedly work at everything they put before me."

One session in which I could see we were actually working on something concrete was in our Cognitive Training sessions. These were scheduled every afternoon right after lunch.

In Cognitive, as it was called, we didn't just talk. We were given specific tasks to attack specific problems. We could document our performance by means of a variety of "games" and electronic devices to improve our organizational skills. A rich assortment of exercises was employed to improve visual-spatial function, hand-eye coordination, and manual dexterity. Through puzzles, games, and computers we strove to develop strategies, were taught techniques for creating and following plans, practiced ways to set priorities, made associations between similar ideas, and increased our efficiency at performing multiple tasks.

The computer exercises were especially useful in improving our ability to concentrate and to speed up our reaction times and our thought processes. In those first weeks, they gave me a better sense of my growth than did the "talking" sessions that filled most of the day. On the computer, I could measure my advancement to progressively more difficult levels. That was satisfying. Sometimes.

"Go for it!" Scott said. He felt his encouragement always had a salutary effect on our performances. However, his hearty slap on my back while my hands were on the keyboard did nothing to improve my score.

I restarted the program and stared at the video monitor, waiting for the red light. Its appearance was a signal for me to press a button as fast as I could. The computer would answer with a number indicating my response time. When I was really fast the computer rewarded me with the sound of heralding trumpets . . . *ba da bum ba da!* Our coaches called this particular exercise "ARC."

As a child, I recall watching a similar game at the state fair. Two contestants sat in drivers' seats, each with a foot on a gas pedal and their hands tightly holding steering wheels, only there was no car—just the seat, the pedals, and the wheel. When, without warning, the traffic light in front of them turned red, the players would slam on their brakes. The driver with the slower reaction time would receive an electric shock through his seat, causing him to jump up in the air. Personally, I'd rather hear trumpets.

I liked ARC, for about five minutes at a time. It demanded a level of attention and concentration that quickly drained my energy and made me feel irritable. We were taught strategies for playing: Sit up straight, feet on the floor; ask yourself if you are paying attention; listen for the tone signaling the start; count three seconds; the instant the red light flashes on, push the button. It didn't take many sessions to learn the strategies, but to remember to employ them all, every time, seemed unachievable. We watched each other play in groups of two or three with a coach offering suggestions and encouragement. It always looked easier when someone else controlled the button.

The red light appeared on the screen and I pounced on the button. Too late. Again. It was an eternity since I had last made the trumpet sound and I was getting frustrated.

"Are you remembering to count to three after the tone?" said Laurie. "It will help you anticipate the red light."

"Oh yeah, count."

I tried again, sure this time that trumpet would validate my efforts. Tone, one, two, three, POUNCE!

Zero score. I forgot to wait for the red light.

"You jumped the gun," Scott said a smile. It was his most common error.

I was tired now. I couldn't have felt more physically irritable if my chair had been wired to electrodes. I just wanted to stop concentrating on that screen. Having to pay so much attention was draining. I no longer cared whether or not I had a fast reaction time. I didn't even care when Scott announced he knew from his Ranger training that he was fast on any trigger.

"Fast is not the point of this," Laurie said. "ARC is one of the cognitive exercises you do to help you increase your ability to pay attention and concentrate."

I didn't want to admit that the tiny bit of concentration this "game" required was a challenge.

I once saw a man leave that electrically charged seat at the state fair looking as if his sudden lurches into the air had never happened. I was just as smooth when I turned the controls over to Scott.

Life was made bearable by my "paper bridge" to Marcia and TuTu and by a blessed peculiarity of my injury that caused me to live in the present tense. My attention was locked on what was happening *now*. Much of the time, I didn't miss my home and family for the simple reason that I didn't notice I had a home and family to miss.

When you watch a good movie you get caught up in the story and may temporarily forget the drama of your own life—your mother is in the hospital, you were laid off yesterday, you're getting married tomorrow. While "living" the movie, your mind is able to set aside such real-life situations.

My mind was almost always at the movies. I was aware of being alone and missing those I loved when their letters and phone calls reminded me they were there. Most hours, however, were spent without the weight of past or future. Conversely, when I was home, on alternate weekends, I accepted that comfortable state entirely, and so my time was not spoiled by my looking ahead to my dreaded departure. I didn't know I was leaving until I was actually leaving. I know now my composure in this regard was a bit unnerving to others.

There was, however, a notable exception. On certain random issues, I would perseverate—lock compulsively on to one idea or concern and not let go. It was a trait that regularly taxed my family's patience and a phenomenon Marcia learned to expect whenever I was returning to New York after a weekend home. It was also a vexation she didn't need on a Monday morning.

When I flew home twice a month for the long weekend, I left New York on the five-forty-five plane Thursday evening and returned at the last possible minute Monday morning. To arrive at HTP promptly at ten A.M. meant catching a seven o'clock plane. On those mornings, my thoughts were riveted on not missing the plane and getting to New York late.

Once I awakened and oriented to the fact this was Monday, I was in my own home, and would shortly return to Manhattan, I would go find Marcia in the kitchen. There, we would engage in an exchange as predictable as Abbott and Costello's "Who's on first?" routine. At least, it was predictable to Marcia. To me, each time was brand-new:

"Am I going to miss the plane?" I would ask.

"You're fine. Go take a shower."

"Maybe I took one last night."

"Maybe you didn't. Take another. You won't miss the plane."

"Okay, but we have to watch the clock."

Ten minutes later I would ask, "Shall we call the airport to see if the plane's on time?"

"You can if you want. I'm eating breakfast," she would say without raising her eyes from her newspaper. "If the plane's late, you'll wait there for it just as you have before."

"Okay." I couldn't catch her eye. "Marcia, what if it's early?"

"Settle down, Claudia. You are not thinking clearly. Have some breakfast."

Nor did the ride to the airport distract me from my preoccupation with being on time.

I craned my head to see the odometer, trying to time it against the second hand on my watch.

"What are you doing?" Marcia said as the car inched ahead, morning traffic backed up for all the reasons it always backs up.

"I'm trying to calculate how long before we get to the airport so we won't be late."

"If your calculations can affect our arrival time, I want to share the patent application for your system. At any rate, we're not late. I always get you there in plenty of time."

"I'm just making sure."

Once I was confident Marcia had this situation under control, I could turn to my notebook and check the calendar. "I figure you'll need to drive me to the airport about seven more times. Then, it will be July thirty-first and I'll be driving myself to work."

"Have you discussed that with Joan?"

"Joan knows that's when I'm going back to work. I've told everyone that."

Marcia negotiated the move around a stalled car, and our speed picked up. "While you're looking at your calendar, what day of the week does HTP finish?"

"Uhm . . . Thursday. There's sort of a graduation party before then."

"Okay, I'll arrange for a long weekend. I can go to the party with you and help you pack. Then we'll have Friday together in New York and come back Saturday. We can make your move home a mini-holiday."

"Yeah. Home for the holiday. Great."

At our conference on Tuesday, I told Joan about Marcia's idea for our weekend and how moving home on Saturday would give me Sunday to settle in before starting work on Monday. She frowned but quickly smoothed her face.

"Why don't you focus on what you need to do now, Claudia," she said. "Don't dwell on your summer plans yet."

Summer plans? What, like Girl Scout camp? I was talking about my life, my job.

"They're forever plans," I said.

Joan smiled. "Well, July must seem like forever. Is there anything else?"

I looked at my notebook. "We made it to the plane on time."

"Good. I'll see you tomorrow."

Memory

Luis Buñuel wrote in his memoirs that "you have to begin to lose your memory, if only in bits and pieces, to realize that memory is what makes our lives. Life without memory is no life at all. . . . Our memory is our coherence, our reason, our feeling, even our action. Without it we are nothing."

If I could label the element of my dysfunctional memory which tears at me, it certainly would not be its practical application. My notes handle the day-to-day trivia. The imperfections of my clerical system are a greater annoyance to my associates than to me. They are the ones who must repeat themselves.

But I do want an ongoing record of the events and emotions that provide the richness, philosophy, and color to my life. I want reflection at will, not just on chance or when jostled by others.

It is a joy to have shared memories with someone you love. I am unable to do so even with myself. I have learned that experiences that I swear by virtue of their very intensity must be indelibly printed in my memory are actually as fleeting as my dreams. When I do jot down notes about events to keep them from slipping away, I later discover only skewed meanings and cryptic fragments. I must become a more serious recorder. If not, my history will seem impoverished.

FROM MY NOTEBOOK, AUGUST 1989

12

In the Same Boat

. . . just remember . . . we're all in this alone.
LILY TOMLIN
❋

We were on an aimless walk outside after lunch, filling up time. Most everyone had gone ahead, but Scott and Richard moved slowly. Lenny and I adopted their pace.

Scott with extravagant gestures was telling us of his delight in having come upon his old diaries from his service overseas.

"This is so great, so great. I haven't been able to remember anything about being stationed in Asia."

He loved the Army and was fiercely proud of being a Ranger captain. That career evaporated one June night in 1988, when a fourteen-year-old child, careening down a Georgia highway in his grandmother's car, collided head-on with Scott's.

We moved en masse across the small side street after Scott held his hand up grandly to stop a car about to make a right turn. Lenny and Richard reached the curb first and Lenny helped Richard up.

"When we're done with this place," Scott said, "I'm headed back to the Army. The Rangers need me." Scott gestured so broadly he lost his balance. I grabbed his arm and supported him while he climbed the curb.

"I'm back to the university," Lenny said. "Soon as I leave here, I'm getting my own place, a fast car, and my psychology degree. Maybe two degrees, one a Ph.D."

Lenny was now in his seventh year of rehabilitation.

We all passionately clutched our dreams, wrapping ourselves in the mantle of who we used to be. We didn't have long discussions about this. We didn't have long discussions about anything. Our knowledge of one another's goals was woven together from bits and threads of conversations and from Interpersonal Group.

The twelve of us were distinctly different. We represented a diversity of cultures, lifestyles, personalities, ages, life experiences, and professional callings. All we had in common was our head injuries, and even those had different causes. Two had suffered crushing blows to the skull from falling objects. The rest of us had had our heads slammed against dashboards, thrust through windshields, or smashed against pavement. Even the length of our postinjury comas varied, ranging from virtually none to as long as six months. Some had had to relearn how to speak and walk.

In six weeks together, we had come to know each other's families and backgrounds. We heard about each other's weekend misadventures, unraveled plans, social mishaps, embarrassing dependencies, and those little losses of dignity too trivial to single out and use as a complaint to anyone, even God.

Through disjointed, halting conversations and, even more, through an osmosis of communal ache, we learned the intimacies of each other's deficits, aspirations, and fears. Shared needs and a peculiarity of circumstance fostered our camaraderie. We were in the same boat even if it had a big hole in it and often seemed in imminent danger of sinking.

Their predicaments mirrored mine, but I more readily understood the experiences they described. I couldn't make sense of my own. I did not possess the insight or imagination to see myself.

Interpersonal Group was the theater in which we played out our parts and revealed our edited and unedited selves. We came to know each other better there than anyplace else, better even than in the lunchroom. It was in Interpersonal Group that we learned Darrow had been an attorney. It was hard to visualize him in that role, but then I didn't look much like a doctor. Sandy-haired, slight of build, he rarely spoke without considerable prodding and had a disconcerting way of looking through people as though they were invisible. He sat stiffly but nervously in his seat. It was not that he moved; rigor mortis could set in and he would still look nervous. It was in his eyes.

He shyly confided to us that his wife had left him after his injury, taking the baby with her. Darrow never appeared distraught over the loss of his wife or his profession or his intellectual abilities, but he seemed to grieve over having been deprived of the everyday companionship of his young daughter.

When we first met, he depended upon a number of tape recorders around the apartment to help him perform simple personal tasks. Each one guided him through a number of different routines. The tape recorder in the bedroom got him dressed, another in his bathroom reminded him to shave and comb his hair, another helped him prepare for rehab. They provided him a measure of independence.

Traveling the short distance from white to blue collar, we had Tommy and Bernie. Tommy had been a truck driver. Wiry, intense, pleasant, but withdrawn, he was proud—in about equal measure—of being Italian and being a truck driver who could "wheel those babies through crowded streets with the best of 'em." But it wasn't a road injury that cost him his ability to be a trucker. It was a pipe that broke loose from its anchors in a loading dock and knocked him out one afternoon as he climbed out of his cab to make a delivery.

Tommy had three children and a quiet, hard-working wife. He found it difficult to accept both his wife working to support all five of them, and his tattered image. "I'm not a player now," he said.

He was never without his very dark sunglasses. He never explained, but I thought he used them to conceal his thoughts. I knew his eyes were blue because I asked him one day to remove his glasses and look at me.

Bernie's career also ended with a pipe. He had been an award-winning supervisor with Consolidated Edison in Manhattan when, while he was perched on a scaffold, a construction worker accidentally dropped a pipe from a platform sixty-five feet above and it crushed his skull. Now he walks with a cane. At age fifty-five, he is two years into a later-years marriage with a devoted woman.

Only three of the twelve of us—Sharon, Beth, and I—were female, which pretty much reflects the male-to-female ratio of head injuries. More men than women experience such trauma. Traditional male lifestyles, with their sports, daredevil stunts, or battles, have made men more vulnerable; and perhaps the injuries of men are more likely to be identified, since men tend to have better jobs and larger incomes than women, which can also mean better medical insurance and more thorough care. These may be the reasons more men than women are in rehabilitation programs. Surely it's not because society sees the average man as more worthy of rehabilitating than the average woman or that his contributions have greater potential value than hers.

Orientation opened the day but Interpersonal Group got it started. It wasn't my favorite session—nothing had that distinction—but as long as I wasn't on the menu, it was stimulating. We never knew what was going to happen. Orientation, in contrast, was routine and fairly boring. There, every morning at ten, we recited our plans for the week and identified what we wanted to accomplish that day. For some reason, I never understood what we were doing. I don't think the others did either. Although the coaches tried to help us sort out our woolly thoughts, we all seemed to just muddle through.

Interpersonal Group was different. The goals were more clear and my desire to achieve was stronger. Every day, one of us was assigned to speak on one of a variety of topics depending upon how creative the coaches were in dreaming up ideas. The trainee who spoke was said to be on the "hot seat."

Following the time-tested idea that the easiest subject on which to discourse is oneself, we were instructed to talk about our families, identify qualities we liked about ourselves and others, and reflect upon our pre-injury achievements. Sometimes we did a role reversal, in which our coach assumed our identity and we, in effect, "interviewed" ourselves. As an initial activity to get us started, we spoke about our backgrounds and how we had come to be at HTP.

Every session was videotaped so we could study our performances later. Throughout the session, our own coach sat next to us to assist us if we ran out of ideas or wandered off the topic or were unclear or confused. "Refer to the question" was a refrain we often heard as our coaches worked to keep us on track, pointing to the big easel and pad which stood at the side with the question written out in large letters. A brief outline was included to keep everyone focused on the subject, in case—which was most of the time—we didn't have a glimmer of an idea as to why we were doing these things.

Although only one of us performed at each session, everyone was expected to pay attention, take notes, and be prepared to critique the performer and the content at the conclusion of the presentation.

Everyone attended—all twelve trainees and all four coaches. Most of us dreaded our turn, not because of a lack of encouragement from the coaches or harsh critiques from our peers, but because these simple exercises were so appallingly difficult.

Occasionally, someone who had forgotten their last experience would be excited at being chosen. *Goody! My turn to be dumped in the tank.* Abe Lincoln expressed my reaction when he quoted the man being tarred and feathered and run out of town on a rail: "If t'wern't for the honor of the thing," the man said, "I'd just as soon not be here."

Today was Sharon's turn. While we waited for the coaches, visitors, and trainees to be seated and the room to settle down so Sharon could begin, I read the notes I had made yesterday on Richard. My records of these sessions are sparse. The videotapes convey far more insights. I marvel at his progress and the seven-year battle he waged to get from his injury to the front of this small classroom. My image of him is the one preserved on tape, a medium-tall, stocky figure with a sweetly smiling face and an open, energetic manner, seated in a patch of sunlight, his cane resting against his chair. He needed considerable assistance from Laurie to tell his story. Even then, his presentation was circuitous and rambling and difficult to follow.

He related how his brother, who was driving, had lost control of their car on the rain-slick road. In the crash that ended the skid, his brother was killed and Richard was severely injured. He spent years in a hospital, the first six months in a coma. Later, at a rehabilitation center, he was outfitted with mechanical aids and taught how to walk and speak again.

"When I was disabilitated," he told us, "I was going to Northwestern University."

"You mean you were going to go there, Richard?" Laurie asked.

"Yes. To be an attorney in the practice of law and this is required that there are multitudes of years of study . . ." Richard lost us in a rambling continuation of his thought.

"So," Laurie summarized, "you are indicating this is the summer after you graduated from high school, and in preparation for your law degree, you intended to study political science."

"Yes, politics and science which is the curriculum to which I had chosen . . ."

Richard's mother had died by then. His father and the six children made their home together. By the time Richard found his way to HTP, his father had also died.

Although never said or even intimated by Richard, my mother believed that Richard's siblings, deeply caught up in starting their own lives, had little time for or patience with Richard. Through the "significant other" family sessions not open to trainees, my mother and Marcia learned that Richard's Aunt Blanche, with remarkable selflessness, stepped into his bleak, orphaned existence. She took him into her own home, prepared his meals, helped him dress, supervised him, and finally got him into HTP.

Blanche's loving care in the face of Richard's considerable physical and emotional need kept her captive in her apartment. Her outings were infrequent and only possible if a neighbor or friend was available to sit with Richard. Her private, personal time was plucked from the late-night hours between eleven P.M. and two in the morning when Richard was asleep.

"Hi, I'm Sharon."

Sharon's bright greeting to the assembled group jerked me back from my notebook. Sharon could have been the prototype of the California girl—tanned, pretty, slim, athletic, casually but well dressed, blond hair fashionably crimped. She had completed her sophomore year at the University of California, San Diego, but she appeared much younger than twenty. That may have been because she was a little giggly and timid in her nervousness. Sometimes she was quite adynamic, but today she was hyperactive, her speech rapid and disjointed.

"I was hurt a year ago . . . by a car . . . I was on a moped . . . he was drunk. The driver was drunk. He tried to drive off and leave me but . . . he had to take me with him . . . my foot was caught in his bumper. He dragged me with his car. My helmet saved my life . . . [*giggle*] . . . not my head, though . . . from being injured."

With Laurie's coaching, we learned that Sharon had been comatose for four days but remained in the hospital for four months to undergo foot and leg repairs. She told us she was waiting to return to her university and that she was going to be a doctor. It sounded like a fine choice to me.

In my notebook I wrote *fine choice*. I was learning to write everything down in my notebook—at first because we were instructed to do so, but eventually because it was so necessary to my functioning that I could not manage without it. Letter-size and thick with sturdy leather covers, my notebook became an appendage. It was my memory. I faithfully noted everything and elaborated on those notes every night. And for many months, everything had equal importance. I flipped back a few pages.

> *I had hummus and tabouli for lunch . . . I didn't eat dinner tonight . . . I live at 69th and 2nd Ave. . . . The radio said alar sprayed on apples can cause cancer. I have come to the Big Apple just when we've learned apples may be carcinogenic.*

"Claudia." Len's voice snapped me back from my reading. "Do you have a comment for Sharon?"

"Yes." I looked in my notebook and read the first line. "I think she should be a doctor. It's a fine choice."

"Good, but we aren't discussing Sharon's career plans now, we're evaluating her presentation. Do you feel you know her a little better? Did she communicate fully, in your opinion? Was she personable? Animated?"

"Yes."

He was waiting.

I referred to the three answers I had written next to the guideline we were to use in our evaluation. "She followed the outline. She was personable. She accepted coaching."

I couldn't think of anything to add. His questions were the best answers.

Don't Make Excuses for Me

I saw the egg begin a slow, wobbly roll toward the edge of the kitchen counter. I could easily grab it before it fell and I did, dropping the casserole dish I was holding to reach for the egg. The dish shattered on the tile floor. It had belonged to my grandmother.

"We all break stuff, you know," said my friend. "Most people wouldn't have even caught the egg."

"Yeah, right," I said, not troubling to disguise my disbelief at what I had done. "I really loved that dish."

"If you think this is bad, you should have seen the mess when Jerry broke the bottle of barbecue sauce."

◦

"Now that you have gotten a real break from the field of medicine, you'll probably never want to go back. All those long hours and stress."

"I loved practicing medicine," I answered.

"Well, you can still call yourself a doctor. That's still more than most people."

◦

"It took me three hours to produce this cake. I had to make three because I kept leaving out ingredients. You should have seen the kitchen," I volunteered in a rare attempt to explain myself.

"That's not so terrible," said my guest. "At least you made a cake from scratch. I can't even make one from a box."

"But," I haltingly defended my point, "I once was a good cook."

Being told my errors are "not that bad" leaves me isolated and frustrated. I crave the understanding of others. I reason that, if a jazz pianist were to develop a crippling arthritis and could play only simple pieces, if she lost mastery of the keyboard and her ability to play elegantly, swiftly, fluidly, would she be comforted by being told there are folks out there who can't even play "Chopsticks"?

I am keenly aware of how much I have to be grateful for in my life, including being alive. However, when my impaired reading skills leave me too confused to sort my mail, it doesn't soothe my pain to record here that I am glad I am not in a coma. Nor do I, who crave my former relationship to the printed word, want to be told there are a multitude of impoverished folks who cannot read.

Please don't trivialize my loss by making excuses for my failures or comparing me to someone who never had what I have lost. It compounds my distress and discounts what I once was without even allowing me the opportunity to express my grief. Though entirely unintentional, it adds insult to injury.

FROM MY NOTEBOOK, JUNE 19, 1989

13

Don't Charge the Battery, Fix the Generator

We were in the car together, riding along.
Marcia turned and asked, "What are you
thinking?" My answer is always the same,
"Nothing." It is not that I have no thoughts
I wish to share. It is that I have no thoughts.
My mind does not daydream, it vegetates.
FROM MY NOTEBOOK, 1989

✛

"The adynamic person," Joan said, "is not dynamic: not spontaneous, not animated."

...not interesting, not fun to be with, not able to carry on a conversation, she charitably did not add.

We were discussing my six-week progress report and the first written evaluation of my deficits since I'd entered HTP. It was actually a copy of the report sent to each of our insurance companies and neurologists. Unlike progress reports used in many other programs, ours were not kept secret from us. HTP regards them as tools to increase their trainees' awareness of major deficits and to enable them to chart their advancement.

Our assignment this day in Cognitive Training was to write down in our own words our interpretation of our reports. We had each been given a copy and told to read it carefully.

The twelve of us labored to do that, some staring at the wall or floor or ceiling for the answers, some tracing every word of the sentence with a finger, quietly sounding out the words, trying to make meaning out of complex language. Our coaches moved from one to another of us, anticipating questions, supplying help, and discussing various points of the content with us.

I read the document several times, combining and recombining phrases in an effort to make it understandable. I could understand the various elements; I had difficulty making sense of the entire sentence and then holding on to the idea. The words "thinking/reasoning" caught my eye, but phrases such as "She has problems ... with adynamia ... attention-concentration ... flooding ... maximalistic thinking ..." held little significance for me.

Also, I felt no emotional connection with their assessments, no "Ah-hah, they have that right." What I read here, with the coaches' help, might have been about someone else.

Adynamia, for instance. By this time, I knew a little about this behavioral expression, but this was the first I had heard "adynamia" applied to me. To me, the term meant Lenny, who was profoundly adynamic. His movements were at times like those of a sleepwalker; his face an impassive, bearded mask; his speech a bass monotone; his manner unemotional and serious. We were at HTP for months before I saw his wonderful, face-splitting grin.

Now, reading my report, I could see how the term might apply to me, but I greeted that dim insight with a shrug of the shoulders. I didn't consider that adynamia or any of the other deficits listed in this ten-page document especially mattered—with the major exception of thinking/reasoning. Yet they gave thinking/reasoning no more emphasis than any of the other problems. I read the report several times to be sure. I even counted the lines of type given to each problem. Measuring the weight of the words by volume, I wrote, *Flooding got 40 lines; thinking/reasoning got only 22.*

Yet thinking/reasoning was my life. The ability to think and reason effectively would determine my future. Six weeks of living in New York had made it very plain to me that I needed this fixed before I went back to medicine.

I turned to Joan and said, "Can we talk?"

We set up an appointment for Monday at three. I felt comforted by the idea that all I had to do was direct this talented staff to work on the right stuff. By the time our Cognitive Training session ended, the report had been forgotten. An hour later, after Community ended and I had gathered my few things, I was in a cab on my way to the airport and my treasured weekend in Detroit.

On Saturday morning, when we had finished breakfast, Marcia asked me to get my notebook while she cleared the table. When I returned, she said, "Let's talk about your progress report. I finished reading it last night."

I explained to Marcia my complaints about the report. "So, I want you to help me line up my ducks so I can show them to Joan."

"When you talk to Joan," Marcia said, "so you don't shoot wildly at your ducks, you may want to leave out your argument that one deficit is given twenty-five more lines—"

"Eighteen," I corrected, disappointed she hadn't liked my strongest point.

"Whatever. Just don't be too quick to discount the other things in this report. Adynamia, for instance, is a significant problem for you. It's not just an infrequent and minor annoyance that exists only when people comment on it, and it's more than being no longer active or energetic or forceful in personality. It also signifies lethargy, a paucity of thought, a depletion of psychic energy and action. It's your enemy, Claudia. Unless you overcome it, you can't be self-sufficient."

I grabbed at her word "paucity." I had included it in my notes. In the report, the phrase used was "a paucity of ideation." This was the only kernel of information with which I could identify—my inability to elaborate on thoughts or generate ideas. It gave a name to what I had not identified but knew was a vast and agonizing problem for me. They included it under the heading of adynamia, but I recognized it as an indispensable element of my thinking that I had just begun to realize was missing and was desperate to get back.

We all have pieces of ourselves that we secretly cherish, that afford us great pleasure. For me, it was the creative aspect of my analytic mind. It had always been playful, inventive, penetrating, intuitive. It was a source of immeasurable joy. As I became aware that it had stopped inventing solutions and exploring ideas, that it could not shift perspective or grapple with more than one thought at a time, I became frightened.

Living without the richest aspect of my intellect would not be endurable. It was akin to having a multicolored kaleidoscope turn to black and white, locked on one pattern.

"HTP has to bring it back," I told Marcia, my voice shaking.

My discussion with Marcia about my report stayed with me. I had gained important insight into actions I could employ. If adynamia was a crippling problem for me, I would try to use the strategies I was learning to address it vigorously—or as vigorously as someone without vigor can manage.

Monday lunchtime provided me with an unplanned opportunity to exercise a conscious effort to fight my usual mental lassitude. It occurred with Lenny, of all people.

For some reason, we found ourselves alone. I would like to think it was I who suggested we carry our lunch out to the dry fountain in the plaza to eat our sandwiches on the steps, but I'm not sure. In any case, we could relax there till it was time for the afternoon session.

Walking out together, I observed Lenny. He was twenty-five now. He had been eighteen when a driver struck his bicycle from behind, throwing his body forward and then running over him. His heart stopped several times in those initial hours, his injuries were massive, and his coma lasted three months. The odds that he would learn to walk and talk were less than poor. Lost forever was the athletic junior Olympian, the gifted college student, the charming raconteur.

Now Lenny rarely initiated conversation. His answers to questions were monosyllabic. He might agree or disagree with an idea presented to him, but he never presented his own idea unless he was prompted and prodded throughout. Nor did he initiate activity unless asked to do so.

It was a lovely, warm spring day. We sat, munching away, oblivious to everything, including each other. He was staring at the wall of the building opposite us. I stared into space. Eventually it occurred to me that, despite my new resolution, I looked as adynamic as he did and we had not been speaking for some time.

I decided to strike up a conversation with him, even though any conversation between two adynamics was bound to be a nonadventure in repartee.

I groped in my empty mind for a way to begin. It seemed pointless to ask what he was thinking. We had both been staring mindlessly into space; I doubted he had any thoughts.

"Nice weather," I said desperately.

"Yes," from far away.

"Interpersonal Group was fun today," I said with too much volume and a contrived, gosh-am-I-having-fun heartiness.

"Yes." Lenny sounded as if he were at an IRS audit that wasn't going well.

Why didn't he help, dammit. Doing this alone was no day at the beach. I couldn't think of anything else to say. We might as well go inside. If I was going to work, it might as well be productive.

I tried again to come up with a question.

Finally I asked, "Are you doing something fun this weekend?"

"Yes." Emotionless.

That good. But I said brightly, now rather pleased with myself for keeping this going, "Well, what are you doing?"

"Well," he said. "We always have plans. What are you doing?"

"Ah, well, ah, hmm. I know I have plans too." I couldn't think of one. Deflated now, I said, "It's time to go back in."

"Yes," Lenny said. We, as one, left silently.

꙳ "That's great, Claudia," Joan said later in her office after I told her of my effort to chat with Lenny. "It tells me you're beginning to see the importance of your adynamia."

"Yes, but, it isn't as important as my thinking problems. I wonder if we can concentrate on those?"

Her eyebrows lifted in an Oh, really? look.

I hesitated. I didn't want to seem to be preempting her role or act as though I were playing doctor. However, I felt a desperate need to communicate my vision of what I needed in my rehabilitation. Anxious to make my point, keenly aware of her valuable time, never in charge of my ideas, I looked to my notes for help.

I wanted to say that I didn't question that all the strategies and programs we were engaged in were valuable, even splendid, but time for me was running out and I felt that we needed to concentrate almost exclusively on the strategies that would improve my thinking and reasoning skills. But I could not sustain, let alone articulate, such a complex thought. So I confined myself to reading out loud exactly what I had written in preparation for this meeting.

"I want to fix my thinking," I said. "Forget the other stuff."

She considered my words thoughtfully. "By the 'other stuff' you mean adynamia, flooding, and so forth? They're all connected, Claudia. We can't address one deficit and ignore the others."

"How does a strategy which is supposed to make me . . ." I groped for the word. Arid? Dry? Is nonflooded a word? Got it. ". . . keep me from flooding, how is that going to help me think better?"

"Are you able to think while you are flooding?"

I shook my head.

"Can you reason in a logical way when you are too adynamic to generate ideas?"

Again the head shake.

"Can you solve a problem if you are unable to keep it in your conscious mind? If you can't concentrate on solving it, or can't pay attention to any of the steps that go into solving it? Do you see how all those things are connected?"

"Yes," I whispered.

"We must work on these other issues, Claudia, for the express purpose of being in a position to attack your thinking and reasoning problems."

"Oh, Lord," I breathed.

There were so many impediments to my recovery. I hadn't made a dent in my adynamia, and my flooding was not only paralyzing, it was occurring with the same frequency. Now, I was being told I had to overcome both in order to fix my other problems. It's like knowing I have to slay a dragon before I can even challenge Cyclops.

I shuddered at the magnitude of the undertaking, but for the first time, I saw the face of the enemy and had a sense of what I needed to address.

That night, in my phone calls to them, I told my mother and Marcia I was overwhelmed by the things I had heard that day but I was now assured I wasn't wasting time.

"I guess they know what they're doing," I said. "It seems the problem may be more complicated than we originally thought."

Bird in a Cage

I recall vividly the *me* I once took for granted. As my dullness and torpor lessens, I am hungry for greater mental activity and expression. At the same time, my very growth has deepened my frustration and disappointment in my performance. I am impatient for more periods of animation and creativity.

At times I feel alive, passionate about the world around me, energized, focused on a new thought. However, I know that other adynamic self will, unbidden, surface from murky depths, reassert herself, and leave me barren of thoughts and energy.

Even then, I retain the memory of freedom and I crave it.

To be adynamic is to be an eagle with clipped wings. It might be more tolerable if I had never flown, or was still so unaware of my situation that I didn't know I could no longer fly.

Misery comes when my cell window is mysteriously opened and I soar briefly, only to learn that the magic that opened the window can apparently control the length of my flight, force me down, and place me back in my cage tormented with desire for the window to open once again.

FROM MY NOTEBOOK, DECEMBER 15, 1989

14

Halfway Home

There are advantages to having a head injury:
For one, you can hide your own Easter eggs.
ANONYMOUS
⚘

I wasn't looking forward to viewing the videotape. I knew at the time I had done a poor job. I had flooded, so my thought processes were completely stalled and with them my memory of what had happened. I had never before seen what I looked like in that state.

The tape was of my third exercise on the hot seat. Our assignment had been to name two qualities we liked about ourselves. The session had taken place two days ago but it took me until today to build up my ego to the point where I could watch it. I arrived at eight, which gave me two hours before the others showed up for Orientation. I got the tape and took it to a session room and popped it into the tape player.

These Interpersonal Group exercises were intended to accomplish several things beyond the obvious ones of our gaining skills in inventing, organizing, and communicating ideas effectively. They also assisted us in becoming more socially adroit and confident, and in learning how to listen to the meaning of words and respond to what was actually said.

The videotapes, which we were encouraged to review as often as we wished—or could bear—allowed us to see how we appeared to the world. Knowing how we composed our faces, or talked, sat, responded to others, or even how much or how little we gestured, enabled us to work at changing our disinhibited or adynamic appearances.

In most tapes there were elements of our performances that we did well, and these were enjoyable to watch. The records of missteps, however, were the ones with the most value. These painful-to-view parts were essential in motivating us to change. They were the answer to Robert Burns's longing for the "giftie" of seeing ourselves as others see us.

When REWIND clicked that it had finished, I pushed PLAY.

It had been raining hard the morning of my presentation, and I had walked from my apartment to HTP without a raincoat or an umbrella. I looked like I had been fished out of a lake. Just seeing the way my wet clothes clung to my body made me shiver. My hair was plastered to my forehead and straggled down either side of my face. The bright red cotton pants teamed with a madras shirt and brown sweater would have been an unfortunate combination even dry and freshly pressed.

The two qualities I picked to talk about were empathy and integrity. I was fully prepared. I had practiced all week the several succinct sentences I had committed to paper, although we weren't allowed to use notes in the talk.

I actually did quite well for several minutes. I defined "empathy" and talked about its role in my relationship to my patients. I gave an example from my practice to show how it enabled me to communicate more effectively with my patients and help them mobilize their resources to get well.

When I finished, Joan, seated on my immediate left, brought my thinking to a halt by asking, "How do you utilize your empathy in relating to your peers in rehab?" She immediately tacked on, "How can you use empathy to help yourself?"

I was caught off guard by her attempt to make me shift gears and by the complexity of two questions. This twist didn't fit into the structure of my presentation. My floodgates opened.

"I . . . what . . . I don't know . . . say it again, please."

"I know I just threw a monkey wrench into your presentation," Joan said, "but I want you to think on your feet. Right now, you're wondering if you wrote this answer on your paper."

I said nothing.

Joan continued saying encouraging things, giving helpful cues, repeating the question, breaking it down. I stared at her face as though I was waiting for her to cue me. Floodwaters had risen so high, I was now drowning. It was a full three minutes—an eternity in any performance—before I spoke again, though my hands were in constant motion, as if their dance could coax my mind to engage. Maybe they were scanning the airwaves for thoughts.

Finally, Joan supplied the answers, which I echoed.

"I, am empathic when . . . ," she said.

I stared at her mouth. "I am empathetic when."

And so I was slowly led out of the flood.

Scott was first to give his critique, with atypical understatement. "Claudia didn't say much."

Looking at the tape, I recognized nothing of myself in that slumped figure with her frozen face, staring eyes, and flat speech; in that automaton who, once flooded, could not rise to the most basic thought or follow the simplest cue. I longed to hear a voice off camera announce that this was a joke, folks, a bad dream, and you are now about to see the real Claudia, who will give a dynamite performance.

How could anyone seeing this creature find two qualities worth admiring? Looking at her, I couldn't find one. It was clear that how I looked when I flooded was as important a change in me as my disruption of thought. It would require a second viewing another day to take me past my self-loathing so that I might develop other useful reactions.

I saw Scott the next morning right after he had screened his own tape of the same assignment. It wasn't only the adynamic among us who needed this mirror. It was equally valuable to the disinhibited. Without it, it would have been easy for him to believe he had done a "good job" simply because he was animated and verbose and so enjoyed center stage. The videotape revealed to him the difference between a lively, well-told, amusing story and a loud, digressive, and pointless anecdote.

His presentation, which was given with excessive gestures and considerable laughter on his part, included a dissertation on his feelings about the Army, how we all had "great parents," the value in a close relationship between Jews and Christians, and his abiding respect for "chaplains and principled Communists."

He seemed surprised to see his expansive gestures, how often he rode over his coach, Ellen, and how carried away he was by the string of topics that had nothing whatsoever to do with his assignment.

Scott, being Scott, laughed it off with "My gift for improvisation may be doomed."

❧ In early May, HTP planned a "midterm party" for its trainees, their family members, and the staff. During the evening social event, we trainees were each asked to make a brief presentation about our experiences in the HTP program.

For my family, who lived so far away, the trip to New York would not only be an occasion to meet my peers and their families, it would also be their first opportunity to attend sessions and to consult with Joan and Yehuda. My mother and Marcia planned their visits in a way that extended my time with them. My mother would come in on Sunday and leave Friday, the day after the party. Marcia would be there from Thursday through Sunday.

Because their visits would embrace the weekends when I could not use my borrowed apartment, my mother hoped to arrange for a room at the Princeton Club on 43rd Street, where my stepfather, Richard, had long been a member. However, a room was not available at the club until Monday, so I spent Friday night with Tina and Anthea, Saturday with Lori, and, when my mother arrived Sunday, I spent the night with her at the Warwick.

Monday morning she accompanied me to HTP and, except for a brief consultation with Joan, sat in on my classes. That afternoon, she moved into the Princeton Club, and I went with her so we could be together. It was the first time I had seen her since coming to New York nine weeks earlier. Perhaps it was observing how I functioned during this double move, or sharing close quarters for a week, but whatever the catalyst, she threw up her hands over my living arrangements.

"You can't keep doing this, Claudia," she said. "I don't know how we all could have gone along with the idea that you didn't need a permanent place to live. This living like a gypsy heightens your dysfunction. You're going in circles trying to cope with this constant change—a borrowed apartment four nights a week, moving hither and yon on the weekend, coming back Monday morning, having to set up camp again, constantly packing and unpacking. All of it, frankly, in a haphazard manner."

She helped me see that I was dissipating my energy with dismal results, that I needed to focus on rehab, eating an evening meal, and performing a few necessary everyday tasks. She pointed out I needed to have a place of my own in which I could leave key items in view so I could be visually cued. She and Marcia understood by now that something in a drawer or a suitcase was inaccessible to my memory. If I couldn't see it, I didn't own it.

"If you lived in a place that's yours," she said, "you would have the freedom to organize your kitchen and the clothes in your closet. You could label things and put signs up so you could manage meals and know what to wear."

I was already buying in to the idea of a simpler life, but she clinched it with "You can be more successful than you currently are."

The next day, while I was in my sessions at HTP, my mother set about researching locations and availability of apartments. The *Village Voice* produced the most promising leads. She checked out several, but only one had the essential ingredients of proximity, security, and simplicity—she had given up on affordability. Its greatest merit was its location at Park Avenue and 33rd: an easy walk to rehab, two blocks from Lori's new apartment, and right at the Lexington Avenue subway stop.

She told them a tentative yes and made an appointment for the three of us to see it on Friday, the morning after the party.

Those eight days with Marcia and my mother in New York were marvelous. All of a sudden, as though someone had waved a magic wand, my life flowed effortlessly and without mishap. Walking through the city with them made it smaller, friendlier, easier to negotiate. Under their guidance, I was well dressed, and well fed and went places—out to dinner, to a gospel concert at Lincoln Center, even to a Broadway play. And on Sunday, Marcia and I went to the Central Park Zoo in the morning and to the Cloisters in the afternoon.

The midterm party on the previous Thursday evening went very well, even though by that time of day I was exhausted and couldn't wait to go home to bed. The party, which was held on the main floor of the dental school building, was festive. Marcia and my mother seemed to have a good time socializing with the other family members and with the staff. I think. My notes are sketchy. It was one of the few times at HTP when I shucked my daily regimen of writing everything down. I only have the copy of my presentation.

At breakfast the next morning, Marcia and my mother enthused about the evening and complimented me on my presentation. After breakfast we took a look at the apartment my mother had identified. The single room was about ten by fifteen. In the corner near the only window was a closet-sized kitchen. An alcove led into the bathroom. The carpeting was hunter green, the walls were white. The furnishings consisted of two hide-a-bed sofas upholstered in rust-colored vinyl, a small pine table, three chairs, two lamp tables, and a dresser.

It had instant appeal. My mother and Marcia remarked on its being bright and airy and clean. I liked it because it was just one room. Nothing could get terribly lost. We agreed it was a find even though, to us non–New Yorkers, the rent seemed exorbitant. I again thanked the Lord for my insurance company, and we concluded the arrangements with the landlord.

Marcia was to meet with Joan at noon. My mother, who had a three o'clock flight back to Michigan, proposed that she and I lunch together. After my mother left, Marcia and I could move my things, which I continued to store at Lori's every weekend, into my new apartment.

My mother and I walked along the bookstalls edging Central Park, luxuriating in the dappled sunlight of a gorgeous early May morning before a leisurely luncheon at the Metropolitan Museum. I had an exuberant sense that I was getting better, but I also knew that my life in New York before they arrived had not gone well. I voiced that idea and explained that although I had learned several strategies to help me compensate for my problems, I wasn't yet adept at utilizing them. I could see incremental improvements in my work at HTP, but very little of that translated to anything practical I could use in managing my personal affairs outside of rehab. I swung widely between optimism and discouragement.

My mother reminded me of how well I had responded to her request two weeks earlier that I speak to a family member undergoing a medical crisis. He needed both explanation and direction regarding his problem, and she felt I had given both admirably.

"When you talk about medicine," she said, "it's hard to grasp that you're injured. You seem to be able to pull the information you need out of memory. Besides, I've read that the brain can continue to improve for up to five years after the injury. I can't see any reason, given how far you've come, that you won't recover fully. But," she blithely assured me, "even if there are a few residual effects, the critical thing is that your medical knowledge and your underlying intellect are intact."

Relief and excitement raced toward my heart. My mother and I were in continuous contact. She of all people could recognize if my intellect was unscathed. Of the nonprofessionals in my life, she better than anyone except Marcia should be able to assess the Me in me, even allowing for my memory and cognitive deficits. After all, it was she who had insisted I cancel my medical board exams and not return to work; she who had urged me to go to HTP.

Her confidence in what she said made me teeter on an emotional and intellectual seesaw, balanced between my desperate desire to be fully healed and my real-world experience of my limitations. In my heart, I knew it was the reality of my ongoing difficulties and my coaches' assessments that were the true gauge of my progress.

I found myself in the curious position of explaining to my mother something about myself I didn't know I knew—that what mattered was not how well I could regurgitate previously learned material or how normal I could appear to others, but how well I could actually think and reason.

We lingered at the table, she making her tea last till it was time for her to leave for the airport. She expressed her sadness about the lost promise of other trainees, saying we had much to be thankful for in my having been spared the awful losses some of them suffered. "At least," she said, wrapping us both in an illusory, gossamer cocoon, "your deficits aren't so bad that you can't compensate." She didn't suggest how or when.

Her rosy view of my future was inspired not only by my growth over this last nine weeks at HTP, but also by how well I fared compared to some of my peers.

She told me of her conversation the previous afternoon with Lenny's and Scott's mothers. When we trainees were doing computer exercises, the three of them were viewing a videotape Joan suggested they watch. It was of a lecture given by the internationally prominent Dr. Muriel Leszak about behavioral changes in the head-injured. More specifically, she was speaking about disinhibition and adynamia—explaining that they appear to be almost opposites. The first, at its extreme, encompasses wildly uninhibited behavior. The second produces a flat, emotionless response.

"I honestly don't know what's worse," said Theresa, Scott's mother. "Not being able to put brakes on your behavior or not being outgoing enough to need brakes. Scott can be so impulsive. I can see how people who don't know him or know about his injury might be turned off by it. Young women, for example. He used to joke that it was the uniform, but whatever it was, he's used to having women be attracted to him. He can't understand now that he turns women off by being overly friendly. One evening, he embraced a woman he was being introduced to."

"You're right about not knowing which is worse," Dean said. She told of going with her husband and Lenny on the previous weekend to a restaurant noted for its spectacular view of the Manhattan skyline from the East River.

"The sun was setting. The sky was streaked in glorious red and gold, the skyscrapers were silhouetted against the light. It was just thrilling to Paul and me, but Lenny was as stony as ever. I urged him to respond, saying things like 'Isn't that beautiful, Lenny?' And he said, 'What's beautiful? What am I supposed to see, Mom?'"

My own mother's eyes teared in recollection even while she confessed her own guilt at my being "spared" so much of what had befallen the others. I again found myself in the curious place of explaining myself to the both of us.

"I am fortunate," I said, "but I can't think like I need to, Mama. I'm adynamic too. Most of the time. When you ask why, in class, I didn't volunteer answers to simple questions anyone could answer, it was because I couldn't find the thoughts in my head even though I know they're in there."

"But you're expressing ideas now," she said. "You are almost like you used to be."

"Yes," I said. "I am different right now. I feel energized, and you're handling the details. It's wonderful. I wish I could always be like this, engaged with my surroundings. But I'm afraid I can't. Yet."

We parted, she to her plane and I to meet Marcia.

Years later, my mother told me about her consultation with Joan. In that conference, she expressed the same views, that she believed I had surface problems but that my "intellect was intact." Joan told her flatly that was not true. My mother could not accept it at the time. Nor, she now says, does she believe it would have been to my advantage if she had.

I met Marcia at Lori's and we walked together to my new apartment. Mentally exhausted by this fully packed half day, so different from my usual HTP routine, I collapsed on the love seat, my legs draped over the end, and napped till dinnertime. While I slept, Marcia put my things away. When I awoke, she showed me the location and contents of closets and drawers. I looked and nodded, but it was information I would have to relearn every day.

My mother was right. I did need a place of my own. But we had yet to grasp the reality that I also needed someone to structure my environment. Till then, nothing would be labeled, nothing would be organized.

Nevertheless, even though I could not take full advantage of an apartment of my own, just staying in one place improved the quality of my life—if not that of my neighbors.

TuTu,

I wrote May 15, this is my first night alone in my new place. It is called a studio. Everything is in one room. I think it's bigger than it looks. One closet is a kitchen. I can't see into it from the sofa.

I wanted a cup of tea. I put water on the stove. I sat on the sofa. Some time passed. I smelled smoke. I thought it must be from another apartment. I thought there couldn't be anything burning in this studio because I could see everything.

The alarm started shrieking. A lot of smoke came from the closet. It made me remember it is a kitchen.

The burner ate a hole right through the sauce pan. I am worried somebody will come and evict me.

Nobody even knocked on the door.

15

Meltdown

There is a pain so utter, it swallows being up;
Then covers the abyss with trance
So memory can step around, across, upon it.
EMILY DICKINSON, *More Poems*
✼

Marcia called me from Detroit to say she had decided to return in two weeks for the long Memorial Day weekend. I was elated at the prospect of having her company a second time that month. I would be free of HTP till Tuesday morning, so we would have four days of play. Using a Magic Marker, I drew heavy black squares around the days on my refrigerator calendar to remind me she was coming back.

It did more than that. Seeing the highlighted days on the calendar morning and night triggered a twice-daily concern—the end of May meant there were only eight weeks before rehab ended. July 31 was approaching fast, but Joan had yet to refer to my plans for my return to my job.

When I told Joan that Marcia would be in town, she said it would be a good time for a family conference—that unlike the brief conferences at the time of the midterm party, we would have a chance for a detailed discussion about my progress and plans. She didn't expand on this, but the proposed meeting had an ominous sound. Marcia told me not to worry about it. That was easy to do. I had plenty to do at rehab and I was beginning to see some results.

The computer exercises and the strategies which I practiced endlessly were teaching me how to focus for longer periods of time. They enabled me to pay better attention to conversation and concentrate longer on activities.

We were also given strategies to help us look more animated, which carried over into actually making us more animated. We learned to quiz ourselves about our alertness: Did we maintain eye contact? Smile? Use body language? It was a juggling act to do all that and think at the same time, but it began to pay off.

I used a battery alarm for specific-time reminders. Timers prompted me to ask myself if I was still doing the task I had begun. Music tapes helped energize my thinking. My brain treated Bruce Springsteen like a wake-up call.

My performance was not consistent or flawless, but my greater productivity was a much-needed boost to my ego, and if I failed to notice any of these achievements, however minor, the coaches were quick to sound fanfares. I was encouraged to elaborate on them in my notebook so I could see them for the benchmarks they were.

One change that excited me greatly had nothing to do with my rehab strategies. It was evidence of a degree of spontaneous recovery. It occurred on the weekend before Memorial Day on a visit to my friends Kay and Edward. I reported it proudly to my grandmother:

> *Dear TuTu,*
>
> *A wonderful thing happened today on the train to Kay's house for the weekend. I daydreamed. I'm quite sure about this. These were random, impromptu thoughts and stories for a prolonged period of time. Mostly old memories I think. I wasn't trying to answer a question. My mind self-initiated these thoughts without any stimulus. I would love to appear to others as "absentminded" because I am daydreaming, rather than vacant.*

The few activities I had were on weekends with friends. For a long time, I saw these as blissful escapes where, for hours at a time, I could pretend nothing had changed in my life. I came to recognize they had another value: with friends to provide the structure and opportunity, I could also be productive, something I had missed greatly during this last vegetative year.

Kay, with whom Lori and I had shared an apartment at college, and her husband, Edward, were especially helpful. They lived in a lovely, large old house in Connecticut and so had plenty of tasks I could do and a willingness to let me do them any weekend I was fortunate enough to spend with them.

> *May 22*
> *Dear Mama,*
> *I painted door frames and furniture at Kay and Edward's in Connecticut.*
> *They took care of all the details. I did the labor, not the thinking. At one point I began to paint a dresser which I had sanded. Kay walked over and removed the handles from the drawer. She didn't look surprised or irritated. Nor did she insult my former skills by stating why handles should be removed first. She just took care of it.*
> *I realize the world can't be restructured so that others will do my planning, organizing, and filling in of gaps I leave undone. But their kindness this weekend made me feel gloriously useful. I spend a disproportionate amount of time on the receiving end of friendship. It was nice this time to leave some painted furniture behind.*

I was writing daily. Between my journal entries, rehab notes, and letters home, I often wrote several pages in a day. By June, my writing skills had developed so that my ability to think and communicate on paper far outstripped my oral skills.

But shopping was still unmastered.

The night before Marcia arrived for the long holiday weekend, I experienced an annoying predicament I was destined to repeat, which I privately referred to as a "meltdown." To demonstrate my improved planning and shopping skills, I wanted to buy the food ahead of time. Marcia loves vegetables, which solved the problem of menu planning. However, I was concerned about how much to buy and how to choose them, and I had yet to have a successful shopping expedition. When I mentioned this during lunch at HTP, Sharon suggested a way to avoid the challenges of the produce department—"frozen vegetables." So, I wrote on my list: *4 bottles seltzer water. 10 boxes frozen vegetables. Don't choose. Buy.*

I did just that and trudged home with two bags of frozen food. I was careful not to set the plastic bags down to rest my hands while waiting on street corners for the lights to change—I had left a few bags stranded that way. I arrived at my apartment door triumphant. I had my key, I had gotten my change, I had not, I thought, overpaid. It had been my most successful trip. I set the groceries down in the hall, unlocked the door, and went inside. Then my nemesis, mental fatigue, overcame me. I flopped down on the sofa for a treacherous "minute" and went to sleep.

The following morning when I was leaving my apartment, I discovered the sodden boxes and bags in their little puddles of water outside the door. I hastily cleaned up the mess. While I was blotting the wet carpeting, my next-door neighbor came out, spotted me, and went right back inside before I could explain myself.

I had only met him once before, the previous week when, just before going to bed, I made a quick dash to the trash chute and locked myself out in the hall. On that occasion, we nodded to each other as he walked rapidly by to his apartment. I had already called the super and was waiting for him, leaning against the wall, stylishly attired in my bare feet with a long T-shirt over panties.

When my mother told my brother of the incident, he said loyally, "Well, clothes don't make the person." On the other hand, naked people rarely command respect.

∾ I was thrilled by Marcia's arrival. Her presence made my new apartment more like home. I knew the weekend would be great. For me. But I was aware she did not especially enjoy coming to Manhattan. It wasn't much fun to be the nanny as she was when we were together. Actually, what she said was "Coming here reminds me how unsafe you are in this city. You don't manage well enough on your own. As for counseling sessions, I'd rather swim with water moccasins."

Saturday morning, Marcia reminded me I had taken up painting in the weeks before rehab and had enjoyed it a lot. The mixing and using of color was the only thing postinjury that sustained my interest. In fact, it excited me intensely. I had had essentially no self-generated activity prior to coming to HTP, yet one day I begged Marcia to buy me paint. Colors so excited me, I wanted to mix my own. Fortunately, she steered me away from the gallon containers of house paint at K mart.

I began painting and I loved every picture with the uncritical eye of a nursery schooler.

I had set my short-lived hobby aside when I moved to New York. Now she suggested that it was time to revive it. I thought it a marvelous idea. Now that I had my own place, I could keep painting supplies.

We went to an art supply shop she found in the neighborhood. I got a basket and drifted through the aisles, buoyant and exhilarated by the colors. By the time Marcia, who had been looking at books, found me, I had filled my basket with boxes of pastel chalks, tiny jars of vividly colored powders, and tubes of every color acrylic and oil paint offered. I, who was normally a very conservative shopper, had gathered hundreds of dollars' worth of supplies. Marcia disengaged me from my riches and sorted out what I needed most.

I almost danced all the way back to the apartment. Marcia was amused. "This isn't the Claudia I've come to know and tolerate. Is there something new in the water?"

The meeting with Yehuda and Joan took place on Tuesday, Marcia's last day. Actually, it turned out to be several meetings—with me, with both me and Marcia, with Marcia alone while Joan took me downstairs for a soda after pointing out to the others that "Claudia has tuned out."

I tuned out a lot. Joan, Yehuda, and Marcia did lots of talking. The verbiage was so complicated and confusing, I had a difficult time paying attention. Also, once they dropped their bomb, I could comprehend nothing.

I was not going to graduate in July.

"We want you to come back for another term, Claudia," Yehuda said in the reasonable, matter-of-fact style he has mastered so well. He could tell a champion athlete that her leg is broken, ending her chance to compete for the gold, and get her to agree that it would be a satisfying alternative to watch the event on big-screen TV from her hospital bed.

Three pairs of eyes stared at me while I struggled for control. Fighting panic, I tried to assimilate the information and mimic their let's-all-examine-this-intelligently posture.

"It's not possible for me to be here next fall," I said. "I'm set to go back to my job July 31."

"I don't think that date was ever locked in, Claudia," Marcia said gently. "What Yehuda is saying is that you're not ready to go back to your job this soon."

"Soon? Soon?" I knew my voice was getting shrill. "July is a year late."

"You are," Yehuda said, tapping the finger of one hand against the palm of the other, "without question [*tap, tap*] or equivocation [*big tap*], not ready to return to work now [*tappity tap tap*]."

Marcia got me out of there with enough grace for both of us. Holding me firmly by the arm, she guided me back to my apartment and urged me to take a nap, saying we would talk later.

For the rest of the afternoon until she left for the airport, she explained the plan again and again. "The bottom line is this. All the trainees including you will celebrate the end of the cycle on July 27 just as planned. Then you come home for a vacation. Then, about Labor Day, you come back for a second five-month cycle."

"But what about my job?"

"Hm . . . let me explain it another way . . ."

It was harder than usual to say good-bye. Marcia got into a cab for the airport and I walked slowly back into my apartment.

The many phone calls after that to Florida and to Michigan provided me an opportunity to talk at length with various family members and friends, trying to work through my distress and accept the derailment of my plans. My pain was raw, but as we all told each other, at least no one had said I couldn't do my job again. All they'd said was that July was too soon.

I took comfort in that but I asked no questions of the HTP staff whenever I thought of it. I felt a sliver of fear in my gut. What else didn't I know? Is there more here than they're telling me? My psyche needed to take their words at face value. "Sometimes," as Freud said, "a cigar is just a cigar." If this was only a postponement, I would learn to live with it.

The extra term was hard to adjust to. It would be spring of next year before I could return to work. My patients and house staff would not even remember me. I didn't question that my job would be waiting.

My disheartenment was limited by my inability to concentrate for long on anything, including my own misery. As is usually the case, the mechanics of daily life took over and kept my disappointment from being crippling.

I also had frequent assurances from my family. Marcia pointed out that an additional term meant I would be "spared the fray of hospital life just now when you're still so vulnerable." My mother said I would have "the summer to practice strategies and thereby ensure that life in New York would be somewhat easier in the next cycle."

"I've finally come to understand," she said, "how difficult many tasks are for you—that you can't do two things at one time, for instance. Your managerial skills are pretty ragged. A full hospital routine would be beyond your ability right now."

Everyone was quick to point out that the very fact of a second cycle meant HTP believed it could do more for me, that I was still capable of greater recovery. I noted those thoughts along with my own.

When I could force myself to think about it, I could agree for brief periods that I was not ready for a frenetic hospital practice. Maybe a postponement while I developed additional strategies and became more skilled in using them was a good idea.

I learned I was not the only one returning. Lenny, Sharon, Beth, Tony, and Scott, five of the seven with whom I had been closest, were also coming back. David was going to the next-step program called Occupational Trials and Bernie was going to retire.

"Yeah, think positive," Scott said. "We'll be together again, and if we spend enough time in these elevators, we can all learn how to fill our own cavities."

～ Marcia's visit and the turmoil that followed caused me to overlook the painting supplies we'd bought. It was several days before I noticed them. I spread them out on the dining-room table and began to draw. My subject was right in front of me on the table—a vase of multicolored anemones that Lori had given me. The light from the window behind them made their colors glorious. I set about capturing their hues on the first page of my large pad.

Prior to my injury, I was no more likely to paint than I was to sing *Carmen* at the Met. Just as I had no voice, I couldn't draw a respectable stick figure. The injury didn't change that, but while it numbed my response to almost all other stimuli, it intensified my perception of color. Certainly I had always enjoyed color. Now I could see hues and tones I had never seen before. Everywhere I turned, I saw a dazzling intensity and diversity of color. I could walk through the gray drizzle of an overcast Manhattan day between the towering monochromatic stone structures and be fascinated by the richness and nuances of the color gray. Put me in a room of impressionistic art and I was oblivious to the pictures' subjects but floored by their brilliant oils.

I painted the flowers in exuberant passion, drawing their long, thin, emerald-green stems topped by small flowers with slender petals in gem colors—ruby, lapis, garnet, topaz. I felt intoxicated by their swaying color. I left the background white to enhance the contrast.

I finished and was just cleaning up when Lori stopped by to invite me out to supper. While I hastily readied myself, she examined my work. "Is this finished, Claudia?"

"Yes." I peered over her shoulder. All the elements were there. "Yes," I said, more confident.

"Why are they floating in the air that way? Shouldn't the flowers be in a vase?"

"They are in a vase," I said. "It's a white vase. Turn the paper a little to the side so its lines catch the light and you can see them better. See? It's white on white. A rather nice contrast."

She hugged me. Art, as they say, is in the eye of the beholder.

16

The Collapse of My Dreams

If I live, I'll be great, I can hardly wait!
CRIS WILLIAMSON
✤

HTP dropped the other shoe two weeks later. It was on Wednesday, June 7, at two-thirty in the afternoon, in Community, our last session of the day.

Scott, smiling and animated as usual, was the one to open our session today. "I volunteer to chair Community. Anybody have a question?"

"Yes," Len said.

"Oh, oh, a coach's question," Scott said.

Len paid no notice. "I propose this topic: How are you coping with the fact that there are things about you that are changed and will remain changed?"

As always, it took me a few minutes to write down the question and process its meaning. I perfunctorily wrote out my answer. After I finished writing, the question began to sink in.

The topic had been presented in a matter-of-fact way.

It was subtle. It was devastating.

It assumed there were things about me that wouldn't change back. This was a message I'd been hearing in various ways throughout rehab. How many times had I been told, "We can't put your brain in a cast and mend it like a broken leg," or "Strategies don't cure problems, they ameliorate them." Why would they say "ameliorate"? When I said "better," I meant all better. For the first time, the import of those phrases registered.

I remember, as a medical student, watching a doctor I admired for his sensitivity explain to a middle-aged woman that she had pancreatic cancer. Her cancer was advanced, he said directly to her, holding her attention. He explained that there were steps we would take to make her comfortable, but we could not cure her.

I marveled at how well the patient took the news. She was solemn but showed no grief. A dying mother with a child still at home, and her composure was more intact than my own.

"Such grace," I later said to him.

"Or denial," replied the doctor.

"What's to deny? You spelled everything straight out."

"She didn't hear me," he said.

The next day, her surgical resident furiously cornered me in the hall. "You said that lady had been told her diagnosis," he said. "I told her Surgery would be signing off her case since she had inoperable cancer, and she became hysterical. She says no one ever told her anything about cancer."

I could understand her unwillingness to accept that she was dying, but I was incredulous that she believed she was learning about her cancer for the first time. I felt I was such a realist I could never be in such denial.

I now learned I was wrong.

Voices droned on, each one answering the question and clarifying its interpretations for himself or herself. My horror widened as I glimpsed deeper layers in Len's question. Everyone? Everyone here has lost his or her old self. Forever? As in permanent injury? *Permanent!*

With each passing minute my chest tightened, my pulse quickened. I began to sweat. When Beth was called upon, she stood up and quickly left the room. Joan followed her.

"Hey, Claudia," Scott said. "Do you want to be next?"

My mouth was dry. I wrestled with my flooding while I found my place on the page. Using my forefinger to guide me, I read my answer in a choppy monotone I hardly recognized as my own voice:

"I . . . don't . . . accept it. I recognize . . . in theory . . . I will . . . never . . . have the same . . . cognitive abilities . . . I once had. But there is nothing . . . about me I . . . am willing to . . . point to . . . and say . . . this is the way . . . it's going to be . . . and I accept it."

If I heard anything after that, it was the blood pounding in my ears. I sat rigidly until we were formally excused. When I became aware the others were leaving, I bolted for the door. My flooding was now a typhoon, engulfing me. I was desperate to flee what had been a haven, to get outside where I could flood in private, my grief witnessed only by the scores of strangers sharing the sidewalks.

Somehow I made my way home.

One word, hiding in my unconscious, lying in wait on the periphery of my knowledge, had stripped me of hope and shattered my dreams. *Permanent.* How could I continue to live with this deficient brain, continue to exist as this unrecognizable, undesirable being? My head injury was bearable only because it was temporary. Permanent injury meant I had already lost. My job. My identity. My life.

I was not this damaged shell of a person. I couldn't be. I remembered and loved the person I was. That was the real me.

I realized the phone was ringing and ringing. It was Joan. I had failed to keep our three o'clock appointment, and apparently my abrupt departure hadn't gone unnoticed. I tried to make sense of what she was saying, but I couldn't take in her words. I muttered something, trying to get her off the phone, and hung up.

I sat for hours, a boneless, jellylike blob with a swollen pain, relieved intermittently by stupor, only to return again and again to consciousness and unbearable grief.

I could not live like this. Without my intellect, I did not want to live. I was a remnant of who I was. I was unlovable. I wanted to end my pain.

There is something to be said for the inertia in grief that can stay us from suicide. I remember a despondent friend telling me how, when he despaired the most, he did not have the physical or emotional energy to make his way to a high bridge and leap to his death, even though if he had found himself in midair with a parachute strapped to his back, he would not pull the ripcord.

Joan called again at some point, and although I again could not respond, I wrote down what she said.

Sobbing in near hysteria, I lay down on the sofa, using the armrest for a pillow. I slept on and off. Mostly I stared at the window, watching it change from the pale glow of the Manhattan night to a watery gray of reflected dawn.

At seven, I got up stiffly. I thought a shower would help revitalize me, but I lacked energy to do more than remove my shoes and jeans. I went into the kitchenette, poured a glass of milk, and took it to the table by the window. Scrawled on the pad in front of me were Joan's words from her call of the night before.

It's okay to hope.

I couldn't believe in myself any longer; I tried to trust Joan. If she was saying it was okay to hope, she must mean there was something to hope for. Clutching at that message, I undressed and showered and dressed again to return to HTP as usual. It was Thursday. If I could get through this day, I would have the weekend alone and time to come to grips with myself.

I felt numb about my self-knowledge. I could never, at least not for very long, slip back again into my former innocence when I believed my losses were all correctable, but I still had a long way to go before reaching emotional acceptance of my head-injured persona.

Joan and I spoke that afternoon at length. We chewed over and over the meaning of "permanent," the thought that even if "real, complete recovery" wasn't possible, I could continue to develop compensatory skills that could help me function at a high level. She told me that what HTP was asking of me was an intellectual recognition that there were parts of me that could never be the same again.

"No one is predicting exactly how far you can go in your recovery," she said. "You should always hope even while you strive to be everything you can be. Just know there will be a ceiling. You won't get everything back."

As we parted, she gave me a poem to read. It was Robert Frost's "Wild Grapes." I took it home, too weary to read that evening. The following night when I did, I discovered in it a wonderful message. I seized on it. It was a talisman.

Frost tells of a child trying desperately to hold, but eventually releasing, a tree branch of wild grapes. She learns that one can let go physically (or

recognize intellectually that total recovery is not possible) without aban-
doning passion and hope. His words told me it was all right to hold on to
desire and dreams.

> *I had not taken the first step in knowledge;*
> *I had not learned to let go with the hands,*
> *As still I have not learned to with the heart,*
> *And have no wish to with the heart—nor need,*
> *That I can see. The mind—is not the heart.*

Please Don't Tell Me You Know What It's Like

The conversation has few variations. They say, "My memory is worthless. I don't know where I'm going half the time. You think you're bad, I'm worse." Or, "Thank God they don't give me those cognitive tests. I'd never pass." Or, "You're lucky you can blame everything on a head injury. You forget that most of us have a poor memory." Or, "Just wait till you get to be 40 (60, 80) like me: You'll know what bad really is."

I understand that people are trying to be nice. They want to reassure me I'm normal, that my problems are no different from theirs. It is a standard way to let me know they feel good about me.

But still, it is inane chatter. It occurs while I am running as fast as I can to stay in place and working to keep alert and energized, to follow their conversation, to consciously direct my mind using every strategy I possess just to do something that for them is automatic.

After twelve years of university education, I labor to read a short story, must ask my high school–trained assistant for instructions on how to do my job, and use an alarm every three minutes while driving to get to the correct destination.

No, people don't know what it's like. People's abilities and inner resources vary widely in degree and kind. That is not the same as being stripped of the abilities one once had and valued. Their occasional absentminded moments and quirks of intellect have not robbed them of intellectual exchanges, separated them from a beloved profession, or made them unrecognizable to themselves.

Without intending to, they discount my struggle to compensate for my losses and minimize the small victories in my day. Surely, it would be outrageous to say to a person with artificial legs that walking is a challenge for us all. I try to take these insensitive comments in the well-intentioned spirit in which they are given, but how I wish others would try less hard to show me an empathy they do not possess.

How much better it is when people act naturally with me. Often, I benefit from their assistance. It feels good to laugh with them when my mistakes are funny and to sense their empathy when they're not.

So, laugh with me, cry with me, but please don't tell me you know how I feel or you know what it's like because "it's the same" for you.

How can it be? You have never lived in my head.

FROM MY NOTEBOOK, AUGUST 16, 1990

17

Waking Up Is Hard to Do

One thing I see clearly. These notes are not thoughts.
They are the creaks and cries of a heart opening slowly.
FLORIDA SCOTT-MAXWELL,
The Measure of My Days
✲

Knowing I would not regain my former self, even with continued rehabilitation, induced waves of depression that frightened me with their intensity. Along with the depression, or because of it, I now had a lower tolerance for frustration.

June 14

Dear TuTu,

This is written on a train ride home to New York from my weekend in New Jersey. I am weary of paying attention, always working on asking myself the how, what, where, and when of every activity and action. I long to be on automatic pilot. I know I am whining and full of self-pity, but I am hungry and too exhausted to find my way through the maze to get food and safe passage back to my apartment door.

I am ashamed of this despondency. I am fortunate in being able to take care of myself, to be on my own. But, I wish someone other than me was in charge here. Knowing I am fortunate and free to make choices isn't making me smile as I screw up the simplest tasks. God forgive my blasphemy, but if this is autonomy, give me subjugation.

Marcia continued to supply me with the daily support of her letters. They were more useful than phone calls because I could review their content and hold on to their meaning. She had been marvelous in helping me come to grips with my depression over having to return to HTP. Now she helped me focus on my strengths and remonstrated with me for being hard on myself about not being more grateful for what I had. In one she wrote, "I ached for your distress, but I confess it was good to hear you sound so alive."

Her words intrigued me. They reminded me that I had begun to experience bewildering new feelings. I realized I was now coloring situations—good or bad—with emotions. Moreover, I remembered an emotion even after I had forgotten the specifics of the situation.

For instance, when Beth asked me if Marcia and I had seen *Harlem Nights*, I said, "I didn't like that movie."

"What's it about?"

"I don't remember that, just that I didn't enjoy it."

This was a step forward. Throughout this last year, my feelings had been anesthetized. I had a diminished visceral response to things I had previously enjoyed—food, friends, athletic activities, movies. I, who had been easily stirred by music, art, drama, books, nature, and poetry, felt nothing when I heard a Puccini aria or viewed a spectacular landscape. I did not delight in the beautiful or thrill to the magnificent or feel awe at the wondrous. Nor was I aware, apart from the complaints of others, that my capability for enjoyment was dampened. Nor did I mind.

Somehow, when I wasn't looking, I had begun to change.

> *June 27*
>
> *Marcia,*
>
> *I am feeling more. I can't explain this clearly, but I feel emotion intensely, on and off, lately. Good and bad feelings, though I often can't pinpoint them more specifically than to say, "I'm excited and it feels good." I want these emotions to stay with me because they make me feel alive. I am, however, having trouble controlling them. The more intensely I feel, the less clearly I think.*
>
> *Today, my cassette player unleashed Bach while I was mixing colors on my palette. The music and colors were so exciting to me that I could barely contain myself to paint.*

July 17
Dear Richard,

I am listening to Vladimir Horowitz. May we all have such enthusiasm in our eighties. He plays notes differently than Mozart wrote them. Not slighting Mozart, his favorite, but allowing himself to play freely. I would like to paint Horowitz's interpretation of Mozart as felt by me. I don't need skill to do that, just what I have, the desire.

My behavior was now growing multifaceted. Bouts of energized activity would surface between periods of vacant silence. However, in either event I was no longer numb. Depending upon the stimulus, I could react passionately. Sometimes too much so, as when Marcia took me to the Detroit Zoo to show me the gardens.

I did not just sit in the park and reflect on their beauty, I thrust my arm high in the air, leapt up, and galloped around the flower beds. My pleasure in being there quickly escalated into such an exalted emotional state that I resembled a hyperactive five-year-old, albeit unusually tall.

Marcia signaled me to come back.

"Claudia," she said through her suppressed laughter, "knock it off. Trust me, it's too much. Come, walk with me for a while."

I agreed reluctantly; I did not want to suppress my joy. I could taste the last day of school, the first day of spring, the ultimate vacation. I loved the sensation of feeling animated and alive without having to use artificial devices to generate the energy. This awakened child embodied old parts of *me* that I missed.

My right shoulder was actively aching from the sudden thrust I had given it. I don't know why it happened, but when my excitement unleashed a surge of adrenaline, my arm would spontaneously shoot up into the air, as though it were an independent entity. Each time, I felt a sharp pain. I wished I could inhibit the action or at least the force of it. I was developing a chronic soreness in the rotator cuff that was damaged at the time of my head injury, but I was loath to consult an orthopedic surgeon. I did not know how to explain the activity aggravating my shoulder.

"You know something, Marcia?" I said as we walked. "The coaches say I'm not spontaneous? Boy, I could show them spontaneity."

"Yeah," she said, "take them to the zoo."

These outbursts were intoxicating, but they caused me some of the same social problems and embarrassment as alcohol would. My intense feelings disrupted my thinking and problem solving and interfered with my ability to stay oriented to time and place. When I was on emotionally, I was easily lost and awash with confusion. It was even harder to deal with because these feelings also left me mentally exhausted. My every response was exaggerated. I could be wildly happy, outraged, or despondent on the slightest pretext, without reasonable correlation to the stimulus. It was the hyperbole of an adolescent whose labile emotions send her soaring over an awaited phone call and crashing over a new pimple.

I wanted Joan's opinion but gave her a censored version of my trip to the zoo, saying only, "Sometimes my mind races. It goes fast. Too fast." To give depth to this profound declaration, I added, "When I feel, I don't think. When I think, I don't feel. I want control. I want to do both—together."

"You can and you do," Joan said.

"No," I said flatly.

I wasn't sure if my problems were understood. On the other hand, I didn't want to elaborate on my disinhibition because I didn't want a solution that would rob me of these newfound and much-desired emotions.

These bouts of animation were not spontaneous. They were provoked by external stimuli: fresh air, art, a piece of music. But I didn't know what piece or how strong the stimuli needed to be. Moreover, I wanted to be animated at will without artificial need.

It was a hard concept to explain even to Marcia.

Christopher [my brother] called last night. I know I was blah. I couldn't budge my adynamia and think of a single thing to say. I don't know how to overcome this. What do I do, say excuse me while I run outside and see the sunset or look at some art books? I don't know what will work or how to measure the dose. And what if I overdose? When I'm excited and bounce off the walls, I'm as unable to think or pay attention as when I'm adynamic.

But I did experiment with my own solutions. My greatest success was with music. I used Bach's *Brandenburg Concertos* or the Brahms "Lullaby" to calm me, and hard rock and marches, among other things, to rev me up. When my energy level reached a certain pitch, I could moderate it by turning off the music. The system was imperfect but interesting. And known only by me.

The greatest problem with it was that I couldn't trust the response—neither its intensity nor its interpretation. My emotions were unreliable. I found it unwise to trust their validity.

Marcia early on stopped asking me how I felt. Instead, she told me so I could know. ("Calm down, Claudia. You're angry and it's because you can't find your car.") And it worked. When I knew what I felt and why I felt it, I could better master the emotion. Yet it was disconcerting to need someone else to tell me what I felt.

The one feeling that was readily identifiable was the consuming depression that followed each jolt of memory about the permanence of my injuries. The trigger was invariably related to my desire to do medicine.

Walking home from rehab one day, I followed my written directions to stop for milk and bread. I identified the things I needed fairly quickly and felt pleased waiting in the short line at the cash register. The man in front of me put down his medical bag so as to free his hands to count out bills and receive change. I noted the bag calmly, recognizing it for what it was but attaching no significance to it until the clerk said to him, "Have a good evening, doctor."

"... you all right, lady?"

The clerk touched my arm and I realized she was speaking to me. I tried to make sense of her words.

"... to sit down? ... need ... help?"

I think I shoved my basket toward her and left the store. I remember walking along the sidewalk, trying to recall what had upset me. What had gone wrong? I read the note in my pocket reminding me about the milk and bread and turned back toward the store.

I pushed the glass door open to enter, when I was slammed by a crushing sense of bereavement. Had my mother died? Then I got it. The doctor. He casually possessed the role I had lost.

I backed out the door and turned blindly toward my apartment. When

I entered the lobby, I averted my face from the doorman so he couldn't see my tears. Once upstairs, I read my note again about the milk and bread. It didn't matter. I wasn't hungry.

◠ In mid-July, two weeks before the end of the cycle, Len told us in Orientation that each of us was expected to give a speech at the final party. I decided my presentation would acknowledge that I was not yet leaving rehab, that I had more work to do. It was a fledgling, albeit intellectual, acceptance of my altered self.

That night, I got out my acrylics and put on Strauss's moving "Death and Transfiguration." Using my left hand, I painted a picture of my brain at work—cobalt-blue "thinking" overlaid with intense scarlet "feelings" and many brilliant yellow disconnections. I think the brain in the picture was more vigorous than the one in my head. I also illustrated my imprisoned language in a second picture.

These acts of creating images pierced small holes in my sense of isolation. The joy I once had in spoken language, the release in confiding and sharing, the pleasure in intellectual exchanges with others, might now have two other expressions, however inchoate and primitive. If I could not speak what I felt, I would draw and write it.

The next morning, I took my pictures with me when I went home to Detroit for the weekend. My paintings felt like speech and I did not want to be separated from those utterances.

◠ "We're at forty-fifteen," Marcia yelled over her shoulder as she trotted after the tennis ball I had hit wildly into the next court. "Go back to playing with your left hand."

"That's what I wanted to do. You told me I had to exercise my right hand."

"Well, forget it. I want some competition."

"Marcia, look at the freighter. She's beautiful."

Our city tennis courts sit amid long, tree-shaded lawns at the water's edge, providing a captivating view of the Great Lakes shipping traffic. I tried to see the color of the smokestack to identify the boat, but the sun was right in my eyes, an hour above the choppy waters of Lake St. Clair.

"Are the binoculars in the car?" I said.

"Claudia, we'll watch freighters later. Play ball."

"But we'll miss the freighter."

Marcia accepted the inevitable and crossed over the net. Once in my view, freighters were unmatched in holding my attention.

My family used to picnic along the Detroit River, into which Lake St. Clair flows. These two waters are connectors between Lake Huron and Lake Erie. As a child, I came to love the long boats and learned their signals and their lore. Their numbers are declining, but I still usually sight one each time I come down to the water.

Marcia squinted at the majestic vessel, a freighter riding high in the water with a crane extended along the deck. "Okay, it's a self-loader, not ocean-going, and it's empty. If you've taught me more than that, I've forgotten it."

"You have to wonder where she's headed."

"Not at match point, I don't." But the game was over.

We went home to shower and dress before going out for breakfast. A year ago, I would have made us cheddar cheese and spinach omelets while we discussed Carl Jung's views on Christianity, or something equally interesting to us at that moment. Today, Marcia picked out my clothes and reviewed my strategies. She never betrayed that she minded the change.

A Pilgrim's Journey through Compensatory Strategies

In General:
Learn to elaborate.
    Speak more completely in conversation.
    Stop telegraphing short messages.
    Refrain from being clipped and blunt.
Show emotion. Stop being flat.
    If I draw a conclusion, I must ask myself what led me to it and how I can
    help the listener grasp my meaning.

Flood Prevention:
Remain calm.
Ask myself if there are any other questions I should ask to clarify the situation.
Stay relaxed when staff poke me with questions during feedback sessions.
They are trying to teach me to shift perspective.
Try to retain an entire unwritten thought in memory. To tell a story:
    a) Hold on to the concept, not the elements.
    b) Relax, allow the idea to flow but not so much that I lose sight of the next
    step.
    c) Do not worry about the words themselves.

Today I reached a level of functional aliveness. It was relatively easy to appear energized, animated, and spontaneous without whipping myself into it. What I would give to feel that way consistently—thoughts and emotion combined without racing, flooding, or vegetation.

Automation is a joke. I learn strategies, practice their use, and try to employ them effectively as a way to compensate for my deficits. But it is not automatic. It is merciless effort.

In physical rehab, a person may learn to walk across a room using braces to support her legs. It takes huge effort and determination, but with hard work the fortunate person may eventually learn to walk, maybe even independent of the braces.

My strategies are mental braces. I have practiced their use until my blisters have become calluses. My early successes excited me as only one in braces struggling to reach the far side of the room can know. My dream was to run, but my progress is slow and laborious.

I never imagined that these cumbersome devices, these strategies, would be something I must forever own. I prayed for a six-month rental.

FROM MY NOTEBOOK, MAY 1990

18

Recycled Brains

My only enduring vision of the future was my
magical date—July 31, graduation. Like me, my
crystal ball has apparently suffered diffuse
neuronal damage.
A LETTER HOME
✱

To HTP, it was the final party acknowledging the completion of our passage through the rehabilitation program. I viewed it as a graduation with the ironic twist that half the class would not be leaving.

Most of those who were actually leaving were going on to the next phase of HTP's program, a supervised work program called Occupational Trials, designed to bridge the distance between rehab and a job. Leaving or not, everyone was going to take part in the nongraduation program, and all the family members and significant others in the trainees' lives were invited.

Because my family lived out of state, my guests were few—my mother, Richard, and Marcia.

My father was unable to come. He is a good man whom I love and admire and from whom I inherited my enthusiasm and zest for life. Our relationship is warm and polite. Unfortunately, I do not know him very well—not even well enough to fight. We never reached that level of intimacy.

He and my mother divorced when I was twelve, and he remarried, but his demanding job in an advertising agency separated us long before that time. He had indicated it would be hard for him to take time off from work and travel from Texas to visit me in New York, and I accepted that. I was not family in that way, and he and his wife, Beverly, a generous and loving woman, knew I had other sources of emotional support.

The presentations, as with the midterm affair, would be given in a small auditorium on the main floor of the dental school. Shortly before six that evening, staff, trainees, and their families began to assemble in the attractive adjoining lounge where a long table held a buffet supper. Guests mingled, sipping their soft drinks and introducing themselves to each other. In a refreshing note of informality, a few seated themselves on the carpeted floor rather than stand and eat while balancing glass, dish, and napkin. In a very short time, they were joined by everyone not occupying the few chairs scattered about.

The mood was festive. The guests were noisily happy and relaxed. We trainees were mildly anxious, concentrating on fielding introductions, making conversation, and thinking about our forthcoming presentations. I was worried that all this socializing would sap my limited vitality.

"I'm fading," I said to Tommy. "I wish I could give my talk now."

"I wish I didn't have to give one," he said. He was resplendent in a beautifully tailored, dark pin-striped suit. A regimental tie and an edge of white handkerchief above his breast pocket gave him a debonair look. I recognized him first by his sunglasses.

Shortly after seven, the group drifted, or possibly were herded, to the auditorium. The room could hold about one hundred fifty people in the steeply banked rows of seats facing a small stage, where twelve wooden chairs were arranged in a semicircle, six on each side of the podium. Someone self-consciously tested the microphone as Len fiddled with the video camera and guests settled into seats. No one directed us. The staff melded into the audience. We were on our own.

Our coifs and attire were dressy and reflected how important the occasion was to us. At my mother's direction, I wore a silk dress in a vivid print. To please her, I let her put a light makeup on me. Between our unaccustomed dresses and suits and given our relative animation, we looked decidedly different, I think, even to each other.

Everyone had to make two presentations. The first was a speech of five minutes about our rehabilitation experience, our progress and accomplishments, and our plans for the near future. In the second part of our program, we each read a brief excerpt from something that had special meaning to us. Our choices varied greatly from rock lyrics to classical poetry. I felt Robert Frost's "Wild Grapes" was a perfect choice for me.

We each did a creditable job. Tommy, despite his fears about this evening, read well. Beth was in high form. Her heavy black hair was piled on top of her head in a Gibson Girl knot that drew attention to her large, dark eyes. Using graceful gestures, she gave the most dramatic performance.

Lenny wore a midnight-blue gabardine suit with a dark red tie. He was perfectly groomed, his beard and hair newly trimmed. Anyone who thought of him as shy, rather than withdrawn, would have been surprised at his easy delivery this evening. He even included a warm, charming acknowledgment of his parents seated in front of him and spoke to the audience in a comfortable, practiced style as though he were used to oration.

Standing confidently like the West Point officer he was, Scott was in a suit and in control. He couldn't resist two jokes, but aside from those two, as it turned out amusing, exceptions, he stayed with the script.

Sharon's peach-colored dress flattered her golden coloring. Her hair was combed back so her face was visible, and she remembered to glance up frequently from her script to look at her audience. Afterward, flushed and radiant from her success, she told me she felt her words exactly captured her feelings. She apparently saw her speech as a vehicle to convey many things she wanted us to know about her injury and rehabilitation. I believe we all did.

I was last. My speech expressed two ideas.

The first concerned my identity. It would be my first public admission that I now understood *intellectually* that, regardless of the outcome, I could no longer afford to put all my emotional eggs in the basket of who I had been. I had rehearsed my words so often that they were devoid of emotional content. I traced the words on paper with my forefinger, looking up at my audience frequently, speaking the lines in a firm voice.

I had held a fixed time table in my head that I would return to medicine in July. Rehabilitation, however, is a much slower process than I thought. I have more problems and they are more difficult than I anticipated. I thought rehabilitation meant a path to take me home, to resume my former life, to return to the person I think of as me . . .

A fragment of a sentence, something, caused the thought to come to life. As I spoke the words, I wanted to snatch them back. While I struggled to not understand what they meant, I scanned the faces watching me, searching for the right pair of eyes.

But successful rehab really means learning to accept this new person. . . . It requires me to reexamine who I am and come up with a less limiting definition than physician.

Regardless of my vocational potential I need to expand my identity beyond my life's work.

I am trying.

I felt icy, my throat was parched, but with that part behind me, my voice strengthened. The end was another kind of admission, but it was richly sugar-coated.

My recent disappointments and depression did not diminish my gratitude for the gifts of my life. I drew upon Socrates to tell of my joy in my reawakened passion. The ability to feel, I said, is the essence of living.

Though there are aspects to the quality of my thinking that still elude me, I have regained the sustaining element in my enjoyment of life—my passion for art, music, nature, love, poetry, and life. . . .

I, of course, would always prefer to be Socrates—discontented— rather than a satisfied sheep. But a more telling question with a joyful answer is, if I could have but one, would I rather have the mind of Socrates or the passion for life I now possess? I would choose passion.

To paraphrase Irving Berlin, I am ready to "face the music and dance."

Those of us onstage had no difficulty discerning where the members of each trainee's family were seated. You had only to see which ones, following a presentation, had their handkerchiefs pressed to streaming eyes and noses.

The party broke up quickly, taking time only for rounds of congratulatory hugs and compliments for each of us. For a change, neither my mother nor Marcia reminded me to smile. I was pleased and it showed. The evening had gone well and it was over.

We trainees had another week together, winding down our work in rehab before we would part. Even those of us returning in another month were conscious of a closure.

Sharon hugged me. "It's not good-bye," she said, echoing Scott's sentiment.

Because the discipline at HTP is unrelenting, our last few days were productive. We were each subjected to the same neuropsychological tests we had been given prior to our admission to the program so our progress could be measured objectively.

On Tuesday, Sharon's mother suggested we celebrate the end of the term with a luncheon away from the dental school. We all thought it was a great idea. After a spirited discussion—well, some of us were spirited—we decided to go on the following day to a Chinese restaurant.

The twelve of us trooped to the lucky recipient of our patronage, the Chinese restaurant a block away. Because it took us so long to make the journey—given our diverse physical limitations and personality considerations—we arrived late, somewhat flustered, and under a time-bound pressure to order quickly and get back as soon as we could.

We were met at the entrance by a man who asked whether we wanted to be seated at two tables for six or one large table. A loud discussion followed until Beth took charge.

"One, please," she said in a firm voice.

"Smoking or nonsmoking?"

"Both, thank you."

After much chair arranging and trading, we settled down and tried to order. All of us had difficulty reading new material. I usually solved my problem with menus by ordering the first item listed no matter what it was. Not everyone was so easy. Many of the group wanted everything explained to them but couldn't remember by the end of the list what had been said earlier.

The waiter returned to the table several times. Finally, he brought another waiter with him. We ordered. We promptly forgot what we ordered. This caused problems when the waiters brought the loaded trays to the table. Asking questions like "Who has number twenty-two?" got only blank stares—at least from those of us who were hungry and paying close attention. Some of the group were noisily arguing and laughing, maybe a bit out of control.

The waiters' helpful efforts to be specific ("Twenty-two is egg foo yong.") were of limited help. The waiters resourcefully tried to slide just any dish in front of us. Most of us didn't object, having no idea what was available, let alone what we had asked for. Those who wouldn't go along with that tactic argued loudly, if without substance, "I don't remember what I ordered, but this isn't it."

We were a kindergarten class without the teacher. When it was almost time to pay the bill (it's best not to dwell on that process), someone noticed Richard's absence. Richard, marvel of locomotion that he is, is awesomely adept in the management of his cane and steel braces but needed help if stairs were involved.

We now remembered he was still in the rest room. In the basement. Proud man that he is, it was hard to convince him he needed our help to get down there. Regrettably, no one thought to make a note that he needed to be brought back up.

We were late getting back to HTP. We could never go back to that restaurant again. But there were lots of others for us to consider another time. Maybe next term.

Next cycle was a long way away—forty days to be exact. I was heart-leaping happy to be going home, graduated or not. It was behind me now as I packed my few belongings and made arrangements to leave the apartment and New York.

Lori agreed to let me store at her place the kitchen things I had bought and some personal items I'd need again in September. The apartment owner said she had a tenant for the month of August, but the studio would be vacated and available again to me the first of September.

None of this was as easy as it sounds. The wrong things went home or to Lori's, my landlady was bewildered by our truncated conversations, and my packing was an unmitigated disaster.

I didn't care, I just wanted to go.

Like many people with a major disorder, I believed in a geographic cure. I blamed New York for my inability to function well. It would be different at home, especially now, armed as I was with my new props and strategies. I boarded the plane for Detroit a little disheveled but high-spirited. I couldn't wait to be home, free and safe.

Back in the Saddle Again

I bicycled my way through adolescence. As a teenager, my blue Raleigh Grand Prix was my most important possession. It offered me heady independence and adventure. My friend Sylvia and I toured our neighborhood and the distant suburbs, proved our mettle on 200-mile, 24-hour marathons, and graduated to the countryside of Michigan.

One week in summer, we cycled off with a backpack of essentials like tuna fish and journeyed up to Stratford, Ontario, 150 miles northeast, to see Shakespeare. Bicycling down country roads in the crisp, wet morning air, watching the sun rise over the tree-lined road ahead of us, I felt invincible.

To bicycle was to be free.

That sense of freedom was harder to maintain as an adult, off on a pre-accident weekend ride. I found myself toting excess baggage of professional concerns and everyday stresses and using the trip to rehash patient problems or mentally draft medical lectures for use in the week ahead. My mind did not always escape into the meadows around me. But by trip's end, my body and sense of well-being were always restored.

Whoever said "It's like riding a bike, you never forget how" is wrong. My natural dexterity for cycling vanished with my injury. Bicycling now takes a level of attention and concentration that is difficult for me to sustain.

After three years of practice, I can follow another cyclist on a bike path away from traffic and usually do well. True, I am easily disconcerted by passing bikes and joggers and am challenged by bumps, cracks, and stop signs. I do not resemble the freewheeling youth heading down the highway, traveling cross-country.

Nevertheless, although I may appear less athletic and relaxed, my body is alive and my mind sees only the present tense. I am stirred and excited by the passing landscape. Colors and scents arouse me. My immediate world has my undivided attention. I am not distracted by a past or future. My disorientation to time and space smoothes away concerns and immerses me in pleasure.

It is then that I regain a measure of the carefree exuberance of youth.

FROM MY NOTEBOOK, AUGUST 26, 1991

19

What I Did on My Summer Vacation

*"Claudia, I want to thank you," said Robert, referring
to my recommendation that he and his wife eat dinner
at Joe Muer's. "We had a wonderful time last night."
"You're welcome," I said, not remembering what we
had done but warmly adding, "I had a great time too."
"Oh? What did you do?"*
FROM MY NOTEBOOK, AUGUST 10, 1989

August started out poorly. And slid from bad to worse.

"What's burning?" Marcia called down to me from atop the ladder I was holding as she cleaned the eaves.

Her words drew my attention to an acrid smell and some wisps of black smoke rolling out of the kitchen window. She hurried down and I raced her to the side door.

"What's wrong?" I shouted over the shrieking alarm.

"Check the oven, that's where the most smoke is."

While she disengaged the smoke alarm, which I privately felt was too sensitive, I grabbed oven mitts and wrenched the door open, filling the kitchen with billowing, black smoke. My eyes were smarting so much I could hardly see the charred mess.

"Uh-oh. It's the meat loaf," I said as I hurried out the side door with the smoking pan.

"Claudia," Marcia's voice followed me. "Why did this happen?"

"You said you like meat loaf."

"I know, and I'm beginning to regret that. You've made three in a row; the problem is we don't get to eat them. Besides, my question is not why are you making meat loaf, but why are they burning? We talked about your not putting anything on the stove without first—"

"I did," I said. "I set the timer."

"We had this conversation two days ago. Yesterday, we talked about you not knowing what the timer meant unless you also wrote a note."

"I wrote a note." I pulled it from my pocket and read its message out loud. "'Timer means take meat loaf from oven.' My timer strategy worked in New York. I don't know why it's impossible to cook here."

"Because this is not a one-room home. You cannot set the stove timer and work in the basement or outdoors or upstairs where you can't hear it. You walk out of the kitchen and forget you're cooking. You have to set your pocket alarm so your prop can travel with you."

Who could argue with that logic? I wished I could. I knew it was irrational, but I loathed hearing that a mystery I could not solve had an obvious answer. I was angry with myself for not seeing it on my own, and annoyed with her for always knowing what I didn't.

When I came back into the kitchen with the now empty, crusted pan, Marcia was leaning against the counter, waiting to continue the conversation.

"Claudia, I know you're upset and frustrated with this first week home, and I'm not going to kid you, you're not doing well. But I think part of your problem is the lack of HTP structure. Your day isn't planned for you here."

"My problem is that none of the strategies I used in New York work here."

"You aren't tailoring your strategies to this environment or using your props to fit your needs here."

"All these situations are new."

"That's my point. These are new situations. You need to either adapt your old strategies or find some new ones. For now, you put away the ladder and I'll go get us some Chinese carry-out. Okay?"

"Such a deal." I was glad to turn to something else but filled with dismay. Adapt strategies? Just how the hell do you do that? Someone ought to invent a do-it-yourself strategy maker.

Fortunately, Marcia had this weekend off, which made life so much easier. Instead of initiating activities, I could follow her lead. After lunch,

Marcia suggested I do the dishes. When I finished, I went looking for her. Noticing that the side door was ajar, I went outside to find her, slamming the door behind me.

Marcia was wheeling the lawn mower out of the garage, heading down the driveway toward me. For her, yard work was a necessary chore of home ownership. It wasn't how she would choose to spend a Saturday.

I loved it and always had. And because I had the opportunity to garden every other weekend, I knew our yard should be blazing in color, the lawn lush, the flower beds weeded. As I looked around I saw only a few tended pockets. It was obvious which areas had attracted my attention. The young peach tree near the garage patio had fresh mulch around it and the impatiens in the flower beds along the driveway were full and healthy. In fact, there wasn't so much as a stray weed in the border edging the driveway.

Everywhere else I turned showed neglect. Rainfall had been sparse since spring and the perennials showed it—thin, wilted, and choked with weeds that always managed to grow, contemptuous even of drought. The lawn was long and shaggy. It needed cutting. Even more, it needed watering.

"What are you doing with the lawn mower?" I said as I trailed after Marcia.

"Taking it for a walk."

"I'll shave the lawn, okay?"

"What a good idea," she said. "Why is it that the only thing that propels you into motion is seeing me do a task? Nothing happens independent of my orchestration. You're like a car in neutral—you need another person to get you in gear."

I had no answer. I functioned best if I copied someone else's activity or worked directly under their guidance. Notes succeeded only to a point. A written instruction to *put the chicken in at four* only made sense at four o'clock. The note would be ineffective if I read it at, say, three forty-five.

"Okay, take over here. I'll go in and do the laundry." She noticed the closed door. "I don't have my key. Can I get back in?"

"Yeah," I said. "It's open. I mean not open, of course, but it's open."

"You mean it's unlocked."

"That's what I said. It's open."

Marcia was called into the hospital Sunday afternoon, cutting the weekend short and leaving me on my own. The timing was good. I functioned much better if I had a nap every afternoon, but because I would rather spend time with her, I tended not to nap if she was available.

Before I could turn to the stairs, the phone rang.

"Hello Claudia," my caller said, "this is Karen."

"Hi, Karen." I slid into the chair behind my desk, where I kept my big notebook. While she made small talk, I flipped through my notes on acquaintances to find Karen's name.

"We need to make plans. What time is the concert?"

"Well, this specific concert . . ." I read down the page under Karen's name. Nothing on a concert, but the last entry said, *Her mother is considering back surgery.* ". . . I'm looking for the details. How's your Mom's back doing?"

"Better, thanks for asking. She's back at work."

"I don't know."

"Know what?" said Karen.

"What we're talking about. I don't recall anything about a concert."

"The DSO at Orchestra Hall Thursday night? I thought you used a calendar of some kind to remind you."

Of course. I should have looked on the calendar, not under Karen's name. "Here it is." I furnished the time and wrote down where we would meet.

"You know," she said, "I think you're getting better. That was pretty good, remembering my mother's back. "

I replaced the receiver and spun in my chair. "It worked!" I yelled. Too loud. Punkin tore out of the room. It was the first time my notebook made me look like I had a memory. I wrote it down so I could tell Marcia.

About six, Marcia called from the ER and said she was finishing up and suggested we salvage the rest of the day by taking in a movie. To ensure that we got there on time, she told me to meet her there. I was pleased and determined to do everything correctly.

The first step was to write down and obey her detailed instructions about when and where to meet. It all went smoothly.

We both enjoyed the movie greatly, even though it was subtitled, which meant I could not read the words quickly enough to comprehend them. As a result, I concentrated on the action and the actors and felt I derived as much sense and pleasure from the film as those who were busy reading.

As we walked out of the theater I sorted out the season and time from the night air. I tagged along as Marcia wound her way through the parking lot, proud of how good I'd become at imitating someone else's lead without showing my disorientation about where we were or what we would be doing next. It took very little to expose my pretense.

Marcia looked at me strangely as I opened the door to get into the passenger side of her car. "Claudia, don't get in my car."

I looked down at my clothes to see if they were soiled. I couldn't imagine why I shouldn't get in and sit down.

"Your car is over there." She pointed down the row.

I was disappointed. I was tired and wanted to go home. Now, it seemed, I must go somewhere on my own.

"Just follow me home," she said.

What a relief. I was going home. I silently cheered, hoping it wouldn't be a long drive.

At dinner the next night, I told Marcia about my phone conversation with Karen and our plans for Thursday and how impressed Karen was with my memory.

"I'm glad the notebook worked," Marcia said. "You don't need to hide that fact. What's important is that your strategy lets you achieve the same goal as memory would. However, don't let people believe you did it unassisted. You don't want their expectations for you to be out of proportion to your ability to deliver. They already confuse your growing ability to compensate with restored brain function."

"I guess." I was deflated. "I don't want people to know all my tricks. They condescend to me when they think I'm less than I used to be."

"Not less, Claudia, different. You're the one who thinks you're less than you used to be. But speaking of tricks reminds me, I could swear I heard you agreeing again to give money to someone who called Saturday. We've talked about this before. You have a hard time—just like most of the population, I must add—with phone solicitors. I typed out a note, sort of a script, that you can read when one calls. Will you try it?"

I nodded. Whether as puppy or puppet, I needed Marcia's guidance. I immediately went to the phone and pinned her note on the little cork board over the desk. I was aware of my vulnerability in interacting with others, especially strangers whose job it was to confuse and manipulate me. Phone solicitors could get me to pledge money for anything, even if I didn't know their organization or had sent them money last week.

I got my first opportunity to try out Marcia's strategy the next afternoon. I was easily outmaneuvered by the warm, friendly voice who proceeded to describe the virtues of a well-known charity.

"I know you represent a worthy cause," I read from the paper, trying not to sound singsong, "but I do not accept telephone solicitation. Your organization is welcome to send me literature through the mail."

"Oh, but this isn't a solicitation," she said. "We don't want you to send us a donation."

Now I was in trouble. Her words were pouring forth at an alarming rate and I didn't have a script for this.

"We are just asking you to buy your magazines through us," she said. "What magazines do you presently subscribe to?"

"I'm sorry?" I said. When did this get to be about magazines? How do I get out of this conversation?

"What magazines do you read that come to your house?"

"I don't know." No, I couldn't say that, she'd think I'm stupid. "I don't read." My God, now I'd gone from stupid to illiterate. "I have a head injury."

"You can't read because of a head injury?" she asked.

"Correct. I am a physician." Why did I tell her that? I could read, I meant I just don't read a lot.

My admissions produced sympathy and a stream of questions: What kind of doctor was I? How was I injured? Her probably well-meant but condescending chatter offended me. I felt exposed. I flooded. Even my anger at both of us could not rescue me. I could not believe I had told a stranger I couldn't read, then told her I was a doctor so she wouldn't think I was uneducated.

But I didn't buy any magazines. And I didn't relate the whole conversation to Marcia when I told her of my success.

We could not insulate me from the unexpected or the stranger, but Marcia and I worked on developing techniques and cues to use in social situations. Before friends arrived for the evening or while in the car on the way to meet others, Marcia would sound a familiar refrain. "Look alive. Don't act B.D." The letters, which stood for brain-dead, were a private if crude reminder to get with it. It always amused me.

When I repeated it to a friend, she didn't see the humor. "It's wrong to use derogatory terms about head injury. You must treat yourself with respect."

She had a point. In the wrong context, or said with the wrong intent or by an outsider, insensitive and prejudicial remarks do hurt, and Marcia would have been the first to jump down the throat of anyone who made one. On the other hand, as I got better at respecting my head-injured self, my use of politically incorrect language about me and laughing at myself would come to be an expression of a growing self-approval.

It was a full year since my injury, but I still frequently wore an absent look and drifted into long periods of silence when I didn't know what was taking place around me.

"It's one of my favorite times," Marcia once said with an irony lost on me. "Seeing your eyes go vacant and hearing your mind come to a grinding halt."

Although Marcia and my family became used to them, these temporary shutdowns disconcerted many friends. Most were supportive. A few couldn't handle it and drifted away.

My ability to maintain social ties was helped immeasurably by my being in my thirties, when my relationships were well established. I had close friendships of many years' standing. It helped also that I lived with a contemporary—unlike, say, the trainees who lived with their parents. Marcia and I had friends in common and she knew or could relate to my friends. Most of my social forays were in her company, and she constantly bridged social chasms and prevented me from falling off conversational cliffs.

My continuing adynamia made me not only act different, but look different—"like no one's in there," TuTu once said after seeing my videos from HTP. Throughout August, Marcia gave new impetus to my five-month-long effort to improve my appearance, sometimes gently suggesting, sometimes pushing. When I grumbled half in earnest that I would shave my head if I had to spend thirty minutes every morning, as she did, just to dry my hair, she said, "It's a burden I bear cheerfully," even though she knew I knew she was lying through her teeth.

"If you'd spend even five minutes on your hair, you could turn around your bag-lady image," she said.

The written list for my morning routine had long included an admonition to *look in the mirror*, but doing so was a futile exercise.

I could, of course, focus on any part of my face, but it took considerable attention for me to see my face as a composite whole. I would look because my notes told me to, but it didn't mean I would recognize that my hair was uncombed or there was spinach between my teeth. Nor did I discern my lack of expression.

Now my notes ordered me to *really look in the mirror. Hair combed? Teeth cleaned? Collar straight? Earrings match? Expression alert, smiling?* It began to make a difference.

So did a similar effort in social situations. At first, the exertion required to appear animated and alert took away my ability to pay attention to the actual conversation. But as I became more practiced in the mechanics of looking animated, I actually became so. This in turn intensified my attentiveness, making it easier to grasp the gist of conversation.

TuTu, always an astute observer, made me feel my efforts were paying off when she said, "I know you're improving. You can now make it look as though you have it together."

Maybe, but whenever I got into a stressful social situation, my animation wore off like cheap deodorant. I had not yet achieved spontaneity or the ability to smile readily, let alone laugh. Nor was I good at initiating conversation. Parties were a misery, but Marcia still pushed me to practice my skills.

In mid-August, we were invited to a wedding in Bloomfield Hills. It was a beautiful day and the reception was to be in the garden of the bride's parents. I had accepted the invitation reluctantly and now wished I didn't have to go.

"You can tell them I have a headache," I said to Marcia, who was in the closet moving clothes back and forth, choosing what she'd wear.

"You're giving *me* a headache," she said, "but I'm not going to lie for you. I'll fix your hair and you can put this on." Marcia produced a dress of hers she knew I loved.

Once we were there, things seemed to go well. For a while. The food was good and all the laughing people seemed to have a lot to say to each other. After thirty minutes or so of trying to smile while I nibbled shrimp, I felt overwhelmed by the crush and needed to be alone. I slipped out the terrace door and wandered to the back of the garden where I could pretend to admire a metal sculpture.

It didn't work. People kept strolling by, making pleasantries, and I felt something more was expected of me than "Hello." While I was trying to figure out what I would say to this latest newcomer who was being so politely and charmingly attentive, my hostess bounced over.

"Oh, good. I see you've met," she said. "Did Claudia tell you, Ian, she was a doctor but she's had this terrible head injury? But you can hardly tell."

Her intentions, unquestionably innocent, did not endear her to me. Nor, apparently, I to the guest, who quickly escaped.

Our hostess talked at me for another few minutes before excusing herself to join her other guests. I stared again at the sculpture whose every nuance I should by now have committed to memory, if I had one. This afternoon was a blistering reminder of my loss of social savvy. Situations such as this shriveled my ego. I squeezed my eyes tightly to seal in my tears.

Marcia wouldn't be lying now. I really did have a headache.

∽ Everything I did reinforced my awareness that everyone else functioned without a need to think out every action. Others thought and moved at lightning speed, leaving me far behind. I never knew what was going on. The best I could do was fake comprehension. It made it hard to fit in.

I didn't have to tell Marcia. She knew.

"I have this great idea," she told me one evening when she came in from the hospital. "I've got some vacation coming and we have yet to do something special this summer. Let's go camping. It's something you love and you're good at. Whaddaya say?"

I was thrilled. Marcia had never done any serious camping, the kind where there are no showers or hot water. She proposed the Porcupine Mountains in Michigan's Upper Peninsula. I loved to hike along the escarpment near Lake in the Clouds and I had always wanted to take her there. I felt a delicious sense of command as I pointed out equipment we needed to bring and packed the car.

Because it was a twelve-hour drive, we started at six the next morning so we could arrive while we still had light to maneuver the car through deep pine forest and along the winding trail to a campsite.

I couldn't remember how to set up the tent and Marcia had never done it. Between us, we managed to half erect it, enough to get our sleeping bags under shelter. We had to use a rock to pound in stakes, as I had not packed the hammer.

"Okay," Marcia said. "Before we kill each other, let's take a break from this. Why don't you set up your cookstove and make us some dinner while I make a fire."

Despite repetitive searching, I could not find the pots or my knife or even a serving spoon. Our mutual assumption that I would pack what we needed was not panning out. I began to regret Marcia's inexperience. I hadn't realized I needed this much help.

I got out the backpacking stove and my kettle so we could eat freeze-dried stroganoff. Try as I might, I could not figure out how the stove worked. I was not eager to tell Marcia. "How about peanut butter for dinner?"

She was wiping ashes off her knee from the fire pit. "Hey, Claudia, where do we take showers?"

"I know there's a place, probably not more than ten miles from here."

"You're kidding, right?"

She hadn't said we needed to go to a campground with more facilities than toilets.

The hiking was beautiful. Camping was beyond me. Especially with missing gear. My skills diminished and with them Marcia's patience.

On the second morning Marcia announced we were going to a motel. "Why?" I said. "What's wrong?"

"You mean besides having to go crashing around in the bushes searching for you without a flashlight in the middle of the night?"

"Oh, that." I had forgotten that I had assured Marcia I could go the lavatory without her guidance, only to get hopelessly lost.

Moving to a motel and eating restaurant meals salvaged the trip, and we spent days hiking, canoeing, and birdwatching. We had traveled down to Glen Haven so we could spend our last day at Sleeping Bear Point. It was a perfect Saturday. Marcia and I hiked over the steep dunes till we reached the shore where we ate our lunch while looking at Lake Michigan. It was one of the few days when nothing went wrong. We swam and she looked for Petoskey stones while I stalked nature with my camera.

Late afternoon, when we were packing the car to leave, Marcia made a casual reference to my departure Wednesday morning to return to HTP. As much as I would dread the day once it arrived, I had never given my return a thought until she mentioned it.

"In three days . . . ?" I lost control. My tears soon turned into hysterical sobbing. I don't remember Sunday or the long drive home. I only know about the exhaustion Marcia spoke of in a letter to my mother.

> *All I need is an occasional eruption by Claudia to teach me not to complain about her adynamia. She was inconsolable. Her only words were "I don't want to go to New York. Please, please, give me my life back." It was such a relief from my own pain when her exhaustion won out and sleep finally overcame her.*
>
> *Ever since she's known she could not go back to her job this summer, she has been less confident. She needs a new goal, a dream she can hold on to about a future which is possible.*

Turkey Dressing

I was sitting on the long, wooden locker-room bench focused intently on tying the laces on my left sneaker, so I did not hear Diane return from blow-drying her hair.

"Uhm, Claudia, do you know you aren't wearing any pants?"

I looked down at my clothes. I had on underwear, my shirt, socks and shoes. Of course I knew my jeans were not yet on. Did she really think I would walk away without pants?

"I'm about to put them on," I said as evenly as possible.

"You'll never get them on over your shoes."

Damn. "I know that," I said and began untying my shoes. Marcia says it doesn't matter what I know if I don't act on it, but sometimes I have to say it anyway.

"So explain this to me." She sat down and propped her foot against the locker. "Why is it after getting dressed for thirty-plus years you can't do it right if you still know how?"

"It's automatic for you. You don't have to think about the steps involved. For me it's mechanical. I can miss a step or go off on a tangent."

"So if your mind is vacant, your dressing is arbitrary?"

"No," I said. "If my mind were vacant, I would just sit here. But before I left here I'd be wearing my blue jeans."

I looked around at the women in various stages of changing and grooming. They all had built-in routines, their next step was marked in mental yellow high-lighter to keep them on track. Their discussions of tort law or shoe sales did not throw them off course. They did not put their sneakers on at first sighting or stow them in their sports bag along with their towel and swimsuit.

"Every 'next step' is an option for me," I said. "Exercising a wrong one's easy, but I usually get back on track."

"Some of what you do is what anyone would do when they're preoccupied."

"Yes, I know. The errors head-injured people make are common. We just make them a lot more often and we don't have to be preoccupied."

FROM MY NOTEBOOK, JANUARY 3, 1992

20

I'm Out of Sorts.
Please Send Sorts.

It is hard to fight an enemy who has
outposts in your head.
SALLY KEMPTON

⊁

It was easy later to see what should have been done. Nothing is obvious from the eye of the storm, but then, nothing was obvious to me in fair weather. My tolerance for stress was low, especially when my plans unraveled, and that happened with ease, like plucking a loose thread and having your whole sleeve fall off. Obstacles the average person would move around or climb over stopped me dead in my tracks.

I arrived at La Guardia at eight-thirty Wednesday morning and took a cab directly to HTP.

The two bags Marcia had packed rode with me in the backseat. Having watched the man in line ahead of me at the taxi stand cram big cases into the backseat and boxes in front made me glad I carried so little. Why were New York cabbies so stubborn about opening their trunks?

I settled into my seat, feeling back in stride. The ride into the city felt familiar; so did the city, except that its scale was more immense. It must have grown by six million people.

I asked my Pakistani driver if he would close the window.

"In the six weeks since I was last here," I said, "they've equipped every truck with a jet engine. I can't hear myself think."

He smiled and nodded. "Yes, yes, big city. Can't shut the window. Enjoy the fresh air. Nice day, nice city."

Just a veritable Garden of Eden.

Marcia had argued that it made more sense to travel the night before so I could get settled before the start of a new term, but I wanted to stay home as long as possible and I was adamant. "Besides, I always take the seven A.M. plane," I had said.

So even though she had misgivings, she didn't press the issue. She never wanted to shake my confidence. It was my plan at the end of the rehab day to move into my old studio apartment. I thought it would be easy. All I had to do was go to Lori's apartment and pick up my things.

When I walked into the HTP waiting room, it felt like a homecoming with everybody greeting each other. Even Lenny was grinning. I was very happy to see them all—I hadn't realized I'd missed them.

At ten, when we moved into Orientation, I took in the new faces. Our total group was twelve again, but six of them were newcomers. Each of us introduced ourselves in turn for the benefit of the new trainees, and I had the opportunity to observe them. Compared to us veterans, they appeared uncertain, confused, disjointed. That's who we were six months ago. We really had changed.

The novices and their significant others included a fashion designer and her husband, a carpenter and his wife, an investment advisor and his mother, a businessman, a college student and her mother, and a hotel manager and his mother, both of Indian descent. In the waiting room, Scott had heartily greeted them with "Welcome to America." I don't know if his reference was to their lineage or the fact that they lived in Queens.

At lunch, we six and Dean were joined by a few of the new people. When Dean prompted us, we talked a little about what we had done during our summer hiatus. For the most part, no one had much to say on the subject.

At the end of the day I rushed off to Lori's apartment to get my things. Everything I owned and needed in New York—from toothpaste to peanut butter, even my underwear and raincoat—was stored at Lori's. When I reached her door, I discovered I had left her key in Detroit.

So I went to my apartment to call her at work and realized I had no key to it, either. I had failed to make arrangements with my landlord to retrieve it.

I persuaded the super, who remembered me, to let me in and immediately went to the phone to call Lori. My phone was dead. Maybe I hadn't arranged for it either, but I was certain I had.

I couldn't figure out how to get toiletries if I couldn't talk to Lori, I couldn't talk to Lori without a phone, I couldn't call for phone repair unless I left the apartment, and I could not do that unless I had a key. I tried to remember where I used to buy food when I lived here six weeks ago. Were there places to eat near here? Could I even find my way there? I didn't know what to do first. I didn't know what to do, period.

I tried to use my strategies but I couldn't remember them or any of my old routines. I simply could not remember what it was like when I lived here before. I was treading water wearing lead boots.

My sense of isolation and confusion quickly escalated. Between floods I wrote in my journal to calm myself, hoping it would enable me to formulate a plan.

> *I can't fight my way out of a paper bag and I can't stop trying. I must calm down and conserve energy. Normal people have trouble living in New York. Siberia has a warmer ring to it.*
>
> *I must stop thinking of a phone as an essential part of survival. I don't even like them—I can't find any words to speak—but I would take twenty disasters a day without complaint if I could have a phone. Maybe I have blown this out of perspective. I'm not climbing Mt. Everest, but I do feel I am suffering from a decrease in oxygen.*

I left my bags where they were and escaped into sleep. The next morning, feeling unkempt because I had no toiletries or fresh underclothes, I went off to HTP, where I learned I had no phone service because New York Bell was on strike.

Because of a family medical emergency, Joan had to be absent this brief rehab week. I was distinctly rattled and out of step. It never occurred to me to turn to anyone else at HTP for help.

By that evening I was exhausted from flooding and unable to function beyond my obsessively trekking up one avenue and down another street in search of a usable telephone.

Working pay phones in Manhattan are the exception, even though their broken counterparts dot almost every corner like decoys set out to lure the innocent in useless directions. Locating an unoccupied phone, having the thirty-six-digit number in hand for a long-distance call, and keeping in mind a clear idea of what I needed to say was like walking on a broken leg to an ambulance company to tell them I needed a ride to the hospital.

I reached my mother at about seven. When I heard her voice my defenses disintegrated. It took a while for her to sort through my incoherence to determine what was wrong.

"Mama, you need to know I'm right here—"

"Right where, Claudia? Try to be calm. Tell me what's wrong."

"I can't hear you." Horns blared as a truck crossed the intersection beating the light. "Trucks are everywhere."

"It's okay, I can hear you."

"What?"

"I HEAR YOU!"

"I can't give up this phone. I don't have one at home."

"Claudia, you've said that many times. Tell me what else is wrong."

It became clear to her finally that I was seriously flooding and unable to function. When I told her I couldn't find the grocery store, she didn't even try to tell me where it was. She knew it wouldn't matter. I wouldn't know what to buy or be able to figure out the money. When my panic subsided, she directed me to Lori's apartment and told me she would call me there.

When she spoke with me and Lori an hour later, she told us she had reservations for the first plane she could get out of northern Michigan, which meant she would be at my apartment Saturday afternoon.

Lori, who was working, wisely packed me off to Connecticut. I could spend the intervening day and a half with Kay, who was on maternity leave from her bank. The notes Lori wrote to guide me on my train journey to Kay's were excruciatingly detailed and covered every foreseeable circumstance, from how I was to dress to the time it would take me to walk to the station and from the station rotunda to the train platform. Her note even instructed me to buy a bagel at Zabar's after I got my ticket.

Don't eat it now! Take it to the platform and eat it there or on the train. Don't make eye contact and don't talk to anyone.

Lori had said there was no way I could screw up. For a change, that was true.

By the time I made the return trip to New York Saturday afternoon, I was calmly vegetative. I was relieved that my mother would be there when I arrived. At the same time I felt uncomfortably childlike in not having saved myself. I had long been independent. My brother and I were responsible latchkey kids. We earned our own money, and I put myself entirely through medical school. I was used to having people lean on me, not the other way round. Now I had suddenly metamorphosed into a confused and dependent child.

When I walked into my apartment building Saturday afternoon, my mother was sitting on the little sofa in the lobby, flanked by four sacks of groceries. After she fed me, she made up the sofa-bed. I collapsed onto my half, gratefully unmindful of her busily putting away the groceries and unpacking our bags—mine were still untouched from my trip from Detroit. I was too benumbed with fatigue to feel rueful that, at age thirty-four, I needed my mother to bail me out.

We were up early on Sunday morning. After breakfast, my mother set about organizing the apartment, which really meant organizing me.

Over the next two days, the bed-sitting room, kitchenette, bathroom, and two closets were systematized to fit my routines and needs. Every space and aperture was assessed for my logical use. With my necessary input and doubtful assistance, we put everything neatly into its appropriate place. She taped or tacked labels on the front of every drawer, cupboard, or closet, listing its contents.

A white placard with a large reminder written in bold black Magic Marker was posted on the door to the hall reminding me to shop on the way home for food and to take one last look in the bathroom mirror before walking out the door.

The ones I liked best were the two sheets pasted to the front of the refrigerator. One, with the headline, "*What Will I Eat Tonight?*" suggested five simple menus and itemized what I needed to buy to produce them. The second was a list of basic supplies I must always have on hand— peanut butter, bread in the freezer, Coca-Cola, toilet paper, canned soups, and the like—to ensure self-sufficiency on bad days when shopping was impossible or forgotten.

We spent the rest of the week devising and practicing some household routines. On the days she didn't attend sessions with me at HTP, she cooked and froze a few main-dish meals for me to heat up. Their recipes were taped to the refrigerator. The supply wouldn't last long, but by the time they ran out, she hoped my routines would be established.

Armed with a letter from HTP saying a telephone was a medical necessity, she went to New York Bell and arranged for service to be instituted, although it was another several days before I was reconnected to my life line—a phone.

As I wrote TuTu,

> *I think the first time a flooded person successfully negotiates their mentally lost self to a working pay phone in New York City, places a call to a correct number and manages to conduct any business however simple, they should be granted a diploma from rehab.*
>
> *I'd rather try to survive blindfolded on a trail in the Grand Canyon than in the streets of Manhattan without a phone. At least I'd be out of the city.*

On the way to rehab Monday morning, my mother and I stopped at the little market on Lexington to buy fruit for our lunch. While she took the bag, I paid the clerk. As I took the change, my mother caught my hand in hers and spoke to the clerk.

"Excuse me, I believe my daughter gave you ten dollars. You've given her change for five."

The clerk apologized and corrected his error. When we got outside, I said, "I was sure I gave him a ten but I thought he would know best."

"Why not try asking? You might be right. Every mistake isn't yours, honey."

I knew the logic of that but I experienced so much misadventure of my own making, that I had begun to assume when anything went wrong it must be my fault. My experiences confused me. I was never sure how much I contributed to any problem I encountered. I worried that my repeated cognitive malfunctions happened because I wasn't trying hard enough.

Failure was a clearer issue when I was younger. Success was a matter of self-application, of will, of heart. When I had done all I could for a patient who died anyway, I grieved but I accepted it. Failure for me would not be that his heart stopped but that my heart had stopped short.

When I told Joan of my adventures during her absence, she said comfortingly that even with plans, things don't always work out. "Be serene," she said. "Accept that you can't control some things."

The fact she was right didn't keep me from a testy response—admittedly not to her but to my journal.

> *Every neuropsychologist should have to experience a simulated brain injury for a year. I wonder how consistently well they would cope; whether they could intellectualize problems and say serenely, "I have the strategies and even though I want desperately to implement them today, I can't. Better luck next time."*
>
> *Would they not rail against themselves, detest their lack of function, and feel incredulous at their unpredictable performances? Could they be calm about their loss of control over thought and emotion?*

Within a week or so, our days settled into the familiar routine established the previous term but with a slight difference. Most of the time, the six of us, whom Scott dubbed "the veterans," were to meet as a separate group. It was another sign that our requirements were more sophisticated. Unlike the newcomers, we six were aware of our deficits—though not of all of their implications—and were familiar with basic strategies and props.

Our key objectives in this second cycle would be to increase and master our strategies, as well as to gain intellectual and emotional acceptance of our new selves. These goals were entwined: strategies help compensate for losses, and the sense of success that comes with a mastery of strategies is an ego boost that fosters acceptance. It was clear right from the outset that there would be a difference in the ideas and the questions we'd be asked to address. We were told we would be challenged to face more emotional issues regarding the significance of our injuries. They lost no time getting started.

On Monday, September 11, the third day of this new cycle, the six of us—Beth, Scott, Tony, Sharon, Lenny, and I—all participated in an Interpersonal Discussion. These videotaped sessions usually brought out the best in us. We were eager to show our coaches we could handle their challenges, and I was pleased my mother was present.

As in past sessions, we were seated in a loose circle. Joan was back and she and Len were the leaders. This day, Yehuda joined us and it was he who stated our topic.

"Sticking to realistic but optimistic possibilities," he said, "describe both what you see yourself doing a year from now and your worst fears about what could happen to you."

It was a dangerous subject, like putting piranha in a tank of guppies. My thinking slowed and my chest tightened. I suspected our most modest dreams might be hopelessly unachievable, our fears quite likely to be realized.

I didn't know what I could hope for. I knew what hopes had been dashed. I hadn't met my July deadline, I'd been in rehab far longer than I expected to be last February when I agreed to come, I'd learned my deficits can't all be fixed.

I feared this question.

Why risk my dreams by airing them? What if putting them into words made them die? I could just hear the emcee heartily saying, "Not so fast, little lady, that dream's been canceled. Choose another one from our neon-lit tree."

I had about ten minutes to construct a response in my notebook while each of my friends took their turn. Their struggles were palpable. My anguish for them heightened my own.

Sharon was first. "I expect to have overcome my problems with adynamia and disinhibition. I want to be living happily. My fear? I fear my memory won't come back enough so I can return to college."

Scott said he would be back as an Army captain in a year. His worst fear was that they might reject him.

Lenny believed he would be living independently and attending university again. He feared "having someone try to kill me again," referring to the accident that caused his injury. "I wouldn't want to go through it again; learning to walk and talk and breathe again."

Beth was the most talkative, and most vague. "I want to be calmly, happily, purposefully pursuing something, having plans to pursue. I fear I could find myself again in a confused state, isolated and alone."

Tommy said simply, "Take day by day. Wish for the best. Whatever comes. I hope to keep my family together. I fear losing everything I've worked for. I've lost my job. I don't want to lose my family."

My turn. I was a little flooded but functional, striving for dignity and poise. The camera reflected neither, but compared to my performances outside the constraints of HTP's structure, I was on top of my form. In a frayed voice with an uneven cadence, I forced out, "I hope to be doing something related to medicine. Something I am good at, something meaningful." I tried to distance my feelings from my words, silently begging them to be true.

I could not formulate my fears. I think I knew what they were when I first heard the question, but I didn't now. I sat frozen, deserted of thoughts. They did not push me.

Later in the afternoon, I awakened from a nap to find a note on the table from my mother telling me she was out at the grocery store.

I was feeling worthless and ungrateful for my life when a call from downstairs announced that Kay was there. She arrived at my door in tears. I drew her in and sat with her on the couch. Through her sobs, she told me that an auto accident had taken the life of a beloved nephew, a high-schooler. I held her in my arms, trying to comfort her.

"Claudia, you could have died last year," she said. "How wonderful you are alive."

I braced myself, not comprehending her point. For a moment, I thought this was a situation I had come to know—a well-intentioned friend telling me how lucky I was not to be in a wheelchair or dead.

But that wasn't Kay's message. She was telling me it was wonderful I was able to be there for her and the others who loved me. "We all treasure who you are. Whatever would I have done without you?"

I was accustomed to seeing myself as a burden to those who cared about me. On all those weekends in Connecticut, when she and Edward had given me so much, I felt my attempts to show my appreciation were woefully inadequate. Now, despite her own grief, she was telling me she felt fortunate to have been able to do things for me, grateful she had the opportunity to show love to someone while that person was still alive.

But her most important words were "You're still in there, the friend I love. You didn't go away just because you were injured."

My ache for her pain was followed by a burst of pleasure. My anima, my spiritual being, was intact, and she could see it.

When she left, I got out my acrylics, put a Kenny G tape on loud, and was in a delirium of laying color on paper when my mother came in loaded down with plastic bags and new menu ideas.

Several days later, I did answer the second question—in my journal.

My greatest fears are:
I will never again be a doctor.
I will lose Marcia.

When I saw my words, I was glad Yehuda had raised the question. Until then, I couldn't put a name to the worms of fear moving below conscious awareness. You cannot fight an enemy you cannot see. Putting my fears on paper might rob them of their power.

Lost in the Women's Room

Because I travel so much, I use a lot of public rest rooms. When I'm alone in an airport, I put a note in my pocket telling me what city I'm in and how to get back to my gate. Today, I have no note and this clearly is not an airport, so I must be with someone, probably Marcia. I lean against the wall outside the door to the women's room and wait.

A *Twilight Zone* skit could be written about rest rooms. You walk into one at an airport in Kansas and you emerge at a gas station in Florida. At least, that's how they feel to me. I can't maintain my orientation throughout those four minutes spent in the women's room. Walking out is always to an unexpected place. But a note or a friend solves the mystery.

Nobody has come to get me. I am beginning to feel uneasy. I should have written down the plan. Waiting for Marcia seems to be a wrong guess.

I look around. This hallway resembles a hospital corridor. I see now that passing strangers are wearing NYU ID badges. My heart sinks. I'm in New York. And alone. Illogically, I feel abandoned.

This women's room is a bad spin of the wheel. I wish I could go back in and come out at a better place.

FROM MY NOTEBOOK, MARCH 9, 1990

21

Getting Better

Mistakes are part of the dues one
pays for a full life.
SOPHIA LOREN
✦

"You're getting better," Joan told me one session. "I know that," I said, and I did too. As I improved, I began doing more things. And the more I did, the more I discovered what I could not do well.

In the flickering light of my growing insight, I could inventory my losses but didn't comprehend their full import. "I have the words," I told my mother when we said good-bye. "I don't have the music." But I did have a renewed interest in trying to perform.

The following weekend when I returned to Detroit, it was with a self-initiated project. Joan had asked me if I knew about a new medication therapy. I did not, but I was pleased to be asked a medical question and I'd always been good at research, so I leapt at the chance to gather information and create a report for her. It was simple on the face of it. I did not make the connection between the project and its parts, most of which were beyond me—finding the data, then reading, organizing, and condensing it into a report.

I always loved medical libraries and I enjoyed exploring their racks. Riffling through stacks of journals, I would find myself pleasantly digressing among topics much distant from my intended research. Now, this long-familiar library at Bi-County Hospital was forbidding. The *Index Medicus* had always been a helpful tool. Today, the long dense lists of alphabetized articles were impenetrable. I was embarrassed to ask any one person for too much help, partly because I didn't want to impose but also because I didn't want to reveal the degree of my ineptitude. So I used five doctor friends and two medical librarians to piece together a one-page synopsis of what was needed. My fifteen-minute project took me all day Friday.

I remember telling students that the most fragile period in a patient's emotional life is not when the illness is acute, but when the patient is getting better. Crisis generates energy. Doctors and hospital staff are employing their skills, the family has rallied round, the patient is lulled, if not by sedatives, then by the sickness itself. Everyone is responding to the battle cry.

Convalescence is another matter. Now, the effort needed is more subtle. The perceived danger is past, yet the patient isn't recovered, not able to do much, and the little that can be done requires more energy than can be summoned. There are doubts. *Will I ever feel as well as I once did?* The patient, no less than the sickness, is boring.

Saturday, after breakfast, Marcia said, "I'm going for a bike ride. Do you want to come?"

"Sure, but I can't go yet. My alarm has ten minutes."

"Oh. What happens in ten minutes?"

"What?"

"What are you going to do when the alarm goes off?"

"Let the cats back in." As soon as I said it I saw the illogic of waiting. "I'll go get them now."

Our cats had only recently begun to go outside again when I was the one opening the door. Over the last year, I had forgotten them for hours at a time on many occasions and they had lost faith that I would think to bring them back in. Since they ranged in age from twelve to seventeen and didn't have front claws, they were interested only in brief strolls about our yard and naps on the patio. It was a commentary on my reliability that my previously loyal trio of furry companions waiting patiently inside the door no longer rushed forward when I opened it. Baby, our seal-point Siamese who was the elder and leader of the pack, would fix his piercing blue eyes up at me as I held the door ajar for a ludicrous thirty seconds, only to pivot and trot away with his entourage in search of Marcia, whose door-opening record was untarnished.

I worked hard to learn to consistently set an alarm and respond to it for tasks throughout each day. It was a relief when my improved skill with timers eliminated the blaring of the smoke alarm before my hearing was permanently impaired. But regaining the trust of my cats was a real marker of growth. My cats had zero tolerance for the eccentricity of others.

When we returned from our ride, I nipped upstairs and showered. I knew we were going someplace but I couldn't remember where. I put on the linen pants and silk blouse Marcia had laid out on my bed, but she hadn't put out stockings and shoes.

"What flavor socks do I wear with this?" I asked.

"The navy ones."

"Have you seen my feet?"

"Yes, they're attached to your legs."

I looked down at my pants, bare feet, and carpeting.

"Where?"

"Shoes, Claudia, not feet. Where are my shoes. You left them at the front door."

"You know I meant shoes," I said to her back as she went down the stairs.

Why was she so testy? Nobody could work on words and strategies twenty-four hours a day. I shouldn't have to waste time and energy at home looking for a word when she knows what I'm trying to say.

I scanned the bedroom again as I put on my socks. Did she ever tell me where my shoes were? I started to call down the stairs and then thought better of it.

Not wanting to face the challenge of the closet, I put my Reeboks back on over the sheer navy stockings. My shoes felt loose without thick crew socks, but I was dressed.

I went in search of Marcia and found her paying bills at the dining-room table.

"What's the plan?" I asked.

"I told you. Twice. We're going to an opening at the art institute."

"Oh, yeah." I sat down. "What are we opening?"

She continued writing checks and putting them into envelopes.

I watched her, trying not to fidget. I would have enjoyed helping her. I liked teamwork these days more than ever, but she felt paperwork went faster without my contribution. I still wrote checks sometimes, thanks to a new Visa card that covered my bounced checks, but Marcia and my mother were in charge of my finances, and my repeated displays of financial initiative were not always well received.

There was not any specific part of managing my bills and checkbook that I was incapable of doing. I simply lacked accuracy and predictability. Check numbers got transposed, transactions went unrecorded. The same charity would receive their annual check from me three times in three months and another charity appeal would be lost in the circular file. Due dates passed, deposits were not made, and just two weeks ago on one particularly off day my ambitious attempt to transfer my savings account from one bank to another bounced a check for $16,000. That special Visa service wouldn't cover that amount. Marcia had to leave work in midday to go talk to the bank.

Publicly, Marcia defended my right to stay involved in my finances. Privately she asked me to utilize restraint. In banking as in medicine, no one is impressed if you perform most of the steps correctly if the end result is wrong. I now kept a low profile.

I forgot about interrupting. "What exactly is the plan?"

Marcia stopped writing and looked at me. "Please cut it out with the questions. How about five bloomin' minutes of silence?"

"I'll forget what I want to ask."

"I hope so."

I folded my hands on the table, willing myself to be quiet.

"Claudia," she said. "Go do something."

"Okay. Like what?"

"Anything. How about opening some of your mail?"

I went into the study and sat down next to a stack of mail because she suggested it. I was better at banking. A medical journal lay on top. Knowing it would take an hour to decide which of its articles I might want to save, I set it aside to look at later. Each new envelope presented a reason to be added to the "later" pile: How did I answer the prescription questionnaire about the variety of diseases I saw each week? Should I buy a

Rototiller? Under what heading did I file each item I should save? Did my car need a tune-up?

Half an hour's work netted me four nondecisions and four empty envelopes for the trash.

When we finally arrived at the opening, the DIA was softly lighted in the gathering dusk and pleasantly filled with chatty, smiling people. I was groomed, coiffed, and suitably attired once Marcia spotted the track shoes I was wearing and made me substitute my pumps. I followed her through the galleries, content until she said, "Claudia, why are you always walking behind me?"

"I'm watching your feet." Uh-oh, wrong thing to say.

"Well, stop it. Walk next to me. I feel like the Pied Piper."

I hadn't known why I tagged behind until that moment. I wanted to tell her that her feet were a focus. They told me where to go. That way, I could filter out these distractions—the voices, the colors, the people.

I moved up beside her.

In the car on the way to the airport Monday morning, Marcia brought up my research activity on Friday.

"Tapping seven expert resources to answer one simple research problem is not a good use of everyone's time," she said as we descended the ramp and she negotiated our entry into the heavy morning traffic on I-94. "That isn't what HTP has in mind when they advise you to use coaches. For a really important question, will you canvass the entire National Institute of Health?"

"No," I said, "but it's a good thing I don't have to pay for medical advice."

Marcia spotted an opening and changed lanes. "If you'd told me about this, I would have taken care of it and saved you time and embarrassment."

"How could I know in advance I couldn't do it?" I said. "Every time I turn around I discover something else I can't do well anymore. When am I going to run out of surprises?"

"Well, you keep me guessing."

The Metropolitan Airport sign flashed into view. She eased the car into the right lane, headed for the exit.

She smiled. "Hey, you haven't asked if we're going to miss the plane."

I shrugged. "Why should I? We always get there in time."

~ My flight arrived on schedule and traffic was light. As my cab approached the Midtown Tunnel I knew that I was going to get to rehab early. I was eager to get there if only so this ride would be over. Plane trips caused a mild motion sickness, a fringe benefit of my injury, and my ride in the back of a cab exacerbated the nausea. I would recall the problem only after I became ill during each ride in from La Guardia. I tried to steer my attention away from my stomach and think up something to say in Orientation.

It was a futile task. Orientation remained a mystery to me.

What's your goal for the day, Claudia?

Gosh, Joan, I'm working to use all my strategies on all of my cognitive deficits.

Goodie, let's get started.

That this wasn't the answer they desired was the only clear rule of Orientation. On Mondays we were expected to add some comment about our weekend. There wasn't the time to say anything with real content, even if I had had the language skills to sum it up. Of course, I was never chided for saying too much, only for telegraphing too little. I was not sorry on the few occasions when my flight was delayed and I missed Orientation.

I was the first to arrive in the waiting room. I settled myself in and stared comfortably at the wall until Scott made his entrance.

"Good morning, everyone," he boomed.

I double-checked the vacant seats around me. "We're the only ones here."

"Tell you what," he said. "Today, you be disinhibited and I'll be adynamic."

"You're off to a great start."

Beth rounded the corner and flopped into the chair to my left. "We're all adynamic and disinhibited both," she said by way of greeting, "though I must say, Scott, you hide your adynamia exceedingly well."

"Thank you." Scott bowed and began a monologue on ways to conceal weapons.

I checked my notebook as the room filled with other trainees and noticed again that I had nothing new to talk about in Orientation. I turned to Beth. "Do you know what you're going to say in Orientation?"

"Not really." She wound a thick strand of hair around her forefinger, coiling and uncoiling it. "I mean, I'll talk about the weekend and probably about getting organized or focused. I'll decide when I get in there."

I missed hearing what Beth actually did say during the session. I was busy looking through past notes to find a new way I could comment.

I volunteered last. A mistake, since we were running ahead of schedule and I had plenty of time to fill. I read my lines. "The weekend went all right. Today I will initiate, be animated, and elaborate."

Joan's hand went up and Tommy called on her to speak.

"Claudia, how are you going to do that?" she said.

"How?" What kind of a question was that? Why didn't they ask something I know, like the pathophysiology of heart failure? "I don't know the answer."

"You'll need to think flexibly. Think about how you got the first thought and then keep rolling."

This seemed familiar, but I wrote it down just in case.

"When you're asked a question, remain calm and think about it in steps. First, what's the question? Second"—she ticked the points off on her hand—"go with the gist of what's asked. Third, don't fight with memory. Fourth, focus on the process, not the outcome. Set aside your concerns about how it sounds. Last, step into the idea, feel it as though you are teaching the answer so you will be more complete and animated when you speak."

It sounded reasonable. "Okay."

At the end of the day, I gave Joan the report I had worked on in Detroit. She seemed pleased and surprised. "Thank you for doing this, Claudia, it's great. Did you put this together yourself?"

I was annoyed. Why couldn't she just leave it at thank you? "Does everything have to relate to rehab?"

"You needed help, huh?"

"I don't understand why I couldn't do this by myself."

"Sit down a minute." She waved me to a chair. She laid my report on her desk and studied it for a moment.

"You had trouble," she said slowly, "because your former organizational abilities are impaired."

"I know about executive function." I held up my hand to stop her. "I've heard enough about my inability to bounce a lot of balls, that is air balls—"

"You mean, you have trouble juggling?" Joan said.

"Yes, juggling balls, but that isn't the point, Joan. How was I supposed to know that trouble juggling meant I couldn't do research?"

"You weren't. It isn't until you try to use a skill and fail that you are conscious of how that particular limitation applies."

"I thought the only problems in my life were the ones we were working on," I said, unreasonably annoyed with her.

"There are a couple things happening here. Many problems have the same root causes. You didn't just discover a 'new' deficit. You just found a new implication of a deficit you already had. To say it another way, the deficit you have wasn't meaningful until you were active enough to try to use a former skill that is now limited by that deficit.

"And there's another wrinkle. You continue to measure your performance against your pre-injury standards. I'm sure your perfectionist tendencies were an asset prior to your injury. Now, they get in the way of the rehabilitation process."

"Swell. I should just lower my standards and I'll be fine."

"Claudia, listen. You are asking too much of yourself. You are engaging in what's called maximalistic thinking."

It was a term I had heard applied to me often enough. I didn't believe it, but I was glad that something about my brain functioning could be described in such grandiose terms as "maximal."

Joan said more but I didn't catch it. I could see she was missing my point, and I, hers.

I chewed over the conversation all the while I walked back to my apartment. This wasn't just a matter of my high standards. I wouldn't have taken on the research this weekend if I had understood I couldn't do it. The problem was that I didn't know my limits. I didn't choose to fail; I had no way of knowing I would.

I spent the next hour composing my thoughts and writing them in my notebook. It was the only way I could clarify my ideas and make them understandable to myself. I would ask Joan to read it the next day. More and more I was giving things I was writing to Joan. It eased my sense of isolation and I hoped it made me more understandable to her.

> *They say I expect too much of myself. Hell, I just continue to be jolted every time my mind slams the brakes on my functioning. I am thrown against the wheel over and over by my costly and unexpected crashes. Just when I think I understand the implications of a deficit and how it limits my performance, I learn of new consequences.*
>
> *I am horrified and, yes, astonished, frustrated, embarrassed, and sometimes despairing about what this injury has done to me.*
>
> <u>*I thought I was better than this!*</u>

The others were at the cafeteria table by the time I went through the line at lunch the next day. I paid for my food and joined them. Dean and Lenny shifted their chairs and trays to make room for me. They were passing around a greeting card.

"I got this card yesterday," Sharon said. I studied it when it came to me. It showed a picture of life's proverbial bowl of lemons with the advice that when presented with lemons, one should make lemonade.

"Do you think it means that my friend thinks I'm not trying hard enough to make the best of things?"

"No," I said. "I think it suggests a positive view of life."

"I wish I knew someone who'd made the celebrated lemonade," Sharon said.

Scott grinned. "It's a secret recipe."

"I'm serious. I'd like some sort of role model."

I empathized with her wish. It would be wonderful to meet another doctor—better yet an internist—who had made it to the other side of rehab. Not that I lacked role models. If you remove head injury from the criteria, I had many. My family is adroit at making the best of what life gives. TuTu could squeeze nectar from bitter herb.

My father spent eighteen months learning to walk with a brace and crutches after he contacted crippling poliomyelitis when he was twenty-three and newly married. As he approaches seventy, he still works in spite of the postpolio syndrome that has fatigued the few muscle cells left in his legs. There is some unwritten rule that prevents complaint in my family—I have sometimes wondered if they were unaware they were bleeding. My father's infectious enthusiasm for life is not stoicism. He seems to believe there is nothing he has been barred from doing.

My mother's corneas were scarred with a recurring viral infection that began in early childhood. There was no successful treatment then, so her eyes were often bandaged tightly shut to ease the pain from light and involuntary movement. Scar tissue and profound astigmatism limited her vision between attacks.

She attended a special elementary school for disabled children that could accommodate her periodic blindness. My mother was the only one in her class of eight who went to high school. The others were too frail or died. My mother went on to graduate second in her college class. A vice president of ABC-TV, she was the first woman general manager of a network-owned television station and the first one in a major market.

TuTu is self-educated. After assuring the state university that her non-existent high school records had been destroyed in a fire, she was allowed to take the entrance examination and attend college for two years. That and high marks on her civil service exam got her a job with the state of Michigan as a social worker. "Lying is never right," she said, pink faced with the admission, "but you do what you must to take care of your children."

When her body failed, shortly after I finished rehab, and she was forced to give up her home, car, and independence and accept life in a hospital bed in Mama and Richard's home, she did it with dignity, grace, and good humor. Her confinement never confined her mind. Approaching ninety, she can still complete a *New York Times* crossword puzzle in an hour, and devour three newspapers a day and five books a week. She matches Marcia's wit line for line until she loses her breath from laughter. She lives life every day to its fullest.

I had always thought I'd inherited their gift for moving past the challenges life presents. That I was still struggling to emotionally accept my new persona made me feel guilty and inadequate. But maybe I was being too literal. Their loses were clearly defined—hardships, but without surprises. I felt I could accept mine better also if they were as clearly defined—that is, if I could grasp the specifics of my limitations.

I wrote Marcia about this and she wrote back with a story my Uncle Patrick had once told her about my mother.

It was winter; your mother was about seven and between eye infections. When she looked out of the window one morning, she saw a snow-covered world. In fact, it was a light dusting of snow and frost, but with her thick, dark lenses she was unable to tell its depth.

She took her sled where it leaned against the side of the door, sprinted down the drive, and with a running leap, belly-flopped the sled onto the bare ground, causing her to shoot off the end and skin her face on the pavement. As she picked herself up, her pain was overshadowed with embarrassment and confusion much as you describe.

How could that not be snow?

My Library Card

There are holes appearing in the dark fabric of my adynamia. Climbing out through them is a slow, disturbing process. Sometimes there are flights of joyous liberation interspersed with occasional, inexplicable postfreedom crashes.

This is a flight. I am giddy, celebrative, and very pleased with myself as I bound down Park Avenue in a triumphant return from the New York Public Library.

I am now the proud owner of a NYC library card. And I have located on the computer, found on the shelf, and checked out from the counter my first book.

Okay, so it doesn't look like much on paper. This is not the sort of news to write home about, especially when my Herculean feat took over three hours to execute. Actually, I can think of no one to whom I could unself-consciously announce this marvelous achievement. How could anyone comprehend my pride and pleasure?

When I look at this event from my usual perspective, I am embarrassed that I view this as an accomplishment. There is, however, no arguing with the emotion I felt walking out of the library with a book tucked under my arm. It was like rounding the two-hundredth mile in a bicycle marathon.

Who says I am not easily self-satisfied?

FROM MY NOTEBOOK, OCTOBER 30, 1989

22

Turning Leaves

*Each one of us has to find his peace from within,
and peace to be real must be unaffected by
outside circumstances. Each thing that I
experience brings me closer to myself. It does not
matter whether I lose or win at the searching. It's
the search that enables me to grow.*

MAHATMA GANDHI,
QUOTED BY JOAN AT THE FINAL PARTY

As I walked to HTP, it felt like autumn. The few trees I passed confirmed the cooler temperatures of mid-October with their early spattering of yellow and red amidst the green, but it was more than that. The air was sweet and fresh and smelled like fall. The street seemed full of energy. I enjoyed the sensation of being swept along by all those purposeful, hurrying people, spilling out of buses or the holes in the sidewalk that led up from the subways, flowing like a tide down sidewalks and across streets into office buildings and stores. I was alternately enchanted, annoyed, and amused by the bustle and the commerce surrounding me, assaulting my senses. My eyes were on the activity, I was not conscious of street signs, my notebook was closed. Yet I covered the distance without a detour or confusion.

Joan had said I would eventually overlearn some tasks to the point where I could focus on the idea behind the action—in this case, getting myself to HTP—without needing to concentrate on the mechanics. I smiled. It was a high-water mark that had nothing to do with flooding.

When I arrived at the waiting room, I heard Scott making vague references to his weekend adventure. My flush of well-being changed to uneasiness. Scott had told us of an earlier adventure in which he was mugged coming up a stairway from the subway—Scott's disabled left side made him appear to be an easy mark. His attacker held him at knifepoint and demanded his wallet. Scott said he needed to reach the landing where he could balance himself enough to get out his wallet. In fact, he wanted the stability of the landing in order to overpower his assailant. Despite his physical limitations, he used his Ranger-perfected judo techniques to disarm his opponent and throw him down the stairs. (We all cheered at this point.) Unfortunately, his hand was cut badly enough in the process to sever a tendon.

As excited as we were by his heroics, I hoped we weren't going to hear a similar tale today. Scott was not one to surrender, and I was afraid he would one day be seriously hurt.

But this weekend's adventure didn't involve bloodshed, only routine frustration. Every day last week we had heard the details of the plan Scott had forged with Len, his coach, to go to the movies on Saturday night with his "buddies." We knew how much he looked forward to the evening, how emotionally invested he was in what was to be his fledgling attempt to make contact with these old friends.

Each of us could identify with that need and the too-common outcome when we tried. We had all suffered the loss of old friends to various degrees. I was grateful for the Loris and Kays in my life. Blessed are the friends who love us as we are.

I could understand how Scott could have trouble with rejection. Scott was attractive and personable. It was easy to believe he once had an appreciative sense of humor and was a good conversationalist who displayed a charming and genuine interest in others, and remnants of that former self still peeked through. But for the most part his conversation rambled and was so focused on himself that he usually paid scant attention to what a companion might say. His voice was loud, his laugh constant, his former subtle humor given way to off-color jokes and crude comments.

By lunchtime, Scott was ready to burst with his need to talk. We were barely settled at our table when he began. With his usual clowning and unself-conscious delight over having the floor, he said, "My problem is I can't remember that I can't remember." But his mother, who had joined us for lunch, could. She supplied the details that helped us understand where he had gone astray.

As it turned out, Scott's weekend didn't fall flat because of rejection. Scott was to meet his friends at six at the theater. Because of his limited skills in executive function, every detail of the plan was written in his notebook so he could maneuver around his memory deficits, and he took care to set his wrist alarm for the first step. But when the alarm went off he exuberantly chose to ignore his written order and the strategy that HTP had drilled into us—to reset the alarm so he would remember to successively execute each additional step. He reasoned he didn't need the help. He changed his shirt several times, which made him late leaving the house.

His notebook was left behind on the dresser.

Worried about the time, he jumped aboard the first bus to come along. By the time he figured out it was going in the wrong direction, he was lost. It didn't occur to him to call home for assistance. Instead, the neon lights of a nearby bar caught his eye and he went in just because, he told us, "it seemed like a good idea. And, who knows, I might have met a woman."

Of course, he didn't. Nor did he ever meet up with his buddies. Instead, he tried to make friends with strangers. He had promised himself never to drink, but his disinhibition led him to make an exception "this time." In a grand gesture, he offered to buy everyone in the bar a drink. Soon after, the bouncer made him leave because he was "wild and noisy." And out of money.

We never asked him how he made it home. We silently regarded him, identifying with his disappointment. He had come face-to-face with a fact we each had to learn repeatedly: If we abandon our plans in wild enthusiasm, we are no longer in control of our situations.

While he philosophically made light of his missed reunion, I envisioned him as he had been—a dignified, tough Ranger who trained soldiers in desert warfare and hostage rescue. I knew how patriotic he was, how he would have relished the chance to prove himself in a Desert Storm.

That afternoon, Joan and Len, who were coaching the six veterans exclusively, told me they wanted me to prepare three half-hour-long lectures on head injury. The first would be based on my medical knowledge and would focus on the anatomy of the brain, the function of each lobe, and how each part interrelated and affected the whole person. Lecture 2 was to be on the different kinds of head injury, their effect on the brain, and how they disrupt function. My third lecture would be on the process of rehabilitation.

The exercises would enable me to try my hand at utilizing strategies for organizing material, working with some new information, and practicing my teaching skills. It was time to find out whether or not I still had what it took to teach medical students.

The plan was that I would give these talks to my fellow trainees. They would be required to pay attention to me, concentrate on the meaning of the material, make notes, try to assimilate new material, and then be tested on it. It would be good practice especially for Lenny and Sharon, who had hopes of returning to college.

I was excited and overwhelmed. It was the first independent project I had had at HTP, and I began to spend all of my free time making the most of it. Each time I hit roadblocks in the two weeks I had in which to prepare for my first lecture, I focused on Joan's confidence that I could do this assignment. Marcia and Joan showed me what questions to ask myself in order to move forward, but they didn't answer them or solve the problems for me.

When I finished the first lecture, I looked around at the bewildered faces of my class. There were very few questions. I learned from their evaluations that I had misjudged their level of understanding. The content was geared too high and I gave too much information, but they liked it. And so did the coaches.

I was a success and I enjoyed the moment, pleased with my achievement and the well-dones from my coaches and friends. That night, I would begin preparing for the next lecture, due in another two weeks, and I was looking forward to it.

But my success had a price. I had spent two weeks preparing material on a subject I knew, material that once would have taken a quick hour to execute. How could I keep up that level of effort? More to the point, if this were a real teaching situation, how could I prepare my material in time?

"You are doing it again, Claudia," Joan said at our conference that afternoon. "You're expecting too much from yourself, judging yourself by a previous standard."

I tried again. "I liked the lecture, Joan. I think it was good. But it tells me teaching medicine would be a problem." The lecture was stuff I knew. Medicine changes constantly. I would have to learn new material in order to teach it, and I was concerned by these implications in terms of a future vocation.

"Write down your thoughts," she said as we parted.

I made a note to do it later and left for home.

As I stepped off the curb at the corner of 32nd Street and Park Avenue, a taxi plowed aggressively through the crosswalk, nearly knocking me down. I charged after the cab, running along Park Avenue, yelling obscenities at the driver. I knew my explosive outrage was out of proportion to the offense, and I didn't know why I was so mad, but I was still seething long after the taillights had vanished in the afternoon gloom.

I retraced my steps. As my rage faded, I felt embarrassed and dismayed, as I always did by my occasional manifestations of disinhibition. I glanced around covertly. Behavior such as this was so out of character for me, but no one around me had noticed. Thank God for New York.

When I went home that weekend, I took the material for my second lecture with me. I never touched it. Once home, I was caught up in my other life.

Saturday morning, I volunteered to go to the post office while Marcia did the laundry. Like shopping, laundry was a chore I had not mastered, but I was successful with errands such as going to the post office. It was a circumscribed job with parts I could quickly check off a list. Because Marcia knew it made me feel productive, she saved errands like that for my every other weekend home.

For a Saturday morning, the line was short. I quickly purchased a roll of stamps and headed over to the mailbox to post a letter and bills Marcia had paid. I had just made my deposit into its yawning mouth and shut the door when the stamped envelopes in my right hand caught my attention. I glared at the box. I'd mailed my stamps. This greedy postal animal that eats indiscriminately had just consumed a $29 breakfast roll.

I went inside to get help. The postal clerk's initial response was, "You're sure they're in there?"

I hated questions like that. "Sure" was no longer a given in anything I did, but this was no time for a shoulder shrug. "Yes," I said confidently as I followed him out to the box. "Sorry to impose on your time, but I did mail them."

"It's all right." He squatted and unlocked the belly of the box. He had a pleasant smile and a kindly, creased face. "We've had people drop all sorts of things in on occasion." He looked back up at me as he handed over the stamps. "Didn't I retrieve some car keys for you a couple weeks ago?"

"Thank you," I said. "That was probably me." New York's anonymity once again looked appealing.

I walked toward the car, only to notice that I was still carrying the envelopes. When I retraced my steps, I almost collided with a man rapidly rounding the car, headed toward me.

"Hey, Dr. Osborn? Claudia?"

I looked up and smiled warmly at the tall, ruddy-faced young man in a football jersey with a toddler slung under his left arm. Since I didn't know any of the Detroit Lions personally, I eliminated one possible identity. There was no question I knew his voice and I was sure I liked him, but I did not know his face or name.

I extended my hand. "Hello."

"How are you? You look great."

"I feel great. It's good to see you." Trying to sound casual I added, "I'm terrible with names—"

"Tom Sattler, it's been a while. I was an intern on your service a year ago last spring."

"Yes." And I did like him. I'd thought he would have made a good internist, but his heart was set on surgery. "How's life in the OR?"

"Good. I picked the right residency, but I'm amazed at how much the medicine you taught me made a difference. You're a wonderful doctor and teacher."

I thanked him and we chatted amicably for a few minutes before I headed to my car.

I glowed with his praise of my work. I wanted to savor it. Once behind the wheel, I whipped out my notebook and jotted down what he had said so I could tell Marcia. When I saw the words on the page I realized they weren't about me. They were about a person I would never be again. Tears spilled from my eyes and coursed down my face.

I started to drive but had to stop almost immediately to wipe my eyes. I left the lot and turned out onto Mack Avenue. What if I was never that good at anything again?

I made myself stop crying and achieved what felt like a composed face and mental clarity before I entered the house.

Marcia handed me some Kleenex before I was through the door. "What happened?"

"I'm just a stamp catcher."

"A what? Is that like a dog catcher?"

"Yes," I said, not sure what part was unclear. "I fetch stamps."

"You said you wanted to go to the post office."

"You're missing the point." Sometimes I wished to God I could just hand Marcia my thoughts as a package instead of as a jigsaw puzzle with pieces missing.

"Okay, what's the point?"

"That's just it. I don't have a point. I'm pointless. I have no purpose. I need to know what it is I can do with my life. I just demonstrated I can't teach new material. Clinical medicine is always new. I don't know what I'm capable of doing."

Or what I could wish for.

I was surrounded by an ocean with an unpredictable tide, erasing each step I took and dissolving my dreams like castles in the sand. I was awash with despair, unable to find an embankment safe from the surge where I could build a foundation. When you run out of dreams you die. I needed dreams.

I didn't realize I had spoken aloud until Marcia wrapped her arms around me.

"I'll buy you some dreams, Claudia," she said while I wept. "Don't worry, I have coupons."

If only she could. If only it were that easy. How long could you run on empty?

I was at my best and worst. My ability to function was noticeably better, but I was adrift. I desperately needed a vision of an achievable future—one I wanted, not just one I could attain. Now that the *me* I knew no longer existed, I had to build another identity and move on, or wither and die. But I didn't know who I was now, so how could I know where I was going? I understood what Scott meant when he said, "I've parachuted down in full combat gear without orders or dog tags. Who am I supposed to attack?"

Being a doctor was what I had dreamed about since I was ten and my mother, brother, and I lived briefly in India. There, I spent one day a week at a village clinic and leprosy camp outside New Delhi that was run by a dedicated, generous physician, Dr. Dorothy Chako.

The on-site laboratory staff was one small man, made smaller by his posture, who sat at a rickety little table outdoors hunched over a microscope looking at stool specimens. The parasites he identified were one of the things we could treat successfully. For the most part, what we really needed was a cure for hunger.

My involvement was limited to running errands, weighing patients, dispensing the pitifully few medications, and staying out of the way. In return, I was allowed to watch Dr. Chako's gentle ministries and hear her diagnoses. These were given in English and recorded on little cards by Mrs. Bowles, the American ambassador's wife, who had long worked with the doctor.

Dr. Chako treated me with the same respectful dignity she gave her patients—I was never excluded from anything because it was too graphic or adult for child eyes. From her, I learned to recognize smallpox scars and kwashiorkor. After a time I could often guess from the symptoms which patients had hookworm and could stay clear of those likely to have TB.

How Dr. Chako handled the magnitude of the bottomless need around her was never clear to me. The passion for medicine she instilled has never left me. I will be ever grateful for her gift. When it came time for me to leave India she sat me down for a final lesson. "Find out what God intends your work to be and do that work to the best of your abilities."

I wish I knew what God intended for me now.

∾ In the weeks following the day at the post office, I began to realize I had a host of new skills and a growing history of small successes. I was also more tolerant of the frailties in my functioning. I recorded my errors— usually in living, red-faced color—in my notebook so I could study them like insects on pins and develop strategies to avoid repeating them. But if a mistake was not financially or emotionally costly to others, I could shrug it off or laugh about it as I had the previous week when, on my way to the basement to wash clothes, I mistakenly threw my laundry down the trash chute. It would have been nice if the maintenance man had looked less incredulous or had said that this happened commonly in my apartment building, but I was laughing with him as we went to retrieve my now truly dirty clothes.

Sometimes strategies, even good ones, fell apart in the unpredictable dynamics of the real world, but I began to measure my progress by my ability to stay with a plan and use backup tactics. If I came through without flooding and actually finished what I had started, I could exult in having beaten the odds.

I had that pleasure at the end of October on a trip to Boston to visit an old friend who had invited me for the weekend. Thursday afternoon, I whipped out of rehab. Carrying my suitcase in one hand and a package for my hostess in another, I managed to hail a cab right at the corner of the dental school despite a drizzling rain.

"Penn Station, please," I said, settling gratefully into the dry warmth. Good cab karma.

Between poor planning and preoccupation with my lecture project, I had missed breakfast and lunch. My stomach felt, as TuTu would say, like my belly button was shaking hands with my backbone, but I had remembered the package, and I should get to the station soon enough to buy a sandwich to eat on the train before the four-hour trip to Boston. I felt I was in the groove and moving well.

A few minutes into the taxi ride, I reached into my pockets to prepare to pay the driver and discovered I had a check, $2.87 in coins, and a credit card.

This was not possible. I had strategies now to prevent this. I glanced at the meter—the fare was two dollars—and quickly asked the driver. "Excuse me, do you ever take checks or a credit card?"

"This is where I should laugh, right?"

"Uh, what I mean is, stop now. I would like to get out here."

"This isn't anywhere near Penn Station."

"I know, but seeing the rain and all, I've decided to walk."

He shrugged. Nothing surprises a New York cabby. I gave him $2.50 and set off into the drizzle at a pounding clip. I was going to be on that four o'clock to Boston.

I bounded onto the train moments before it pulled away from the platform. I settled my damp, hungry self in the only bench seat available. One half was occupied by a smartly dressed matron who withdrew into her corner as if to distance herself from my rain-soaked clothes. Her gorgeous brown gabardine coat and Ferragamo pumps and bag were unspotted by the rain, her ash-blond hair dry and perfectly coifed. As she watched me try to catch my breath I was confident she had never run for anything in her life.

Her visible distaste did not lessen my triumph. I had abandoned the cab without flooding, gotten to the station in time despite the rain and suitcase, found the booth and bought the correct ticket with a credit card, then located the track and boarded the right train. And I still had the package. In four hours, I would be in Boston and the sanctuary of my friends' home.

I had won, dammit, *won*.

Before I realized what I was doing, I let out a whoop of joy and thrust my right arm up in the air. I startled myself with this show of exuberance. I decided against glancing toward my neighbor.

Basking in contentment, I resorted to my time-tested way of ignoring the pangs of hunger. I fell asleep, fingering the thirty-seven cents left in my pocket.

Acceptance of an Afterlife

I am worried about the recent casual references made by Joan and Yehuda in our conference. Yehuda said, in a careful not-promising-anything style, that the cognitive training I was getting now might have a future career application. It might be possible one day, he said, for me to give structured, basic lectures on introductory material to nursing or maybe even medical students.

"You will," he said, throwing me a bone, "still have the title of physician. There are physician-type things you can do without the medical, legal responsibility that goes with the primary work."

I try not to wince visibly. It is not "acceptance" if I explode.

I can imagine Joan in my shoes. She is good at her job as a neuropsychologist and she seems to reap many emotional rewards from working with head-injured people. What if Joan were told she could not practice her profession but she could still be called a neuropsychologist? She could administer some of the more basic tests, although not analyze them—that would be done by "real doctors." And she could coach ARC. Of course, she would have someone else making the important decision as to when trainees could advance and she would never again act as a group leader or personal counselor. Her role might advance as far as that of her medical secretary.

Not to fear, however; she could still call herself a neuropsychologist!

I just bet her joy would rival mine at this moment.

Although I cannot yet detail the specifics of my future job, I can and will practice and/or teach medicine at some level. Even if I'm wrong about that, I will do meaningful work somewhere. What a tragic waste of eight years of work and graduate schooling, of love of my healing profession, if I could only end up with worthless medical scut work just so I can say I am a doctor.

There is no danger I will turn into Yehuda's story of the "bitter has-been." I have never had that potential. On the other hand, my ability to practice medicine is not a pipe dream.

Please, God.

23

Not as I Wish, but as I Am

*What's terrible is to pretend that the second rate
is first rate. To pretend that you don't need love
when you do; or you like your work when you
know quite well you're capable of better.*
DORIS LESSING
✳

The weather had turned bleak and quite cold, the skies were a dirty gray. My walks to and from HTP now required a warm coat. But I liked it that the city lights were coming on earlier in the evening, making everything softer and prettier, lightening my mood. It was hard to believe we were more than halfway through November, halfway through the second cycle.

I'm not sure exactly why HTP had us prepare speeches for the midterm and final parties, but I knew they worked for me. Having to prepare what was, in effect, a public statement about myself helped me assess my progress and dissipate some of my fears. In so doing, I could move on.

This second cycle's midterm party fell on the Thursday before Thanksgiving. It was pleasant and uneventful. Marcia came for the long weekend. At my urging, my mother did not. I would see my parents, TuTu, and my brother, Christopher, in Florida at Christmas.

As on the previous two occasions, I had a hard time writing my speech. It seemed impossible to sort out my feelings, to put into words my questions about my future, to define the dragons I had been wrestling with— what was it I had to accept? What were my abilities and potential? Could I be loved and wanted as an equal and not as a dependent? The easy part was to recount my progress. To do that, I compared my current function with that in the previous cycle using the classic story of the blind man and the elephant:

> *Six months ago when I gave my first midterm speech I explained my problem of adynamia by saying that if I was blindfolded and left next to an elephant, it might take some prompting for it to occur to me to reach out and examine his trunk. I might miss completely the fact that his trunk was connected to anything or explore the rest of his body. Not recognizing the elephant, I might never ask how or why he came to be there.*
>
> *Now if you put me back with the elephant, I will energize myself and reach out to examine his trunk. I will initiate a barrage of self-directed questions to help me identify my companion and I will ask where he came from.*
>
> *It is still true that I might not recognize the elephant, but if I identify his trunk as a vacuum cleaner, I can at least laugh at my own misperception.*

The time between Thanksgiving and the start of the Christmas break rushed by. Our days at HTP were packed full. We were doing much of what we had been doing right along, only now we were plowing deeper and moving faster. We worked on mastering strategies designed to retailor our behavior and advance our productivity. We engaged in more demanding role-playing to practice performing in real-life situations. In our daily group discussions, we tackled pointed questions. "How do I protect myself from bitterness and a sense of defeat?" "Why am I depressed?" "How might adynamia or disinhibition or flooding (take your pick) affect my performance?" "What do I find the most difficult thing to bear?"

We polished our use of props such as timers and alarms, tape cassettes, lists, and notebooks. I had become a master of the latter, which continued to be my memory and organizer and was essential to my functioning well. Joan helped Lenny develop a system whereby he used a red dot on written work to keep him focused and attentive.

We were becoming more self-reliant. While our trust in our coaches was undiminished, we were developing a growing confidence in ourselves.

Slowly, and jerkily, my focus changed and grew sharper. I had given up my hopeless quest for my old job. I tried to look around, to objectively size up my strengths, to lay a recognizable foundation for a new identity.

I remember an alcoholic patient of mine who refused to consider a treatment program or attend AA meetings. His enlarged heart, sexual dysfunction, and liver disease were all caused by his alcohol and I counseled him repeatedly about his addiction. It seemed in vain. Then, one day he started attending AA and stopped drinking. I asked him why he decided to quit.

"You said the booze caused my ulcer. I didn't want a messed-up gut."

I often didn't know which things I said to patients would be taken to heart. Maybe they were smarter at HTP and knew which phrases held power to change us. For me there were three simple mantras that brought light. Len's words, "You can't be devastated if you're the one in control," pushed me to gain independence with strategies.

When I was disgusted with the worthless person I had become, Joan's admonition to "change your lens" encouraged me to see myself through the kinder and occasionally more objective eyes of others. And it was Ellen's advice to "learn to measure yourself by a different yardstick" that helped clear the way for new dreams.

The two lectures that I had presented so far in HTP proved to me that I could teach. The preparation was awful and tediously slow, but the result was palatable. My audience could learn from me and I did not put them to sleep. True, new material overwhelmed me, but I was able to fall back on previously learned medical knowledge and incorporate the rote-learned material from rehab. Lecturing, it seemed, was a challenge but not impossible.

I realized something else that changed my approach to examining future job possibilities. I had had my fill of failure. I did not want to pound against a closed door unless there was a reasonable expectation that it might open. I needed to be productive, indeed I thrived on it, but I knew my future employment had to match my present talents, which did not include walking on water. My ego enjoyed provocative challenge, not mission impossible.

My philosophy was sound but I lacked a tangible goal. I still had no idea what jobs I could actually do or what skills I could reliably count on.

Still, my altered outlook inspired hope, albeit a delicate one. I lost it easily; like a distant lighthouse beam shrouded in fog, but just as predictably it would reappear and stay my course from the reefs. While I journeyed, I tried to develop patience about my destination.

Christmas vacation was ambitious. Marcia's parents invited me to Carthage, Missouri, for the first days of the holiday, then Marcia would accompany me to Florida to celebrate a second Christmas with Mama, TuTu, Richard, and Christopher.

Christmas Eve was spent in Carthage in the home of Marcia's parents, a retired pastor and his wife. After services at their Nazarene church and a bountiful dinner, we turned to the beautifully wrapped presents under a large tree fairly dripping with handmade and treasured ornaments. I looked around at the loving group, feeling blessed to be there, swelling with the joy of the moment.

The eldest grandchild was given the honor of opening the first present. My happy mood was now escalating dangerously. When the youngster confided to me that he had already sneaked a peak into every package, I impulsively and loudly exclaimed with delight, "You little shit!"

The shock in the room was palpable. Eyes widened and mouths gaped in a telling but silent response. It was unquestionably the first time such language had ever been used in their home. But our activities quickly resumed as though nothing untoward had been said. It was not the time to explain that my outburst, however inappropriate, was an expression of my happiness at being with them.

Marcia later told me she had warned her family that I might swear when I was excited or unable to think of another word. It's a common phenomenon for head-injured and aphasic people. Under stress, an obscenity may be the first word the brain supplies. This may be akin to the overuse of imprecations in people with limited vocabularies who use them for nouns, verbs, and adjectives.

As Goethe said, when ideas fail, words come in very handy. I evidently needed some sanitized four-letter ones.

Christmas in Florida went less well. My exhaustion was taking its toll.

"One hour," my mother was saying, "before we leave for the Everglades, okay?" She was trying to energize me and was not having much success. "We'll have lunch at the Rod and Gun Club like we always do, okay? At breakfast, everyone thought this would be fun."

"Jeanne, why don't you go with TuTu and Richard?" Marcia said.

"The point of this trip is that the two of you go," my mother said. "This is your holiday, Marcia. And, you love going, don't you, Claudia? Claudia? You love the trip, right?"

"Yeah, this is a good trip."

"No, the Everglades," my mother said. "Going to the Everglades."

"Let's go one day," I said. "We could have lunch at that place."

We went, but our excursion to one of the country's most precious natural resources was less than my mother had desired. My persistent aphasia, lethargy, and unawareness of the conversation or my surroundings put a pall on everyone. It bewildered TuTu and withered Richard. Marcia was annoyed with her own inability to rise to the occasion. Finally, my mother alone kept up the conversation.

TuTu sat in back between Marcia and me. Each of us held one of her hands. I slumped at the window, my unfocused eyes on the canal edging the road.

I adore the water birds, and although their numbers have severely declined, making them harder to spot, I had a keen eye and had once delighted in pointing out each new sighting of a roseate spoonbill, ibis, osprey, or wood stork.

"Tell me when you see a good bird," TuTu said to me repeatedly.

Surely I must have tried, but it takes concentration and constant scanning of the landscape.

"Isn't that an eagle, Claudia?" TuTu said.

I didn't respond.

TuTu nudged Marcia, her expressive eyes searching. "Doesn't she see the birds? Doesn't she care about them anymore?"

"Her brain is resting."

"Are you crying, TuTu?" Marcia asked a short while later.

I registered her words and turned to see.

"Allergies, pollen," TuTu whispered back, releasing my hand to wipe the tears on her cheeks with a snowy hanky. She was not of the throwaway tissue generation.

"We can fix that, TuTu," Marcia said. "Remember, you have two doctors in the family."

I put my arm around her and she nestled against me, her tears more pronounced.

"Two doctors," I said.

After I was in bed that evening, my mother and Marcia talked. Mama spoke of her and Richard's love and gratitude for Marcia, and how frightening it was for them to see me so dysfunctional in a familiar environment. My mother said something about the precariousness of life, about any one of us being five seconds away from the unforeseen disaster, "A matter of luck," she said, "of circumstances."

"There is no one, no thing I can get angry at." Marcia punched her fist into the sofa pillow. "Everything is just a matter of circumstance and I'm sick of it. I'd like to take a circumstance and throw it up against the wall."

My last lecture, the one on rehabilitation, was scheduled for the second week of January and would take about forty-five minutes.

"Third time and you're out, Claudia," Scott said, then laughed heartily and alone while I looked at my notes. The room was stuffy. In addition to our usual assemblage of six trainees, Lenny's mother, and Len and Joan, there were two visiting therapists, one of whom was from Poland.

Even with my need to concentrate on what I was saying, I was acutely conscious of the trainees' attention. This material was relevant to their lives. Despite their having heard it in various guises throughout this last year, I wanted to give them a meaningful summary.

"Rehabilitation at HTP is a holistic process," I told them. "We are striving to gain function and competence in every area of our life, be it cognitive, behavioral, or personal. In order to do so, we need to meet three over-lapping and interdependent objectives."

I pointed at the easel where I had written:

1. *Awareness*—must identify and understand deficits
2. *Compensation*—develop strategies to compensate
3. *Acceptance*—some things about us cannot be restored

"These three objectives combine to make one whole rehabilitated person," I said. "Take awareness. Yehuda says we must be able to 'stand the pain of discovery' of our losses. When I say that, I have this image of myself clinging by my fingernails to a window ledge. What he is saying is that this discovery cannot just be an intellectual one. We must also understand our losses on an emotional level. That understanding is assisted by our growing ability to compensate for our deficits and by our regaining some control over our lives."

My eyes roved the group, trying to read them. Sharon was busily taking notes. Lenny's eyes were fixed on me, as were Beth's, who continued winding her hair. Scott was squirming, trying not to crack a joke—I broke eye contact with him quickly.

The coaches were nodding encouragingly, which did not necessarily reflect on my presentation. They would have cheered me on if I were reciting "Bo Peep." Their critiques would come later.

"You would think one must first recognize and understand one's deficits before learning how to compensate for them. It doesn't work that way. A certain level of learning has to come first, before awareness can be achieved. If a trainee is unable to be alert and focused, learning may not take place. Therefore the first thing we worked on in rehabilitation was attention/concentration. Unfortunately, there's a catch-22.

"It's difficult to pay attention and concentrate if you are markedly adynamic and/or disinhibited. But to attack the disinhibition and adynamia—especially when we are unaware that the problems exist—we must first learn how to pay attention and concentrate.

"Therefore, even before Scott grasps that he is disinhibited"—that got his attention—"he is instructed to put on the brakes, settle down and listen, not to speak until asked to do so and then only to read the answers he has first written in his notebook. While learning how to control his behavior, he begins learning, through computer exercises, to pay attention and concentrate. Only after Scott's attention and concentration are improved is he able to develop an awareness of his disinhibition.

"It is not enough for me to intellectually understand that I am adynamic and that I flood. I must also learn to live with this knowledge, adapt myself to compensate for my deficits, and feel okay about who I am. True acceptance is more than the calm resignation that our injuries have permanently changed our lives and put a ceiling on what we can achieve. It doesn't have to be all negative."

Home stretch. "With growing competency there is improved self-esteem, enthusiasm for realistic options for the future, and in Yehuda's dramatic words, 'a healing of one's shattered sense of self.'"

I sat down to their applause. If nothing else, I knew how I would talk about acceptance in my speech for the final party.

That night, I told my notebook, and thus Joan,

> *I want to do whatever I do well. I hate functioning at the fringe of my abilities. I want a tolerable level of stress and a job I enjoy and can do successfully. I believe I can grow more and it is a mistake to resign myself to my present level of function. But whatever I achieve, the real test of acceptance will be whether life is worth living and has meaning and pleasure.*

In my conference with Joan the following afternoon, she complimented me on the lecture again, saying HTP might want to use taped excerpts from it. We then rehashed my concern about my difficulties in preparing the lecture, which led to our discussing my employment limitations and gave her an opening to introduce a topic on her mind.

"Claudia, you have heard us mention a post-HTP job-training program called Occupational Trials. Have you given any thought to entering this program?"

"No." I felt flustered. It was déjà vu all over again. "Six months would mean my delay in going home." Wait, I said that? I said *home,* not *getting back to work?* When did that shift occur?

Joan was saying something I didn't catch.

"I'm sorry?"

"I was saying it doesn't have to be six months. It can be as short as three. I wish you'd meet with Saralyn Silver, the director of the program." She opened the NYU phone directory. "You would have a much better feel for what it entails."

"I'd be put in some Mickey Mouse job, wouldn't I?"

"Not at all. Saralyn would try to place you in a job at the NYU Medical Center. It would seem like a familiar environment to you and would help you identify for yourself what you can do."

She turned the open book toward me, and I wrote Saralyn's name and number in my notebook.

"Besides," Joan said, "along with getting insight into the level of your job skills, it will impart skills. You would be given a job coach who could help you build strategies. And the situation would allow you to stumble and try again without losing a job. Best of all, it's a wonderful bridge for you between here and home." She stood, ending the conference. "Please talk it over with your family but also talk to Saralyn."

I called Occupational Trials the next day and spoke to Saralyn. Like Joan, she felt I'd find the program helpful. I discussed it with Marcia and my mother that night. And the next night, and the one after that. We kept changing each other's mind.

"I thought a lot about what you said last night, Claudia," my mother said on one occasion. "I'm reversing what I said earlier. I now agree with Marcia's view."

"Refresh my memory, Mama. Is that for or against?"

"Against staying. What more is there to be learned that's worth your having to stay there through May? You will have been absent for over a year. Better to come home and get on with your life. Why not get your job practice in a real job?"

"Two days ago, I wanted you to say that, Mama. Now I'm not sure. I think Saralyn's right. I would be working in a hospital, though not high up, that's for sure. And I would have a net underneath to catch me if I should fall. I can't get that in a real job."

"I think there's a part of you that's saying you need this," she said slowly. "That's reason enough to do it, Claudia. But you've said you don't have to tell them before the end of January. Why don't we postpone the discussion till then when you and Marcia and I can talk it over together?"

"Okay. I'll write down to think about it on January 30."

It's nice to be able to stave off one's worry with a notation.

A Brief Quiz to Assess Head Injury
(in Lieu of Neuropsychological Testing)

1. A man walks up to you on the street, pulls out a gun, and demands your wallet. Your response is to
   a. Ask him to repeat himself. You were not paying attention.
   b. Hand over your wallet because he asked for it. You do not realize you are being robbed.
   c. Wrestle him for control of the gun, even though your arm is in a sling from your last similar street encounter.
   d. Hand over your wallet while assessing your situation and thinking through your next move.

2. A friend loaned you his video *The War of the Roses,* a dark comedy about a couple fighting over their divorce settlement. Later, when he asks you what you thought of it, you tell him:
   a. You have heard of it and would like to see it one day.
   b. It was a good war film [said without humor].
   c. You love war movies and recount at length your favorite battles in history and act them out.
   d. Thank him for letting you see it and laugh with him about its funnier scenes.

GRADING YOURSELF
In each scenario, if you answered **a,** you have attention/concentration and memory deficits.

If you included **b,** you are also adynamic.

If you included **c,** you are also disinhibited.

But, if you only picked **d** (and it wasn't a blind guess), you don't need rehabilitation.

FROM MY NOTEBOOK, SEPTEMBER 12, 1990

24

Moving On

Life is easier than you think. All that is necessary
is to accept the impossible, do without the
indispensable, and bear the intolerable.
KATHLEEN NORRIS
⋎

A few weeks later, I was searching for a tampon in my hall locker after lunch when Lenny stopped next to me, watching my unsuccessful rummaging through shelves and pockets. High school revisited.

"Some of what you said had its merits," he said, swaying slightly as he spoke.

"Thank you," I said, figuring I would eventually guess what we were talking about.

"It's hard to trust those guys, but this doctor I went to was all right."

"Doctor?" I said.

"En-do-crin-ol-o-gist." He emphasized each syllable in turn. "Says my hy-po-thal-a-mus doesn't work right. You know what that is, don't you?"

"Yes, it regulates many different functions, like your thyroid and—"

"Thyroid. That's one of the things he's giving me medication for."

"I'm glad you saw him."

"So am I, now."

Endocrine problems are often a part of head injury because the pituitary and hypothalamus, which regulate hormones, may have been injured as well. This can result in multiple problems: thyroid dysfunction, an inability of the body to regulate its water/salts balance, a growth impairment in some children, menstrual irregularity, sexual dysfunction, even acne.

Sometimes the symptoms are ignored or assumed to be coincidental.

Checking thyroid function or other hormonal imbalances may be forgotten in the face of more overwhelming losses. Still, a young person whose social world has diminished after an injury should not have the added burden of severe acne caused by the increased production of steroids and testosterone.

"Doctors saved my life," Lenny said, "but, you know, I've been poked and prodded and tubed everywhere. I've suffered too many indignities to trust your profession, Claudia. You never know what's going to happen. Anyway"—he shrugged his shoulders and looked embarrassed—"I wanted you to know it worked out this time."

"I'm really glad, Lenny." I squeezed his arm and, when he left, returned to my locker search.

An injury to the brain is, first of all, a physical injury. It may affect any part of the body, not just cognitive skills and behavior. Each of us had problems as a result of our head injuries, the kinds of problems everyone thinks of as "physical."

Bernie's hearing was affected, as were Scott's left arm and leg and Sharon's vision. For me, it was my right arm and neurogenic bladder. Lenny's and Richard's problems were so many and varied, they had spent years of their young lives in intimate contact with medical professionals.

Even as we praised the heroics that had saved our lives, we all told stories of the frustrations and indignities that resulted from medical experiences. Each of us could recall moments that loomed larger in our minds than the physical loss we could not undo:

Six doctors—only one of whom needs to see your chest incision—crowd around your bed while your breasts are exposed. A resident tells you how lucky you should feel because you didn't die in the accident with your beloved husband. You stare at the bedpan and call-light—both just out of reach—while you soil your sheets. The procedure that they never explained to you except to say it would feel like a little pinch feels like a root canal without Novocain. The lab tech who needed three tries to draw your blood ten minutes ago is back for more because the intern forgot to order a specific test.

My own special moment came when my bladder was tested.

My bladder does not completely empty and the process of urinating is slow. Testing bladder function is unpleasant, even when expertly done, as it was this day, and small, insensitive practices can easily make it needlessly worse.

I was put into a large room divided into two parts by a drawn curtain— I later learned the part I couldn't see contained a desk and dictaphone. I was barely acquainted with the hospital nurse who would do the procedure, but I knew she was efficient and experienced. After I emptied my bladder in the attached bathroom, she instructed me to undress from the waist down, which I quickly did. I am not especially modest but I was surprised not to be given a sheet. I lay down on the examining table as she directed, and within a very few minutes she had inserted a catheter into my bladder to check for residual urine, and a second tube into my rectum.

Perhaps she thought a doctor would know what to expect, but I was unprepared for her next move, which was to pierce the area around the urethra with sharp wires. I jerked in reflexive pain.

She patted my shoulder. "I'm sorry, it's to measure nerve function. That step is the reason nurses ask for transfers or quit. They hate it almost as much as the patients." She helped me down from the table and to a portable commode inexplicably placed in the middle of the room. After I lowered my naked, tubed, and wired behind gingerly onto the seat, she connected the catheter to a bag of saline fluid suspended from a pole and began filling my bladder until I indicated it was uncomfortably full. She then told me to empty it.

I knew this was so she could measure the reaction of muscles and nerves, but my understanding of why I needed these tests didn't help. I hated this procedure, not for its discomfort but because it made me focus on my body's failing and because it rendered me temporarily powerless, in someone else's control.

Just as I began to concentrate on trying to empty my bladder, I was startled by a brief knock. Then, without waiting for an answer, a white-coated man entered the room.

"I'm going to dictate," he said to the nurse, who neither protested nor gave me a drape.

Marvelous. We might as well be doing this test at Tiger Stadium. His eyes met mine and I realized he was a former colleague, a urologist.

"Claudia? Well, uhm, hello." He refrained from adding, "You're looking great," settling for an outstretched hand.

"Hi there." I gave his hand a brief shake. Are there rules of etiquette for greeting colleagues while seated on a toilet? "How are you?"

"Fine, thanks. And you?"

"Fine, just fine." I only stopped in to pee.

I attempted a smile.

He nodded and moved on.

Lenny had said he'd "suffered indignities" while doctors poked and prodded him, in albeit sincere attempts to save his life. Doctors, I could have told him, are not always spared either.

❦Graduation day arrived that year on February first. I was assured it would be my last one at HTP. As with the previous final party, this one would be held in one of the small auditoriums of the dental school and my guests would be Mama, Richard, and Marcia.

Again, each of us would give a speech on aspects of our rehabilitation and read a brief poem or prose excerpt. But the mood was different this time. We were really leaving and I was eager to be out of the gate. I took it to be one of HTP's chief virtues that, unlike many group programs for various maladies, its coaches did not foster our dependence on them. They encouraged my desire for independence.

I was so focused on preparing my speech and self-absorbed in completing some closure at HTP that I hardly knew my family was in town. I didn't even join them for luncheon. While they went off by themselves, we trainees dined as usual in "chez dental school" after a morning of rehearsing aloud to each other.

Scott was grinning as he put his tray down next to mine on the lunch table. It was delightful to be around someone who made it so easy to smile.

"Your speech is really about Humpty Dumpty," he said.

"Well, it's clear I think they should have scrapped the idea of patching that guy up. They should have rebuilt him."

"If it were my army, we would've redirected the king's men."

"Maybe you should rewrite the poem."

That evening at the party when the speeches got under way, Scott was the first of us veterans to speak.

He approached the podium and arranged his notes. I waited for him to crack a joke or laugh or do something clownish, but he maintained a dignified control. He spoke of the deficit that troubled him the most, the damage to the part of the brain that inhibits and controls behavior. He recounted his struggle to master the uncontrolled expression of his feelings, saying the two cycles at HTP were "the most winding road of my life."

His poem was "The Prayer of an Unknown Confederate Soldier," whom he likened to himself in that he was given the opposite of what he sought in a supreme test of what he might become. "I asked for strength, I was given disability."

I thought Scott would have felt more heroic had his injuries occurred on a battlefield, but his fight to create a new life after devastating injury was truly his finest hour.

Beth read her lines effortlessly, like an actress, looking up at the audience frequently. Her speech concerned her struggle to gain control of her life and was, she told us, both a "dedication to those who helped" her develop and harness her resources and a "declaration that to use other people's guidance, advice, and support is not a sign of weakness but of strength and growth." Dark eyes flashing, she finished by asserting with a proud half smile, "My irrepressible spirit will prevail."

I was confident that she was right.

Tommy wore his protective armor—the dark glasses he was never without. He was nervous, I knew, but nothing in his voice or manner betrayed it. He swaggered just a bit on his trip to the podium and stood in a relaxed, spread-leg way. I sat on the edge of my seat and silently cheered him on. He didn't need my help.

"When things got hard," he said, "I stuck to it. . . . I am back on track, I made it. I want to show my kids that this is the way to act when things get tough." His poem reflected that theme. It was three lines long: "I made it through the good times," he read. "I made it through the bad times. But mostly, I just made it." I was unclear as to its authorship. I wondered if he had written it himself and I forgot to ask him later.

By now, I could see most everyone in the audience had tear-streaked faces or were blowing their noses. But they were smiling.

Listening to my fellow trainees voice their feelings and experiences was therapeutic. My own struggle paled in comparison.

Sharon moved to the podium quickly while Amy was still introducing her. She spread her notes on the little desk under the light, squared her slender shoulders in a "let's get to it" gesture, and began to read. Sharon was at her best, and thus our best speaker.

"I was confused about myself," she said. "I didn't know who I was or what I stood for. In place of the Sharon I knew, there was a big gaping hole. I was confused about my injury. I didn't know what was wrong with me, but I knew I was very different. I was confused about other people. . . . I would hide myself from them. I had a lot of guilt about what had happened to me. I blamed myself. I felt I had lost everything in my life. I found out about myself, who I really am. I am learning to accept help. I am beginning to find myself. The hole is filling in."

Her poem has enabled me to regain my footing many times.

> *Daylight.*
> *I must wait for the sunrise.*
> *I must think of a new life.*
> *And I must not give in.*

I felt my own eyes smart.

Lenny outdid himself. He walked up to the podium and spoke as though he were on the creamed-chicken-and-green-peas speech circuit. He spoke of this year of rehabilitation and what his parents and HTP had helped him accomplish. Some of us knew the sacrifices his parents had made to be with him and how they had devoted the last seven years of their life to his recovery. As he spoke, his words were directed to his parents, Paul and Dean.

He felt he had made real progress in his knowledge about his problems and his situation. Whereas he once was labeled, he said he felt those labels had been dropped. He had to devise and follow strategies that were limiting in their own way but that now gave him a measure of independence.

"They are a paradox," he said, "their bonds have helped make me free." He finished strongly by expressing his gratitude to his mother and father. "I feel assured there is an end point to the chaos in which I have been living. This is a question for my parents." He spoke directly to them: "How am I doing?"

They were nodding through their tears.

Of all of us, it was Lenny who had improved the most during our rehab year. A person had emerged from that automaton and I admired him greatly.

In my speech, I drew upon Yehuda Ben-Yishay's words that a head injury produced in a person a "shattered sense of self." I likened my process of rebuilding myself to an incident in my childhood when I broke my mother's porcelain vase.

"Although pieces were scattered everywhere across the floor, I was unperturbed—after the initial shock. I used Elmer's glue and began a laborious process of patching that vase together. Periodically my brother would draw my attention to a stray piece under a chair or to a gaping hole in my reconstruction.

"It was some time before I could see the futility of my efforts, and I was only reluctantly dissuaded from my next bright idea of supporting the structure with transparent tape. My patchwork efforts bore some resemblance to the original art. It might fool an admirer at fifty yards. It also had a delightful new quality of letting in streaks of light, which I hoped might mitigate my mother's reaction.

"Despite the fact that I had used all the available pieces in my repair, there was a flaw—the vase could not hold water. I now saw little to love and admire. It did not even have a useful function.

"Rehab has shown me that there is a second approach to shattered objects—whether a vase or a sense of self. It is to construct a new image rather than patch the old one. I do not mean from scratch, but even so, it is a formidable task. The new image would incorporate much of the old sense of self. One would not discard any valuable qualities and personality characteristics that are still available; that is, not lost under a chair. The end result will certainly not be identical to the original, but there will be lots of similarity. It might be as beautiful. It will definitely be functional. Since I am rebuilding, I might intentionally alter the pattern and let in a few of those streaks of light. After all, they may be delightful. . . ."

I concluded by saying, "If I could return home knowing I could again contribute, that I would be a whole person able to give to others and be an equal partner in every relationship, it would be the greatest gift I could give to myself and to those who love me."

Rehab Analogy

I found myself journeying through a frightening wilderness, dark and dense with trees. It was an unexpected, accidental trek—I am not courageous or foolhardy enough to plan such an adventure. It was but a quirk of fate that took me from my hearth, away from the comfort of my family.

My forced march was made harder by my grief, but it was a nightmare that enriched my life.

I was not particularly brave out there. As a matter of fact I was often frightened, confused, and despairing. But what I remember most now about my sojourn are its gifts: finding an adroit guide and dragon slayer, the exhilaration of growth, my reawakened spirit, the sustenance of strangers, and of course, the pieces of comedy.

My heart has not become braver. I do not strike boldly out where angels fear to tread. But again I look forward to the experience of the day—rather than seeking its end. I am willingly caught up in life's adventure, willing to risk new trails, to see the humor of my life and laugh loudly.

I sit here tonight enjoying the fire, listening to Mozart. I am content but it is not because of Mozart. I attribute the peace I have acquired to that trek through the wilderness. I will long be grateful for it.

FROM MY NOTEBOOK, FEBRUARY 2, 1990

Occupational Trials

*This thing we call failure is not the falling
down, but the staying down.*
MARY PICKFORD
⊁

There is an English proverb that says "a stumble may prevent a fall." That argument convinced me of the merit of Occupational Trials. It would give me a way to make mistakes without harming my reputation or risking an employer's loss of confidence in me. Then later, I would be able to undertake a "real" job with better insight as to how my deficits played out in a work environment and have some idea of how to ameliorate them.

I sometimes suspect that if I had gone directly home, I would have had an emotional collapse. Certainly, my progress would have been slowed enormously. As it was, OT allowed me to fail gracefully, helped me stand again, and enabled me to heal before I went home in May.

HTP, which is a subsection of The Rusk Institute of Rehabilitation Medicine, assigned me to work at the NYU Medical Center on East 34th Street, in the admissions office of Rusk. Patients were transferred to Rusk for rehabilitation for all sorts of reasons—spinal cord injuries, neuromuscular diseases, strokes, amputated limbs, and the like. To determine if the patient could benefit from being at Rusk and was stable and ready for transfer, Admissions first needed to call and interview the patient and the legion of people caring for him or her: primary doctor, nurse, social worker, family, and physical, occupational, and speech therapists.

The nursing coordinator of the department was Eileen Kowal and her colleague was Robyn Hoffman. My job was to assist in making these phone calls and to record the patient's status. My medical background equipped me admirably—I could interpret medical jargon, read the patients' medical records, understand what the transferring medical personnel were trying to communicate (or conceal), and define terms when asked by the office staff. It seemed an ideal match. In addition, Eileen and the staff were warm and supportive and made me feel useful and included.

I learned the routine in a couple of weeks. I never learned to cope with the individual situations no matter how many times I was confronted by them.

This was my fifth attempt to reach this physical therapist. On one occasion, she had been unavailable. The other three calls I categorized as "other." Either I had called the wrong hospital or the wrong department or had no hospital at all, had inquired about the wrong patient, or had missed essential questions. These are the sorts of calls that are best forgotten, and my head injury always obliged. Everyone has made these missteps; the volume of mine was impressive.

I had a number of lists of questions I was expected to ask various people concerning the course of hospital stay, medications, diagnosis, cautions, and significant factors. In preparation for each call, I spread the patient's file out in front of me along with the relevant names—that of the patient, his mother and sister, the hospital, doctors, a nurse. Each list of questions was tailored to fit the person I was calling. In this case, I needed to learn the distance the patient could walk, his endurance, his motivation, his prognosis. I silently rehearsed asking the questions just before I dialed. My index finger pointed steadily at the name of the physical therapist so I would not confuse it with the patient's or doctor's name. That always worked at HTP, keeping my finger glued on a cue for speech or action.

I dialed correctly, got the right department, asked for the right physical therapist—and was placed on hold. I didn't do "hold" well. I felt like an amateur tightrope walker—I couldn't stand in the middle and wave to the crowd. I had to keep moving until I reached the far side. Today, even my finger got up and left its post. I lost the name.

"Hello," a voice said at last, "this is Sally."

"Hi," I said, wondering if I knew a Sally. "What can I do for you?"

"I don't know. You called me."

"Oh . . . right." I stalled, looking for her name. "This is Claudia Osborn from the Rusk admissions office." Still no name. I took a guess at her identity. "I just want to ask you a couple of questions about your brother Michael."

"I don't have a brother Michael."

"Michael Johnson?" I began shuffling papers on my desk. A big mistake, as I scan badly and the physical therapy questions sheet was no longer on top.

"He's my patient."

"Oh, sorry. I meant patient." At least I did now, but I couldn't find the questions. I seized a list and finally asked, "Is he eating well?"

"I don't know. You'd have to ask his nurses."

My heart sank. I thought she was a nurse. Maybe I should just hang up.

"Listen," she said, "I'm in kind of a hurry. Why don't I just summarize his progress in PT, okay?"

"Okay." I was so rattled now, I could not record much of what she said, but it would have to do. I was not calling back.

> *Tu Tu,*
>
> *As its name implies, OT tests our work skills in real-life work situations, through trial and error. With a great emphasis on the latter.*
>
> *Only in the real situation do I come face-to-face with the implications of my deficits. It means much more when I see myself malfunction in a busy office than to just have an intellectual understanding of my limitations.*

As at HTP, coaching was an integral part of OT. Saralyn Silver was the director of the program and my coach. She was a silver-haired, plump, motherly woman who was respected for her research and her success in bridging the worlds of rehabilitation and employment.

Each week I met with Saralyn at lunchtime or before or after my workday to discuss glitches in my performance and strategies to overcome them. In addition to Saralyn's coaching, Eileen and Robyn were key supports and effective on-the-job teachers. Once weekly, we six trainees met as a group with Saralyn and swapped ideas and experiences, although we trainees did more of the latter in our frequent lunches together alone.

The big, noisy cafeteria of the dental school was now replaced by an even larger, noisier hospital cafeteria. We not only had to use our maps to find the place, we had to meet outside the entrance to find each other.

Today, we loaded our trays and found six seats together at one of the long trestle tables. We were all employed in the hospital complex. None of us understood or knew much about each other's job, but I knew that Tommy did photocopying, Lenny and Sharon did clerical work in different clinics, and Beth sat at an information desk in an outpatient chemotherapy clinic. Scott was unassigned, waiting to get into some sort of residential program.

"Let's eat quickly." Tommy dropped his tray heavily on the table and took a slug of Dr Pepper while still standing. "I gotta get out of here and get some air. Where I work a guy could get claustrophobic. I need a job outdoors."

"Not in a New York winter," Sharon said. "But trust me, I'm never getting a job again where I have to stuff envelopes. It doesn't have much to do with going back to school."

"Well," Beth said in a reasoning tone, "stuffing envelopes isn't the point. We're learning good job habits."

"I have good job habits," Lenny almost snapped. "It's boring work. Are you bored, Claudia?"

Scott slapped me on the back. "You look like you're lapsing into a coma."

"Sorry," I said. "I never seem to do the same thing twice at my job, though I guess I'm supposed to. I could use some boredom."

"You're lucky." Beth took the plastic wrap off her sandwich. "Does anyone know how to transfer a call to another phone?"

Sharon shook her head. "I don't really believe it's possible at this place, but it's a good idea to say you're trying to right before you disconnect the call."

On this we all agreed.

∿ My schedule was simple. My job was not. I was drained. I worked two hours in the morning and spent most of my lunch hour in the Glass Garden, a large enclosed greenhouse attached to Rusk, where I would alternately stare into space or nod off. I worked another two hours in the afternoon, then went home and to bed as quickly as I could. The intensity and concentration required by these four hours of work consumed all my mental energy, leaving room for nothing else in my life. My writing declined; I stopped painting; I engaged in no activity except going to the grocery store. Although I was not physically tired, I escaped into sleep each time an opportunity allowed. My mind could perform only a finite amount of work before it shut down.

Although I was overwhelmed by the job, there were intermittent satisfactions, as when I would play doctor when the staff asked me to explain a medical case. But mostly, being on the periphery of medicine made me feel just out of reach of an old friend. It produced a gnawing ache and sadness, and occasional confusion about my role.

I liked where I worked and the idea of working, but I felt as though I had only one arm and was trying to dig a ditch with a spoon. The task was beyond my tools and abilities.

Obviously the coaches thought so too. In April, two months into the job, they changed my assignment. I was told I would be given a combination of mental and physical work. I was relieved. When my mental stamina was taxed, I craved physical work. It made me feel productive, and I liked the evidence of my effort, the satisfaction of seeing a finished job. When I learned that my new assignment meant doing gardening and related tasks, I was jubilant.

The plan was that I would continue to work in Admissions for two hours each morning when I was fresh, then spend two hours each afternoon working in the Glass Garden. Officially known as the Enid A. Haupt Glass Garden, this is actually an enclave of enclosed and open gardens full of exotic and native plants, orchids, birds, and a pond with a fountain. In addition to being a beautiful retreat for patients, visitors, and staff, these tranquil areas are used for an innovative horticultural therapy program.

I was given a variety of tasks, all of which I found delightful. Some days I was assigned to paint small sheds, transplant perennials, or sundry other small jobs. Several times a week, I assisted patients in the horticultural therapy program. For the most part, these were physical rehabilitation patients—paraplegics or amputees in wheelchairs, among others—who welcomed an extra hand or direction to pot a flower, create a dish garden, or prune a plant.

My afternoons never failed to be a source of pleasure, in part because I loved what I was doing, in part because I was so happy to be spared the alternative of working the whole day in cerebral work beyond my ability. More important, horticultural therapy allowed me to learn. It embodied the concept of the Native American adage "Tell me, and I'll forget. Show me, and I may not remember. Involve me, and I'll understand."

One day, I assisted a seventy-year-old stroke patient in a wheelchair. I was practically in his lap as, head to head, he guided me in potting a cutting. He knew exactly what was needed; I was his hands. His pleasure in teaching me how to wrap and handle a tender root was greater than in the finished product, which he insisted on giving to me. He overrode my protests and thanks with a gesture, saying, "I've got to get back to my room. I'm hungry enough to eat the plant and maybe the dirt too."

We laughed at his joke as I guided his chair to the waiting attendant. I sat on a bench dappled in sunlight, holding the little pot, savoring the damp, flower-scented air. My thoughts drifted to the village in India.

Although Dr. Chako picked up my mother and me when it was still dark, patients were already waiting when we arrived at the clinic. People would line up as early as four A.M. One day a pregnant woman fainted at my feet. The verbal exchange in Hindi with Dr. Chako when she recovered was beyond my comprehension.

"Is she going to be all right?" I asked.

"I've told her she must stop eating dirt," Dr. Chako said. "Pregnant women do that sometimes when their bodies are begging for certain nutrients. Tomorrow morning I'll make that my lecture topic. Now fetch me whatever's left of those canned supplements."

We were nearly out of supplements; Dr. Chako never ran out of optimism. Since most people in India were hungry, my ten-year-old mind thought eating dirt was a logical way to stop an empty gnawing in one's belly. I didn't say so then.

I smiled at the recollection. I would eat it now if it would stop the craving inside me.

∾ With less mental fatigue from my job, I could resume doing other things in my life. When my friends in Maine invited me to spend the weekend with them, I jumped at the chance. The prospect of being in their good company, away from New York, and the delicious opportunity of riding a sweet horse named Kazablanca was as heady as new wine.

I arranged for a Friday-morning flight connecting through Boston and returning Sunday evening. I was now a seasoned traveler, well able to use my strategies. However, sometimes overlearned strategies are impossible to contradict. That explains why I told my cab driver to take me to La Guardia, even though I knew quite well I was flying out of Newark. *La Guardia* was a set phrase for me, my internal code word for *airport.*

When he did as I asked and took me to La Guardia, I realized I had a problem. I was disconcerted but not worried. As usual, I had allowed considerable time.

I ran to the taxi stand to catch a cab to Newark. I was an experienced taxi rider by now. I had endured drivers who spoke no English, gave me—usually without my protest—incorrect change, made unscheduled stops, and took innovative and circuitous routes. I learned from each experience and my luck with drivers improved.

This day I learned a new lesson. Never underestimate the perversity of New York cabbies.

I knew I was in trouble when we had gone a hundred yards and my driver pulled over to consult a map. I shoved two dollars at him and tried to get out so I could run back to the taxi stand for another cab, but he floored the accelerator as soon as I opened the door. Only the weight of my suitcase on the seat next to me kept me inside.

My antiflooding strategies were not equal to this challenge. I regained my bearings a few times for brief periods but not enough to notice the meter until we were forced to a screeching stop by a red light.

At the time, the fare from La Guardia to Midtown Manhattan was $13. How calm could I stay when we passed the Empire State Building and the meter read $30? As he made an incorrect turn, I desperately explained I was catching a plane, and Newark was in New Jersey, not Brooklyn.

"No problem, madam," he said, but he reversed his direction.

When he finally allowed me to exit his cab at the Newark terminal twenty minutes after my plane had departed, I actually said thank you in reflexive relief. He insisted that, with the tolls, my fare came to $130, but after we quarreled loudly he agreed to accept all I had—$100—in return for my assurance I would not call the Metro Transit Authority.

Despite the missed plane, the trip was salvaged by my calling Richard in Florida. He calmed me down and walked me through the steps of using my credit card to get cash and instructed me to go to any counter and find out the next flight to Portland, no matter what airline. That turned out to be USAir, where a sympathetic counter agent put me on a direct flight to Maine. I had been scheduled to take two Northwest planes to get there; now I would arrive an hour earlier without paying a cent more. When I later explained my $100 cab ride to Marcia, I hastily emphasized my good fortune with airlines.

The weekend in Maine was glorious, and to cap it off, Marilyn allowed me to ride Kazablanca by the shore. I was in heaven. I adore horses and the exhilaration of riding. Kazablanca was a young Morgan with little ocean experience, and I relished the invitation to help her lose her fear of running beside the breaking waves.

The day was cool but the sun was warm. As I cantered along the beach, I could feel Kazablanca calming down, which probably relaxed my heightened attention. I don't know what caused me to lose my balance. As I lurched forward, my only hope of staying on would have been to grasp her mane, but I couldn't risk breaking her trust. It would frighten her and undo exactly what I hoped to accomplish.

I jumped off to clear her hooves.

Kazablanca stopped running and came back to my call. She had never lost a rider before, so she was likely confused. It seemed a small plus to weigh against my pain to say she did not look scared.

My left thigh and shoulder swelled rapidly. Marilyn spotted her riderless horse and came running to my aid. To transport me to her home, she hoisted me up onto Kazablanca. The trip back was the only ride I had ever had that I didn't enjoy. I wished fervently the horse could turn into a down-filled gurney.

My friends iced my ribs, shoulder, and arm and insisted I stay over and go to a hospital in Portland. I was just as insistent that I return to New York that night so I could go to work Monday morning.

My notebook entry Monday night was sketchy.

> *I have this fantasy request: I want one day a month without head injury. This morning is a blur. All I know is I wound up in the ER in a full flood and unable to communicate intelligibly. It is a precarious and expensive situation in which to be. I know the potential for trouble in a hospital.*

I don't know what set off my flood on Monday morning. The unused plan that Marcia and I had drafted Sunday night on the phone had been for me to get an X ray of my posterior ribs and shoulder first thing in the morning.

Maybe I tried and failed. I don't remember. I learned later from Eileen and Robyn that I "came limping into the office" about ten in the morning, holding my left arm across my chest, confused and unable to tell them what was wrong. They had never seen someone in a seriously flooded state, so they assumed the worst—that I had suffered an acute neurological episode such as a brain hemorrhage. They called for a wheelchair and took me immediately to the ER. It was a logical thing to do.

ER by its very definition assumes the worst. They didn't know me or my history. They only saw someone with an injury who was confused and unable to communicate. The emergency room "cookbook" dictates the protocol: CAT scan of the brain, drug screen, IV fluids, multiple blood tests, a neurological consultation. I should be grateful they remembered to X-ray my shoulder.

Saralyn arrived and claimed me, then guided me out of my flooded state. After I could communicate effectively and my situation became clear, my physician—a gentle, very pregnant internist—was able to cancel some of the most costly and embarrassing orders. The whole fiasco took about seven hours.

In retrospect, I can't say I much minded falling off the horse. Physical pain and injury are one thing—I can explain those to someone else. Pain has not yet forced me to relinquish dignity or command. Flooding is another matter. I looked and acted incompetent. I had to abdicate choice and control. So far, physical pain has been trivial compared to the humiliation of my floods.

I was determined to redouble my efforts to control my flooding. I would stop believing it was not possible, that I could not do it. I vowed to ploddingly practice the strategies that could make small inroads and build on those. I would do anything to never again be at the mercy of a flood.

My interim report arrived a few days later. Even though Saralyn had been gently preparing me, I was alarmed when I read the summary words: "She has not attained the competence to resume competitive employment even in a capacity far reduced from her pre-injury status."

When the pounding in my ears stopped and I could gather myself together, my eyes picked up another phrase: "One of her major strengths is her calm acceptance of her existential situation."

This was calm? Well, what the hell, I might as well accept the compliment. It was sometimes true.

Go to sleep and deal with it tomorrow.

I spent the weekend alone, wrestling with my thoughts, trying to reconcile and articulate some disparate ideas.

Occupational Trials succeeded in doing exactly what they were designed to do. They let me fail in a protected environment. It spared me the painful judgment of colleagues if this failure had occurred in Detroit.

There was a certain irony to these Trials. If I had had only the greenhouse experience, I would have felt underused and untried. Instead, by trying and failing at the Admissions job, I could welcome the relief of less challenging work. No one had to point out that a job in a greenhouse was not on the road to reestablishing my career, and I still grieved for that loss. But the loss was now tempered by reality. It was as if my leg were crushed in a vise and the pain was awful. Amputation would be a welcome solution.

I had always known pleasure in doing my work well, including simple work. I wanted to arise each morning knowing I would go to a job, even a nonmedical one, that I could do well. But I now understood that it was likely my ego needs would not be met through any job I was currently capable of doing. Satisfaction of those needs would have to come from other sources.

In this last year, my greatest intellectual pleasure and sense of achievement had come from writing and painting. Writing, especially, was satisfying. It allowed me clear and orderly communication, a chance for the new *me* to be known by Joan, my family, and friends; to feel understood; to bridge the emotional chasm between myself and others. I wondered if writing could help fill the gaping hole left by my loss of the practice of medicine.

I wrote in my journal:

> *For the first time in a long while without grandiose illusion, I think more of my potential than does HTP. I believe I can lead a life that is intellectually, spiritually, and emotionally rewarding.*
> *Still, I would not mind if proving it looked a little easier.*

A few days later, I got a job offer from Detroit. My neurologist, Dr. Shatz, had arranged for me to work as a volunteer at Henry Ford Hospital in a drug study on Alzheimer's patients. I would have a medical assistant helping me. I knew none of the specifics, but if she thought I was capable, I was.

I couldn't wait to get home. Now, knowing a job would be waiting, I was elated. I called everyone—family, coaches, friends.

Not everyone saw the significance of this job.

"Wait . . . wait, let me get this straight," my friend Deborah said. "Your practice job in a hospital was gardening, not working with other doctors? Now you're taking an unpaid job, right? Your hospital would most likely take you back. Why not just jump into medicine and see how it goes?"

Why not indeed.

Role Reversal

When Marcia and I left the movie theater and reached the glass doors of the lobby, we could see the rain splashing on the parking lot, forming puddles that reflected the colored lights in the mall.

"Where's the car?" I said, shivering in anticipation, hoping we had managed a close spot.

"We drove separately. I'm down the row to the right."

I reached in my pocket, pulled out the map I had drawn when I parked my car, and I studied it for a moment. "I'll see you at home," I said and charged out into the rain.

I backed out my car and drove around toward the exit. To my left I saw Marcia running back toward the theater. I swung down her row and picked her up. "Problem?" I said as she leapt into my passenger seat.

"I must have parked over further than I thought. I can't see a thing through my glasses in this rain."

I tried not to smile too broadly. "We'll find it."

FROM MY NOTEBOOK, JUNE 1991

Living in the Real World

Whatever you can do, or dream you can, begin it.
GOETHE

Life after rehabilitation was uneven, as I should have expected but naturally had not. I was so fixated on the idea of being home, I had not considered that my deficits caught the same flight and returned with me.

When I was with Marcia and my other friends, the pace of their activity and conversation was too fast. I was always off balance, scrambling to follow, fatigued from trying to guess an answer or sort out where to focus my attention. In seeking a way out of my confusion, I asked too many questions. I bred irritation, disappointment, and sometimes incredulity.

"Stop with the questions, you're driving me crazy," my friend Ginny said in the car. "I'll tell you again, but pay attention. We don't want two cars, so we're picking up Randy. Joe will go on his own and join us later . . ."

Join us where? Joe who? I should have written down the plan, but when had there been time? I didn't know if I had enough money for where we were going. Where were we going? I sure couldn't ask her again . . .

"Claudia, for Pete's sake, are you listening?"

It was worse when there were four of us in the car. The conversation took more turns than the road. I couldn't keep up.

". . . he has the programs in place. It should work. Right?"

"Matthew?" I asked.

Randy gave me an odd look.

"Bill Clinton," Ginny said. "We stopped talking about Matt ten minutes ago."

Their voices were animated, clearly enjoying the moment and each other's company. I retreated and watched the road.

". . . he's the best writer since Faulkner. He should get a Pulitzer. Right, Claudia? You always liked him."

"Bill Clinton?" I asked, to their embarrassed laughter.

I told Joan about it in a letter.

> *I am most lonely and isolated when I am with my friends. The person they look for doesn't live here anymore and I don't yet know how to establish new, and equal, relationships. I don't seek a life which is quiescent or predictable; I do want to be able to cope with the unexpected.*

With all that, I was seeing progress. A quality of normalcy was gradually creeping into my life. "But," I told Marcia, "it's creeping in too damned gradually."

The Alzheimer's project was delayed for two months. As eager as I was to begin, the break was a blessing. It gave me time to establish daily routines and rework strategies. Marcia and Saralyn were a great help in that area.

To my notebook, alarms, and lists, I added maps, which not only told me where I had parked the car but also things like how to cook. "Recipe maps" were my invention to graphically steer me through a multiple-step recipe or meal, and thanks to them, Marcia and I began eating better. We also worked out procedures for things such as handling mail (mostly, "Don't open the mail when I'm not here, Claudia, upon pain of death") and organizing my clothes.

For the latter, my mother, using three-by-five cards, made a file that I kept on my dresser. Each card showed which clothes combined to make a suitable outfit for work. After I wore an outfit, I moved that card to the back of the file. That technique kept me from wearing the same clothes every time and saved me from having to make clothing decisions. To overcome my tendency to wear the same combinations again and again, she made an inventory that we posted on the inside of the closet door. This reminded me what items I owned and the occasions for which I should wear them.

Household tasks depleted energy needed for learning my job at Henry Ford Hospital. After much discussion, I agreed to Marcia's proposal that we hire someone one day every two weeks to do general cleaning; Marcia would do all the laundry and grocery shopping. It was not only faster than when I did it, it was easier on her than salvaging my botched efforts.

I ignored unsolicited professional advice regarding our approach to our household chores.

"I think it's important you learn to master shopping and laundry, Claudia," one person told me. "Let me be frank. Marcia could leave or die, then where would you be?"

"If that happened," I said, "I would have far more serious concerns than dirty clothes."

In the Motor City—where children teethe on steering wheels and freeways like giant spider webs link the metropolis to far-flung satellite cities and suburban communities—public transit is limited and rapid transit doesn't exist. Driving yourself is critical to all but the simplest lifestyle.

I was relatively safe on the road. My problem in driving a car was in remembering my destination and staying on course. I would take an early exit or pass the correct one each time my orientation slipped. If I left from somewhere away from home, heading toward a third location, I automatically drove home no matter the note on the dash announcing the correct destination. I could be thirty minutes along a freeway to Toledo before discovering I belonged at my neighborhood bank, and the only way to get back on track was to go home and start again.

Postrehab, I still pasted a note to the dashboard and told my tiny tape recorder my destination, but I added Marcia's idea of setting a timer to ring every three minutes. When it beeped, I automatically (nice word) started asking myself questions about where I was versus where I wanted to be. As a result, I was never more than three minutes off course.

At the end of summer, I was called to my job at Henry Ford Hospital, a very large medical complex in the inner city of Detroit. Rhonna Shatz, my doctor and now my boss, was the director of the Behavioral Neurology

Department. She had a realistic grasp of my limitations and felt confident my duties were well within my abilities and that she could capitalize on my strengths. The job had structure and variety. Short bursts of activity with patients and families were followed by quiet work when Cathy, my medical assistant, and I would chart patient records.

Cathy was a supportive person who could handle routines and solve organizational problems efficiently and cheerfully. Together, we tested patients in areas such as comprehending and expressing language, memory, orientation, and following multistep commands. The beauty of it was that I could ask patients what day it was and record their response even though I didn't know the answer to my own question.

The best part of the job was that most of my time was spent with patients and their families. I could not have dreamed up something so enjoyable or so vital to my well-being. Well, I could have envisioned a salary.

Cathy could do my job better than I, which was a problem at first. Because she acted as though there was nothing difficult in the work, I had trouble acknowledging that I was learning it slowly. During the several weeks of practice it took for me to learn how to administer baseline-function tests to the patients, she kept innocently pointing out how poorly they performed. Since I knew some patients were doing better than I could have done, my initial intention to be candid with her regarding my weaknesses took a long detour around my pride.

I changed my mind after my first flood. After I explained my deficits and how best she could assist me, we really became a team. Honesty is not only right, it is less embarrassing and much more productive.

My head injury afforded me insight into the needs and problems of my Alzheimer's patients, for whom my empathy was acute. This intuitive approach made my interviews richer and deepened their trust in the program.

September 15, 1990
 There had been an attempt in June to test Mrs. B that failed when she began hyperventilating and crying. I was told we could expect her to do this again.
 I could not have told someone else how to decrease her anxiety and

fear, but I was able to do it myself. The patient completed all of the tests.
She felt good about herself and the experience. I did too. I always knew
I practiced medicine as much for me as for my patients.

It was satisfying to be working even two half days a week. I learned during the summer that I derived considerable pleasure in writing essays and beginning work on a book. I also enjoyed planting and tending my garden and cooking for Marcia, who has always been an appreciative eater. But none of those activities ranked with getting up in the morning knowing I was going to a job. Even in the worst moments of my Occupational Trials when I most longed to escape, I was in love with the idea of going to work.

I was aware my social life had become rather thin. Marcia was as popular as ever, but I had less social contact and generated infrequent invitations on my own. A few friends simply disappeared; some acquaintances drifted away. It is a routine consequence of head injury, one I understood. I had little in common with former colleagues. Some friends were uncomfortable with my deficits or felt I was boring, less informed, less energetic, different.

Even as deep and close a friendship as Marcia's and mine was not immune from aspects of this socially changed me. By year's end, we were getting along easier than in the first months, but I was wary of her space, acutely conscious of how my dependency on her shaped our daily routines and impinged on her freedom. We both earnestly sought ways to balance our relationship, to put ourselves on a more equal basis. But true equality—financial, social, or intellectual—was not possible, at least not then.

I often wondered when I was at HTP if it would really be possible for couples—whether married, lovers, or domestic partners—to survive the head injury of one mate, if it might not be in the best interest of both to separate. I have since come to believe that you can achieve a healthy relationship after a successful rehabilitation if both partners have a realistic view of their changed roles and are able to make accommodations for each other without anger or martyrdom by one and docility or obsequiousness by the other.

Such relationships still raise troublesome, sometimes frightening, questions: How much chafing does it take to fray a bond? How hard is it always to be the coach or to overlook embarrassing public conduct? How many times can one partner forgive and the dependent suffer humiliation and beseech forgiveness? It's asking a lot of your partner to keep in mind that the mislaid checks, burned meals, lost car keys (or cars), forgotten appointments, and unreturned calls or library books are all the fault of the head injury and not the person. It's understandable if one partner seeks social activities outside the home and relationships that do not include the head-injured partner. But it will be a problem if done in a manner that makes the dependent partner feel excluded, unwanted and unloved.

I counted my blessings. I lived with someone of intelligence and humor who respected, loved, and knew me "when" and who had the willingness to accept the new *me* "as is." Even so, it took effort and time for us to establish a relationship that did not ring of parent and child.

In my first year home, Marcia's almost palpable sense of loss of her best friend undermined my efforts to accept myself. I was almost jealous of Marcia's admiration for and wistful regret about the loss of an energetic Claudia who took care of everything, argued philosophy, generated ideas, made things happen.

I would love to be that woman again, but she died in 1988. While I shall always miss her, I do not idealize her. She wasn't much fun. She steeped herself in her work and was often unavailable to her friends and family; she was so attentive to her patients' needs that there was not much left for herself. She could not paint and she wrote nothing that was not medical.

I began to value the fledgling parts of the new *me*. I learned to use a new yardstick in an old world while others continued to measure my performance against their memory of me and weigh their losses. It was sometimes disconcerting when my best efforts produced a good result that others saw as disappointing. Granted, I did it too, sometimes—but I also came to appreciate my new accomplishments.

I willed myself to be serene about my limited social interaction and about my mistakes and failures, real or perceived. In retrospect, I understood that the efforts by the therapists at HTP and Rusk to strengthen my ego were more successful than I'd realized at the time. Inasmuch as dysfunction is a reality for me, I came to value the sense of humor, self-tolerance, and *c´est la vie* approach they helped me develop.

I needed it during a beautiful party in Birmingham, just prior to Christmas. People I had not seen in years greeted me warmly and told me sincerely that I looked wonderful. "I wouldn't know you had that accident."

To a person, they wanted to know what I was doing and, once I told them, why I was doing it. Chunks of the evening were spent in one-sided conversations. "Think how much neurology you've learned. As long as you don't have a real job, why not do a neurology residency?" Or, "I know a small hospital that would love to have you part time if a whole day's too much. This is right up your alley."

I found myself momentarily intrigued and excited by these pipe dreams until my vision cleared with the pain of fact. While I was trying to get my bearings, a man listening to the conversation offered his theory.

"Maybe you haven't gone back into medicine simply because you really don't want it bad enough."

I forgot Richard's dictum not to rise to such lures and not to defend myself. In trying, I flooded.

"At least," I said to my mother and Richard on the way home, "my dreams have a foot in reality. People talk about clinical medicine as though the chief requirements are showing up and wearing a white coat. Before I know it, they've made my hunger ravenous without throwing me anything edible."

When I got home that night there was a message on the answering machine letting me know that Beth had disappeared. Her family was looking for her.

In a note to Joan, I said:

> *I'm worried about Beth dropping out of sight and I'm very sorry for her family. Sadly, I am less surprised by bad news than good reports about my fellow trainees.*
>
> *I know I'm lucky. After all, I have a happy job, it looks as though I will be teaching, my writing is progressing well, and I still make my home with Marcia. Even so, Joan, despite my blessings, despite rehabilitation, I find my life difficult. How much harder it must be for the*

others.

If I had been younger at the time of my injury, without long-term, strong relationships with supportive people; if I had lacked vocational ideas and life experiences; if I'd had greater impairments, I doubt I would be okay. I was once uncommonly resolute and resilient. I am no longer either one.

So I wonder. If I cope so poorly with all my good fortune, how do other trainees survive? They can't all be that much tougher than I.

In May 1991, I went to New York to visit friends. I arranged to divide the time between Kay and Edward's house in the country and Lori's apartment in the city. On Friday, my first day, I made a lunch date with Tina.

My plan for the day was straightforward—pick Tina up at Christie's at 59th Street and Park Avenue, and go to lunch. Afterward, I would stroll up through Central Park and stop by the Fauve exhibit at the Metropolitan Museum.

I decided not to write out a tediously complete plan. I simply jotted down:

> *Start out @ 11:00 A.M.*
> *12:30, 59th & Park*
> *Fauve Exhibit at Met*

I had hated living in Manhattan, but walking around the city on a glorious morning in mid-May is always exhilarating. New York's cement-gray sameness softens in the clear, rosy light of spring. The sky was a brilliant blue, trees were in full leaf, ornamental trees with slender stems and blossoms of lavender, white, pink looked like giant bouquets. The scent of moist earth and sun-warmed spring air was intoxicating. It diffused my focus. I didn't know where to look first.

I had not walked two blocks when I spied the cart of a street vendor on the corner. I enthusiastically wolfed down a hot dog with mustard and sauerkraut. I liked the walk, I liked the people, I liked how I felt. I was eager to reach Central Park. When I passed a subway entrance, I impulsively decided a train would speed me there, forgetting the park was not my destination.

Although the train ride had not been in my plan, it could have worked. There is a subway station at 59th Street, just a block from where I needed to be—had I remembered I was meeting Tina. However, after glancing at my notes, I concluded I had written "59th St." merely because I thought it was the best place to enter Central Park. Now, I had a better idea. I would stay on the subway to 86th Street. It made more sense to see the art exhibit first and then walk back down through Central Park.

Inside the Metropolitan, I thought warmly about Tina, that I must call her sometime.

Wait, I did call her. We were having lunch.

It is fortunate Tina is an art expert or I might not have remembered her until hours after our appointment. As it was, I still had ample time. I could even have walked through the park to Christie's, but I panicked and rushed back to the subway. With half an hour to spare, I exited at 59th Street—right into Bloomingdale's Department Store.

I enter stores with trepidation. I am not up to the bustle—the decisions, stimulation, distractions, and confusion. This day, as a visitor to New York, I felt confident, like the kid who had made good returning to the old neighborhood—well, a very elegant neighborhood. It was time to sally forth and confront the intimidation of Bloomie's. I was beguiled by the romantic lighting, the glittering displays, the smartly dressed shoppers all around me.

My bravado faded in less than five minutes and I was searching frantically for an exit when a saleswoman—whom I mistook for a mannequin—sprang to life and stopped me dead-on by spraying me with perfume.

While I was recovering—"Yes, it's heavenly, yes, I like it, yes, it's a great price"—I was within sight of the exit. I could have run for it but I didn't. Instead I said, "Yes. Charge it."

I could hardly chide myself for impulse buying when it was my first independent, nonedible purchase in nearly three years. However, although I never wear perfume, I now had a $75 bottle of "Knowing."

I slid into the seat next to Tina right on time, if not hungry. While we ate, I spoke of my purchase. I was a little rueful, but Tina was philosophic.

"Be glad you weren't in Tiffany's," she said.

⌒ Besides the expensive shopping spree, spring brought with it a closure to the civil suit against the driver who had injured me. Sometimes closure is the best you can hope to have.

In his initial hearing in Grosse Pointe Traffic Court, the driver's attorney had asked me if I would allow him to plead no contest. I refused. He chose to plead not guilty of careless driving. He was convicted and fined $100.

He was insured for $20,000, the minimum required in Michigan, but the insurance company balked at paying me. Our recourse was to go to court. My attorney moved to sue for my lost wages.

I was ambivalent about taking legal action. I knew that the only pain arising out of a civil action against a twenty-year-old who had nothing to lose would be mine. I agreed finally because I did not want the man who injured me to forget me or to believe the only thing he destroyed that July evening three years earlier was an expensive bicycle.

I could not have borne a trial. I need not have worried. Our petition to the court resulted in the judge's asking to see the defendant, me, and my mother alone in his chambers.

The judge discouraged our suit.

"You have an excellent case, but there's nothing to win," he said. "I would expect this young man has learned his lesson." In what respect was not explained.

"Your Honor," my mother said, "you and I are about the same age. My daughter's life, to say nothing of the loss of her earning potential, has been dramatically lessened. If it had been me or you, Your Honor, who caused her harm, we would have voluntarily gotten a second job or a loan, done everything possible to try to make up even a fraction of her loss. This young man has never even apologized."

The result was that the insurance company paid me the $20,000. My mother sought and it was granted that the defendant would pay me from his earnings—$5,000 initially and another $1,000 each year for three years on the anniversary of my injury. My mother reasoned it would ensure that he remembered me for a while.

Sometimes I wonder if it was a meaningful penance or if he just resented me for it.

In July 1992, my old friend Terrie Taylor, a professor at Michigan State University College of Osteopathic Medicine, called me with a job proposal. Terrie is an internist who specializes in tropical medicine. Half of each year is spent in Malawi, Africa, doing research on children with malaria.

"Claudia, I have an idea," she said. "What would you say to teaching first-year med students how to take a history and perform a physical exam? It's all rote material. You know it well."

"It sounds wonderful." Was it? I had heard so many pie-in-the-sky ideas about employment, I tried to keep my enthusiasm in check. "May I think on it and call you back? Tomorrow? Thank you, Terrie, thank you."

That night, Marcia endorsed the idea.

"It's great," she said. "Teaching clinical medicine was your forte. I can't think of anything more ingrained in you. It's, if you'll pardon the expression, like riding a bicycle. In fact"—she grinned—"you'll teach it far better than you could formulate a plan for cooking eggs for breakfast."

I called Terrie on the spot.

On the basis of my past reputation and my assistant clinical professorship at MSU, she sold the committee on the idea of using me. I was offered an unpaid position beginning in September. I would teach two successive two-hour classes of eight students once a week.

The drive to the East Lansing campus was a hundred miles each way. To optimize my teaching performance after a long drive, I would put my sleeping bag on the floor of a vacant office and take a nap before and after my classes.

There is nothing like sharing knowledge, which is a combination of information, instinct, and experience. Teaching these receptive, eager young people to have a passion for what they will be doing gives me pleasure and, I hope, helps them find greater satisfaction in their work. The twelve-year journey to become a doctor is a long way to travel if you don't like the destination. When I was with my class, the difficulties in my life over the last four years evaporated. It was a good thing that MSU didn't know I would have paid them for the privilege of again teaching medicine.

Every head-injured person enters a rehabilitation program hoping to be fully restored. No such program exists.

Joan told me that there was a ceiling on recovery. No one could predict where it would be, but you could be certain there was one and it would stop you from gaining back all you had lost. This ceiling idea is important. It's disheartening to chase rainbows. We understood that before our heads were injured; we should keep it in mind now. I have no potential to become a soloist at the Metropolitan Opera (as those who have heard me sing can attest) or to be the quarterback for the Detroit Lions.

At the same time, it is important that this ceiling idea not limit your dreams. It is healthy and reasonable for me to seek lofty goals as long as they're rooted in reality. It is only in aspiring to the improbable that one can achieve as much as possible. I do not—and neither do my counselors—know how far I can stretch.

TuTu is still expanding her knowledge at age ninety. I always envisioned for myself a lifelong intellectual, emotional, and spiritual growth. I still do. I am just using a different yardstick to measure my progress.

⌒ I had lost my car at the post office two blocks away and had trudged home through the deep snow. I was upstairs changing out of my wet clothes when I overheard Marcia's sister discussing me with some wonder.

"I thought Claudia was doing better than this. She can't practice medicine, they didn't fix her memory, she can't even keep track of her car. What's better?"

I was curious about Marcia's answer.

"Claudia is better," she said. "Her ability to use props and strategies is so good most people don't guess her deficits. Of course, things still go wrong. She's worked terribly hard for what she's accomplished, but some of the most important things she achieved in rehabilitation are not visible. She has had to alter her expectations but she has regained her sense of self. I don't know what Claudia will yet do in her life, but she now sees her promise, not just her inadequacies."

That is only one reason I like Marcia.

Lewis Carroll said, "It's a poor sort of memory that only works backwards." I agree. If nothing else, I have regained a forward memory—my dreams—and with them, a future.

March 20, 1997

GROSS POINTE

Life is a verb.
CHARLOTTE PERKINS GILMAN
❖

Nearly nine years have passed since my injury, a full seven years since I said good-bye to my friends at HTP.

I continue to improve. The underlying reasons are strategies and discipline in using them. Others have been inventive in helping me expand my productivity. My mother, who now lives full time in Florida with Richard, has stayed with me twice a year for two weeks each time and has helped me retailor strategies to put my life in order.

She has also helped with things that are beyond my abilities. Last year, she packed, unpacked, and administered Marcia's and my move to a larger house. She organized every drawer, closet, shelf, and cupboard in our house and catalogued my clothes. Together, we set up a file system for my personal papers and household records. These organizational practices cover every aspect of my life—record keeping, mail sorting, phone calls, and designing effective-action lists of what to do, buy, or fix.

The most important part of this is not her labor, however much I value it. It is the strategies that emerge out of it, strategies that shore up my skills. Some of these are new, but most are old ones that have been refocused and retailored to fit new situations, or restored because I had corrupted them through misuse.

None of these ideas would be useful if I were unwilling to go through the tedium of endless repetition and constant mistakes in order to use them. It has rarely been the case that the idea behind a prop is bad, but my skill in using it can take years to develop. Patience is required. Fortunately, patience too is learnable.

For example, I have a device to tape my business and important phone calls so that I can concentrate on the conversation without the distraction of taking notes. In the first two years of owning the recorder, I taped two calls. Now, I record fully half of them.

There are different limits on what each of us is capable of mastering, and strategies are not perfect. As Saralyn often reminded me, they can't be in the real world. There are too many variables modifying each situation. Quite simply, people seldom ask the question for which you have prepared the answer.

Occasionally, repeated and vigorous practice leads to internal change. My language skills have improved tremendously, no doubt the result of the years I have spent writing at my computer. Also, I consciously use my right hand for everything except sports—we all need a break from rehab and I like to win at tennis. Every year my right arm too shows objective improvement. It is not a matter of resurrection of my dead nerve cells. Different cells are learning the job.

I have kept abreast, more or less, of the changes in the lives of my fellow trainees and coaches.

Lenny Dean is a volunteer assistant to the staff at Crumby House, a rehabilitation center. He is taking art classes and spends his free time on painting and photography in his home state of Tennessee. He has made great strides combating his severe adynamia and his resonant laugh is heard more often.

Beth Ravitz, when she disappeared, was trying to escape her "label" by running off to Australia. After returning to the States, she graduated from a program in massage therapy. She lives independently and works in Manhattan.

Scott Paoli retired from the Army but would still like to return to it. He is becoming involved in a mentoring program, working with children and teaching them judo.

Sharon Schaffield took her life fifteen months after leaving the program.

Tommy lives in New York with his supportive wife and their three children.

Bernie Skiba and his wife are in New Jersey, where he is a volunteer in the gift shop and mail department at Palisades General Hospital.

Richard Siller is concentrating on his talent for art and attends art classes. He has his own apartment in the same building as his remarkable Aunt Blanche.

David Dermer ran a day-care center for a while but is looking for a less stressful career. He has married and is raising his stepson.

Joan Gold and Len Travaglione left HTP and formed their own rehabilitation group in upstate New York. Yehuda Ben-Yishay and NYU's Rusk-HTP continue to be a stellar influence in head-trauma rehabilitation. Ellen Zide is still there. Laurie Freeman went into private practice following the birth of her daughter. Saralyn Silver retired from her longtime work at Occupational Trials.

TuTu died in her own bedroom and in my mother's arms March 23, 1995, a month after her ninetieth birthday party.

Marcia is in private practice, a calling and professional situation for which she is eminently gifted. We still live together, and she still insists on being the first to touch the mail.

I still do research one day a week in the Department of Neurology at Detroit's Henry Ford Hospital and teach first-year medical students at Michigan State University, where I was recently promoted to the unpaid position of associate clinical professor of medicine. I lecture and write about head injury. I have a wonderful garden. I am in love and loved.

In my first speech at HTP, I said my head injury had been my greatest challenge and overcoming it would be my greatest achievement. I prayed, then, that sheer hard work in rehab would restore me to my former self. Some continue to look for that person in me and are disappointed in my progress.

This would be a great story if I had been able to return to the practice of medicine. It would be great, too, if the blind could see and the paralyzed, walk. Because HTP deals in the practical, they helped the new me develop, and showed me a way past my unfulfilled hopes so I would not remain immobilized by grief. At the same time, it would be simplistic to think that grief ends—it is neither finite nor simple. Longing for what one had has a way of popping up at unexpected times. But over time, the intensity eases.

If I were asked, I would counsel someone with a devastating injury not to focus on their loss and what might have been, but to fully live the life they have now and to carve out new and achievable dreams to fit it.

This new life is truly mine. I own it and I am earnestly trying to learn, as Dr. Chako advised, what God intends me to do with it.

I was a happy woman before my injury, I am a happy one today.

Special Thanks

Becoming the most one can be is simply not possible without professional help and the active support of others. My journey through and beyond rehabilitation was accomplished with a large cast of family, friends, and professionals who pulled or cajoled me along, lifted me up and wiped me off when I stumbled, and sometimes carried me on their shoulders.

My debts of gratitude are large and owed to many.

Foremost to Jeanne Findlater, my mother, whose indefatigable energy, patience, and talent in organizing me and editing my work made my writing of this book possible. Her contribution to my well-being cannot be described or quantified.

Marcia E. Baker, whose high expectations kept me on a challenging upward path, and whose love and encouragement willed me along it and directed the way.

Gertrude Sullivan, "TuTu," who loved us all unconditionally.

Laurie Kamaiko, my lifeline during those months in New York, who always gives the richest possible interpretation to friendship.

Richard Findlater, my stepfather, who enriches and nurtures intuitively and inventively.

Rhonna Shatz, D.O., my gifted and caring neurologist, and to her husband, Mark Shatz, Ph.D., who led me to Rusk.

The extraordinary "coaches" who staffed the NYU Head Trauma Program: Drs. Joan Gold, Ellen Zide, Laurie Freeman, Len Travaglione, and their brilliant leader, Yehuda Ben-Yishay, who founded that program, which is a model in head trauma rehabilitation.

Saralyn Silver, who led me through Occupational Trials and was a needed and available counselor long after my transition to Detroit.

My fellow trainees, who generously allowed me to portray them in this book without masks or makeup.

My parents, William and Beverly Osborn, and the Rev. Wilson Baker and his wife, Elaine, all of whom gave me their love and prayers.

Christopher Osborn Findlater, my brother, whose electronic savvy wedded computer word processing with head injury and kept me out of technological quicksand.

Kay Gauthreaux Lee, Shirl Weaver, Tina and Anthea Zonars, Dean Dean, Michael and Dee Schaffield, Terrie Taylor, Cindy Kregoski, and Cathy Cafini—all of whom went far out of their way to help me and did so over and over and over.

Christina Ward, my agent and advocate.

State Farm Insurance, which underwrote the full cost of my training at NYU's Rusk Institute, gave me a computer so essential to writing this book and managing my life, and provided me with Caroline Haire, R.N., of Medical Care Coordinators, Inc., my rehabilitation nurse in Detroit and my liaison to the medical support community.

Those who read and critiqued the drafts of the manuscript, but most especially Sylvia Cantoni, Kathleen Kirschenheit, Dick and Joyce Mittenthal, Molly Sapp, Bridget Sullivan, and Robert L. White.

David King, the coauthor of *Self-Editing for Fiction Writers*, who showed me how to employ his techniques in real-life writing.

Thank you all. Helping me was often heroic, frustrating, expensive, and disappointing. I pray it was never considered thankless.

⊹ ⊱

A Head Injury Primer

Adynamia (See *Behavioral Manifestations*)

Amnesia A partial or total loss of ability to recall events or experiences. (See also *Retrograde Amnesia* or *Post-Traumatic Amnesia.*)

Anhedonia Loss of a sense of pleasure; for example, an inability to be thrilled by a glorious sunset or respond to music that formerly was passionately loved. *ex. page 106.*

Behavioral Manifestations Three common organic behaviors associated with head injury are adynamia, disinhibition, and flooding. These are the result of injury to the frontal lobes of the brain as well as to the temporal lobes and the hypothalamus. Current medical technology enables doctors to pinpoint specific areas of brain-tissue damage causing these changes in behavior.

1. *Adynamia:* apathy, loss of drive. The individual is no longer dynamic or energetic and may appear to lack motivation. Responses to others or to situations are dull, flat. There is slowed mental functioning, a marked decrease in ideas, activity is rarely self-initiated. *ex. pages 92-98.*

2. *Disinhibition:* a decrease in the ability to control impulsive behavior. Disinhibited individuals may speak and act without considering the consequences. They may appear impatient, quick to anger or to laugh. They may race off on a tangent, interrupt others, speak loudly, and say inappropriate things, and have difficulty inhibiting sexual, aggressive, and antisocial behavior. Disinhibition, a noticeably active behavior, may be said to be the opposite of adynamia; however elements of disinhibition and adynamia frequently occur in the same individual. *ex. pages 101-102, 124-125, 167-168, 174-175, 177.*

3. *Flooding:* overwhelmed by, or awash in, one's emotions. This can take place even though the flooded individual does not appear upset or distraught

or even consciously aware of being under an emotional overload. In a flood, thought-processing slows, and thinking, language skills, and actions may be severely impaired. Flooding may be triggered by external events—the need to make a decision or immediately solve a problem; or from internal pressure— the awareness of one's own confusion, a sense of helplessness, the pain of one's loss of self. *ex. pages 100-101, 166-167, 212-213.*

Aphasia The inability to comprehend and/or to express language. This may include written or spoken words, ideas, or sign language. It may be a partial or complete impairment.

Apraxia The inability to perform a well-known, purposeful action in spite of having normal mobility, attention, and comprehension. As an example, a person wants to answer a ringing phone and nothing is wrong with his arm, yet he is unable to correctly bring the receiver to his ear.

Brain Stem That part of the brain which connects the spinal cord with the hemispheres of the brain. The brain stem also regulates consciousness, heart rate, breathing, eye movements, and swallowing. "All sensations going to the brain, as well as signals from the brain to the rest of the body, must pass through the brain stem." [1]

Closed Head Injury (CHI) (See also *Traumatic Brain Injury*) Damage to the brain that is not accompanied by a fractured skull or a penetrating injury (such as a bullet that pierces the skull). CHI usually causes diffuse damage to the brain and affects many areas of function.

Coma An altered state of consciousness in which the eyes do not open even in response to pain, commands are not obeyed, and recognizable words cannot be spoken.[4] Once individuals become more responsive in any of these three areas, they are technically no longer in a coma. The Glasgow Coma Scale is used to measure the levels of coma, which are defined by the individual's ability to respond. A return to full consciousness may occur swiftly or take place gradually over years.

Concussion A disturbance or impairment of neurological function caused by a TBI that is transient and reversible and often accompanied by a brief loss of consciousness. Sometimes a concussion will produce ongoing symptoms of minor neurologic dysfunction that may last several months. This is called a postconcussional syndrome. [5] Concussions may be graded in severity according to the degree of confusion, length of unconsciousness, or amnesia experienced.

Consequences of a TBI *Physical impairments* can include speech, seizure disorders, hearing, vision, and other sensory losses. An individual may show partial or severe lack of coordination, balance, muscle tone, and movement, including paralysis.[1]

Cognitive impairments can include changes in thinking and reasoning skill and diminished learning ability. Varying degrees of problems may exist in long- and short-term memory, attention, concentration, and communication skills, planning, problem solving, and abstract reasoning.[1]

Emotional and behavioral impairments (see also *Behavioral Manifestations*) These may include sleep disorders, mood swings, restlessness, lack of energy, anxiety, depression, inability to cope, agitation, sexual dysfunction, inappropriate behavior, inability to self-monitor, self-centeredness, low self-esteem, poor emotional control, crying and laughing excessively, lack of motivation, and difficulty relating to others.[1]

Disinhibition (See *Behavioral Manifestations*)

Executive Function The ability to organize thoughts and work, to create plans and successfully execute them, to manage the administrative functions of one's life. Individuals with impaired executive function may appear to live moment to moment, fail to monitor their activities or social interactions to make sure plans are carried out (or even made). With diminished ability to create strategies, to handle more than one task at a time, to be effective, reliable, and productive, the simplest job may be too challenging. *ex. pages 161-162, 163-165, 205-206.*

Flooding (See *Behavioral Manifestations*)

Head Injury (HI) (See *Traumatic Brain Injury*) The term is applied to damage sustained by the brain—not the bony case (the cranium) which surrounds it.

Incidence and Scope of TBI Each year, about 373,000 Americans are hospitalized as a result of TBI. Nearly 100,000 of those injured sustain moderate to severe brain injuries resulting in lifelong disabling conditions. Males sustain nearly two times as many head injuries as females, and 50 percent of all head injuries are experienced by those under age 35. Motor vehicle accidents cause nearly half of all TBIs; falls are the second leading cause. After one TBI, the risk for a second injury is three times greater; after a second TBI, the risk for a third injury is eight times greater.[2]

Open Head Injury Traumatic damage to the brain in which the skull is broken or penetrated as can happen with a bullet, knife, or blow from a sharp object. Damage from an open head injury is often more localized to the particular area of impact or the path of the internal wound. Specific deficits result without necessarily involving diffuse (broad) areas of the brain.

Post-Traumatic Amnesia (PTA) The inability to remember continuous, day-to-day experiences or events that occur after the injury to the brain. The duration of PTA is "the best guide to the severity of the diffuse [brain]damage."[3] PTA may last from minutes to months.

Prop A device used to carry out a strategy or function. Common ones are tape recorders, beepers and alarms, notebooks and lists. (See *Strategy*)

Retrograde or Pre-Traumatic Amnesia The inability to remember events or experiences that occurred before a head injury.

Strategy An operating plan designed to assist the individual in carrying out a task. A strategy may involve using one or more props. (See *Prop*).

Traumatic Brain Injury (TBI) Known also as head injury, a TBI is damage to the brain that is not degenerative or congenital in origin but was caused by external force. TBIs commonly occur in vehicle accidents, falls, assaults, and sports injuries. When there is rapid acceleration and deceleration of the head, as can occur with a sudden impact to it during an auto accident, the brain is bounced back and forth against the inside of the skull causing bruising and later swelling. Nerve fibers can be stretched and torn diffusely throughout the brain causing physical, cognitive, and behavioral impairments.

Significant injury can occur without a loss of consciousness, but usually, in a TBI, the brain stem is injured and produces a period of coma that may last a prolonged time. Not all outcomes of head injury are obvious, which is why TBI is called the silent injury.[1]

Today, the *closed head injury* classification has been expanded to include other injuries to the brain such as are caused by encephalitis, meningitis, anoxia (loss of oxygen as can occur during cardiac arrest or near drowning), metabolic disorders, poisoning, brain tumors, and seizure disorders.

References and Resources

1. Basic Questions about Brain Injury and Disability, Brain Injury Association, Inc., 1776 Massachusetts Ave., NW, Suite 100, Washington, DC 20036; phone: 202-296-6443; fax: 202-296-8850; Family Help Line: 800-444-6443. In addition to providing invaluable information and research materials, BIA serves as a national clearing house able to put individuals in touch with rehabilitation facilities, support groups, educational help, and other resources in every state in the U.S.
2. Fact Sheet/Traumatic Brain Injury, BIA (formerly National Head Injury Association, Inc.).
3. Jennett, Bryan: Scale and Scope of the Problem: *Rehabilitation of the Adult and Child with Traumatic Brain Injury*, Edition 2, F. A. Davis Company, Philadelphia, 1990, Chap. 1, p. 4.
4. Jennett, B., and Teasdale, G.: Aspects of coma after severe head injury. *Lancet* 1:878, 1977.
5. Miller, J.D., and Jones, P.A.: Minor Head Injury, *Rehabilitation of the Adult and Child with Traumatic Brain Injury*, Edition 2, F. A. Davis Company, Philadelphia, 1990, Chap. 17, *p*. 237.
6. Rosenthal, Mitchell, et al.: *Rehabilitation of the Adult and Child with Traumatic Brain Injury*, Edition 2, F. A. Davis Company, Philadelphia, 1990.